DEAF CHILDREN: DEVELOPMENTAL PERSPECTIVES

This is the first volume of a series entitled

DEVELOPMENTAL PSYCHOLOGY SERIES

Under the Editorship of Harry Beilin,
Developmental Psychology Program
City University of New York Graduate School
New York, New York

DEAF CHILDREN: DEVELOPMENTAL PERSPECTIVES

Edited by

Lynn S. Liben

The Pennsylvania State University
College of Human Development
University Park, Pennsylvania

ACADEMIC PRESS   New York   San Francisco   London   1978

A Subsidiary of Harcourt Brace Jovanovich, Publishers

ACADEMIC PRESS, INC.
111 Fifth Avenue, New York, New York 10003

United Kingdom Edition published by
ACADEMIC PRESS, INC. (LONDON) LTD.
24/28 Oval Road, London NW1 7DX

Library of Congress Cataloging in Publication Data
Main entry under title:

Deaf children: Developmental perspectives

Includes bibliographies.
1. Children, Deaf——Addresses, essays, lectures.
I. Liben, Lynn S. [DNLM: 1. Deafness——In infancy and
childhood. 2. Deafness——Rehabilitation. WV271 D489]
HV2390.D48   155.4'5'12   77–77237
ISBN 0–12–447950–2

PRINTED IN THE UNITED STATES OF AMERICA
78 79 80 81 82   9 8 7 6 5 4 3 2 1

Contents

II LINGUISTIC ISSUES

IV EDUCATIONAL AND CULTURAL CONTEXTS

List of Contributors

Numbers in parentheses indicate the pages on which the authors' contributions begin.

URSULA BELLUGI (43), The Salk Institute for Biological Studies, San Diego, California 92112

PENELOPE H. BROOKS (87), Institute of Mental Retardation and Intellectual Development, George Peabody College, Nashville, Tennessee 37203

ADRIENNE E. HARRIS* (217), Department of Psychology, Glendon College, York University, Toronto, Ontario, Canada M4N 3M6

ROBERT I. HARRIS (137), Mental Health–Hearing Impaired, St. Paul–Ramsey Hospital and Medical Center, St. Paul, Minnesota 55101

EDWARD S. KLIMA (43), University of California, San Diego, La Jolla, California 92093

LYNN S. LIBEN (3, 195), College of Human Development, The Pennsylvania State University, University Park, Pennsylvania 16802

KATHRYN P. MEADOW (21), Kendall Demonstration Elementary School, Gallaudet College, Washington, D.C. 20002

DONALD F. MOORES (173), College of Education, The Pennsylvania State University, University Park, Pennsylvania 16802

R. S. NICKERSON (115), Bolt Beranek and Newman, Inc., Cambridge, Massachusetts 02138

HILDE S. SCHLESINGER (69, 157), The Langley–Porter Neuropsychiatric Institute, San Francisco, California 94143

GEORGE SPERLING (103), Bell Labs, Murray Hill, New Jersey 07974 and Department of Psychology, New York University, New York, New York 10003

* Present address: Department of Psychology, Rutgers–Newark, Newark, New Jersey 07102

Preface

As one mechanism for fostering the interdisciplinary goals of the Society for Research in Child Development, the Long-Range Planning Committee, with funds from The Grant Foundation of New York, began sponsoring a series of interdisciplinary study groups and summer institutes in 1974. The present volume is an outgrowth of one such study group that was formed to consider "Theoretical and Practical Implications of Research on the Development of Deaf Children."

As originally conceived, this study group was organized to provide (a) an impetus for critical reviews of past work related to deaf children; (b) a forum for the exchange of theories, issues, and methodologies across disciplinary boundaries as they relate to deafness; and (c) an opportunity for systematic identification and dissemination of the important variables and controls that should be considered in planning research and services for deaf people.

An additional goal of the study group was to identify new areas of research, evaluation, and application. This goal seemed particularly important because when working within a special population it is common to become "inbred" in approach, automatically accepting traditional theoretical and practical assumptions. In order to facilitate the identification of the kinds of information needed by the "uninitiated" and to encourage the application of new perspectives to old issues, several discussants were included in the study group. These discussants were scholars who had had relatively limited contact with deafness prior to their participation in this study group, and who were, therefore, in a good position to question fundamental assumptions of the field and to raise new issues and questions.

The study group consisted of 11 persons, drawn from several disciplines. Ursula Bellugi, presently at The Salk Institute for Biological Studies, represents the disciplines of linguistics and psycholinguistics. For several years she has been involved in the study of American Sign

Language (ASL) and the acquisition of ASL by deaf children. Adrienne Harris, trained as a developmental psychologist, served as one of the discussants. She is particularly interested in how concepts of verbal control, and of societal control more generally, apply to the development of deaf children. Robert Harris, himself deaf from the age of 8 months, is trained as a clinical psychologist. He has also been interested in deaf children's and adults' control mechanisms, particularly in impulse control. Kay Meadow, currently in charge of research at the Kendall Demonstration Elementary School of Gallaudet College, is trained as a sociologist. She has been active in studying sociological aspects of deafness and, in addition, has worked with Hilde Schlesinger in research on the development of deaf children. Donald Moores, an educational psychologist who taught for many years at the American School for the Deaf and at the Rochester School for the Deaf, has more recently worked on a national, longitudinal program to evaluate a variety of educational programs for deaf children. In addition, he has been interested in how the approaches of verbal control and ethology may be useful in the study of deaf children. Ray Nickerson has worked with deaf children at the Clarke School in the development of a computer system for speech training. However, most of his work has been in the area of experimental psychology, particularly in information processing and memory; thus, he served primarily in the role of a discussant. Richard Nowell, an educational psychologist, served during the study group as an interpreter for Robert Harris. He has been in charge of the interpreter-training program at the National Technical Institute for the Deaf in Rochester, New York and is interested in issues of communication more generally. In addition, he has conducted research on memory processes in deaf college students, and is now involved in developing educational services for multiply-handicapped deaf children. Penelope Brooks, a cognitive psychologist, has conducted research on both linguistic and affective aspects of deaf children's development. Hilde Schlesinger, a child psychiatrist, has developed (with Kay Meadow) a project in which hearing parents are encouraged to use total communication with their deaf children. She has been active in evaluating the effects of this program, particularly with respect to the reciprocity of parent–child communication and to the acquisition of language. George Sperling, an experimental psychologist particularly interested in information processing, also served as a discussant. Finally, I have been trained as a developmental psychologist, with particular emphasis on cognitive development. My own research with deaf children and adults has concerned the development of memory strategies.

Given the goals, organizational structure, and members of the study group, the formal product of the group—this volume—should be of interest to a diverse group of researchers and practitioners. Insofar as this volume provides a review of past literature and enumerates important variables and controls related to deafness, it should be a valuable resource for people who are planning or participating in research programs or services for deaf children and adults, but who have had relatively little experience in this area. Since the book delineates new issues and areas for research, it should also prove useful for those already well versed in past work and methodologies related to deafness. Finally, since atypical populations provide a means of testing the adequacy of theories originally developed on "normal" or "typical" populations, scholars interested in more general issues within disciplines such as sociology, developmental psychology, linguistics, psycholinguistics, experimental psychology, communication, clinical psychology, psychiatry, and education should also find the book of value.

It is obvious that an endeavor such as this one is indebted to many people and organizations. First, I would like to thank The Grant Foundation, especially Phil Sapir, president, for providing financial support to the Society for Research in Child Development for these interdisciplinary programs in general. Second, I would like to thank the Long-Range Planning Committee of the Society for Research in Child Development for their decision to support this study group in particular. Although I am grateful to the whole Committee and the entire Society, I would like to express particular thanks to Harold Stevenson—Chairman of the Long-Range Planning Committee—and T. Berry Brazelton—liaison between the study group and the Committee—for their help in the establishment and implementation of this study group. In addition, Dorothy Eichorn provided invaluable assistance in business and financial matters. I would also like to thank the many people at the Rochester School for the Deaf and the National Technical Institute for the Deaf (particularly, Milo Bishop, Michele Boyer, Bill Castle, Ralph Hoag, Ross Stuckless, and Len Zwick) for their continued cooperation in my personal involvement and research with deaf children and adolescents. Thanks are also expressed to my colleagues at Penn State and at the University of Rochester for their encouragement; to the secretarial staffs at both institutions for typing this volume; to Debbie Heilbrun, Elisa Klein, and Marcia Welterlen for help in indexing; and to the staff at Academic Press for their help in its production. Last, but most important, I would like to acknowledge gratefully the role that my husband, Richard Nowell, has had in the study group from its inception. Without his support—both intellectual and personal—the study group would never have become a reality.

I

INTRODUCTION

1

The Development of Deaf Children:
An Overview of Issues

LYNN S. LIBEN

INTRODUCTION

To understand the development of deaf children, it is necessary to consider not only the classic variables of developmental research and intervention (e.g., intelligence, sex, social class, ethnic group), but also the many individual and environmental variables that are uniquely associated with deafness. This chapter provides an introduction to the relevant terms and concepts associated with these variables and provides an overview of the major methodological, social, linguistic, cultural, and educational issues that are discussed extensively in the remaining chapters of this book.

INDIVIDUAL DIFFERENCES IN DEAFNESS

"Deafness" is a term sometimes used to refer to any hearing loss. Using this criterion, about 2 million people in the United States would be classified as deaf. Within this large group, however, there are many

3

DEAF CHILDREN: DEVELOPMENTAL PERSPECTIVES

important subgroups that must be distinguished for planning professional services (e.g., mental health facilities, educational programs) and
research.

Probably the single most important distinction to be made is between
prelingual and postlingual deafness. Children who are congenitally deaf
or who lose their hearing prior to the acquisition of language ("prelingual") are in a very different position vis-à-vis the hearing world than
those who are deafened after the development of spoken language
("postlingual"). In the former case, the language of the majority hearing
culture cannot be acquired naturally in the course of everyday living.
Thus, prelingual deaf children typically have impoverished language
skills and little opportunity to communicate meaningfully with those
around them. In contrast, postlingually deafened people already have
language and communication skills and can use them subsequently in
educational and social contexts. Although the *speech* of the postlingually
deaf person typically deteriorates with the loss of auditory feedback,
language competence is maintained.

A second important distinction concerns the degree of loss. Hearing
loss is typically classified as moderate, severe, or profound. Those with
moderate losses are generally able to function relatively normally in a
hearing environment, while those with severe losses generally cannot.
Details on how hearing is measured, the terminology used to describe
hearing losses, and the behavioral consequences of differing degrees of
loss are discussed by Meadow (Chapter 2 of this volume).

Degree of loss is not the only variable that determines how successfully
the individual uses residual hearing. Success also depends on the pattern
of loss (that is, at what frequencies the losses occur); on the individual's
ability to discriminate, and not simply to hear, sounds within a particular
frequency and intensity range; on motivation; on training, and on similar
factors. In addition, there are individual differences in tolerance for
amplification: Some people find amplification exceedingly painful and
thus cannot use powerful hearing aids even though they would be useful
mechanically.

These variables are important insofar as they determine the extent to
which an individual can participate normally in the educational and
social settings of the hearing community. In the chapters that follow, the
children and adults referred to as "deaf" are generally those who cannot
function normally in such settings, rather than those with any degree of
hearing loss at all. That is, they are people who have profound, prelingual hearing losses that are not eliminated through amplification and are,
therefore, people who require special education, services, and so on. It is
estimated that only about 10% of deaf people, or 200,000 Americans,
meet these stricter criteria of deafness (Meadow, 1975).

Even within the "educationally" deaf population, it is still important to distinguish among the causes of deafness. First, different etiologies are differentially associated with other physical and mental handicaps, which themselves have profound implications for development (e.g., see Vernon, 1968). Second, parents' reactions to their deaf children also vary as a function of etiology. For example, when the etiology of deafness is unknown, parents are more likely to feel guilty about their child's deafness (Meadow, 1968). Deafness caused by rubella may also be associated with particular parental reactions. In an extensive study of rubella children, Chess, Korn, and Fernandez (1971) found that parents are likely to consider rubella children to be more "fragile" than nonrubella children, even when no identifiable handicap is present. This might result in different parental treatment of rubella children that, in turn, may underlie the observation commonly made by educators of deaf children that there is "something different" about rubella children. Third, one etiology—genetic deafness—is more likely to be associated with parental deafness than are other etiologies. Parental hearing status has pervasive effects on the deaf child, some of which are discussed in the next section. Additional discussions of etiologies and historical changes in these etiologies are included in Chapter 2 by Meadow.

In summary, when trying to study the deaf child it is necessary to consider not only those individual differences that are recognized as important for all developmental research but also several variables that are related specifically to deafness. Many researchers—due to insufficient knowledge of such variables—have ignored them, and thus their research is inconclusive. Even when researchers are well informed about these variables, however, it is difficult to control for all of them properly. Some of the obstacles that can be faced when trying to use multiple criteria for selecting deaf subjects are illustrated by Meadow in Chapter 2 of this volume.

FAMILY ENVIRONMENTS

As already noted, children whose deafness is hereditary are more likely than other deaf children to have deaf parents (although it should be noted that because of recessive inheritance patterns, not all genetically deaf children have deaf parents). Contrary to popular belief, however, the combination of a deaf child with deaf parents is rare: Only about 10% of deaf children have deaf parents (Rainer, Altshuler, & Kallmann, 1963). More commonly, then, the deaf child is born into a hearing family that, prior to the discovery of the child's deafness, had little or no knowledge about hearing loss. The hearing status of the deaf child's parents has profound implications for development.

First, insofar as deaf people comprise a subcultural group (Vernon & Makowsky, 1969), deaf children with deaf parents have a shared subculture, whereas deaf children with hearing parents do not. Some of the ramifications of this situation are discussed by Adrienne Harris in Chapter 12 of this volume.

Whether the deaf child's parents are hearing or deaf also affects the availability of appropriate role models. Deaf children with hearing parents often have little or no regular contact with deaf adults, and may think that deaf children either disappear, or somehow outgrow their deafness. Insofar as modeling and identification are important, social and cognitive development may be more difficult for the deaf child with hearing parents than for the deaf child with deaf parents.

The hearing status of parents is also associated with different patterns of parent–child communication. Most deaf children with deaf parents are exposed to some form of manual communication from birth. Consequently, they learn manual language in the same natural way that a hearing child normally acquires spoken language, sharing a common communication system with their parents. In contrast, deaf children with hearing parents typically have only limited communication with their parents, because linguistic communication for these children must wait until oral skills develop through formal instruction in English. In addition to the linguistic and cognitive consequences of these different environments (reviewed in the following sections), there are serious consequences for emotional development. Hilde Schlesinger (Chapter 4 of this volume) discusses the developmental consequences of impoverished parent–child communication, and Robert Harris (Chapter 8 of this volume) considers the effect of parental hearing status on affective development—particularly on the development of impulse control.

LINGUISTIC ENVIRONMENTS

As already noted, most deaf children have hearing parents, who, traditionally, have been discouraged from using manual communication. In a survey conducted in the 1960s, Stuckless and Birch (1966) found that only 11% of hearing parents reported using manual communication with their deaf children. The expectation in these families was that the deaf child would eventually acquire sufficient oral–aural skills through formal education to permit meaningful communication with the hearing world. In some programs, formal speech therapy is begun when the child is 2 or 3 years old, so that at best, the deaf child's language begins to develop later than the hearing child's. Unfortunately, however, the deaf child faces not only a *delay* in the acquisition of oral–aural skills, but faces quantitative and qualitative deficits as well.

First, the speech produced by most deaf people is difficult to understand, particularly by listeners unfamiliar with the speech of deaf people. Problems include abnormal pitch, abnormal intonation patterns, faulty timing, and poor control of intensity (see Nickerson, 1975a, for a thorough review of these and other deficiencies). Similarly, deaf people's comprehension of spoken language also is usually poor. Findings by Lowell (1957–1958, 1959), for example, indicate that even the best speechreaders understand only about one-fourth of what is said even in dyadic conversations. Many of the children tested understood as little as 5% of what was spoken.

The nature of spoken language is largely responsible for people's limited success in extracting information from the visual information in speech. That is, many of the distinctions among sounds are not visually observable. In English, only about 40% of the sounds are visible on the lips. Although some consonant distinctions are observable (for example, the difference between /b/ and /f/ as in "bell" and "fell"), others are not ("bell" and "pell"). Similarly, vowel distinctions are not visible since they are made by changes within the mouth rather than by changes on the lips ("bell," versus "ball"). Consequently, much of speechreading depends on filling in the gaps in available information. In turn, this filling-in process depends on a firm grasp of the vocabulary and syntax of the language being spoken. For the deaf person, this semantic and syntactic knowledge must be derived from impoverished visual information in the first place, thus closing a vicious cycle.

Given the insufficiency of the phonological information normally available to the eye from spoken language, several methods have been designed to provide supplementary information. The most common system for supplementing information about the spoken language is fingerspelling. In fingerspelling, each letter of the alphabet is represented by a distinct hand configuration, so that each English word is spelled out L-E-T-T-E-R--B-Y--L-E-T-T-E-R. Fingerspelling should not be confused with sign languages (discussed later) in which single signs represent whole ideas (analogous to single words rather than to single letters) and in which direct correspondence to English orthography is not necessary. (Some sign systems with close correspondences between signs and English have been developed, also discussed later.)

A second system that has been used to supplement phonological information is "cued speech" (Cornett, 1967). In cued speech, 12 hand positions are used to provide information about phonemic distinctions that are not otherwise visible. For example, when saying the words "bell" and "ball," two different hand configurations (hands placed near the face) would be used to distinguish between the two vowels. The hand positions used in cued speech—unlike those of fingerspelling—are not, by themselves, interpretable as language. Instead, the visual information available in the accompanying speech is also necessary. Given the difficulty in mastering cued speech in both productive and receptive modes, it has never been very popular.

There also have been attempts to add information about the speech signal by the use of electromechanical devices. Such devices are particularly valuable because they potentially allow the deaf person to understand speakers who do not know any of the communication systems designed specifically for use with deaf people.

One approach has been to create devices that transform information in the speech signal to tactual signals. Pickett (1963), for example, developed a device in which 10 vibrators (arranged to stimulate each fingertip) are driven by transformed speech signals, each vibrator corresponding to a different frequency band. Evaluations of the use of this device has shown that, although some distinctions are easier to make through visual cues available on the lips (e.g., /a/ versus /y/), others are easier to make tactually (e.g., /m/ versus /b/), and thus the device does appear to provide useful supplementary information.

A second approach has been to use various kinds of visual displays to provide information about the characteristics of the speech signal. Upton (1968) developed a device to display information on a pair of eyeglasses to be worn by the deaf person. Five miniature lights, embedded in each lens, flash to indicate voiced frication, frication, voicing, stop, and voiced stop. Lights appropriate for the particular speech signal appear to be superimposed on the face of the speaker, so that, for example, when the word "sat" is spoken, three of the lights come on in turn (frication, voicing, stop).

More recently, computer technology has been applied to the problem of providing detailed information about the speech signal. Nickerson and Stevens (1972, 1973) have developed a computer-based system in which information from the speech signal (acquired from a voice microphone and from a miniature accelerometer attached to the throat or nose) is filtered, analyzed, and stored in a computer. Various information about the speech signal (e.g., pitch, loudness, voicing, nasalization, tongue position) may be displayed in real time or may be "frozen" for study on the cathrode ray tube (CRT).

Various instructional games using this speech information have been developed. In one game, the speaker must direct a ball through a hole in a wall shown on the CRT. The ball moves at a constant speed from left to right, with its height determined by the fundamental frequency of the speaker's voice. By changing the size of the ball and the size and position of the hole, the criteria for acceptable voice pitches may be varied. Similar games have been developed to teach other aspects of the speech signal. Evaluations of this training have revealed improvements in the timing of sentences and phrases, in controlling inadvertent jumps in pitch, and in several other specific skills. However, comparable improvements in overall intelligibility of speech have not been found (Nickerson, 1975b).

Thus, various devices have been designed to transduce information from the auditory to the visual mode. Such devices usually have been developed to supplement the reception of speech or to aid formal speech instruction. A related issue is how (or, indeed, if) visual representations of speech may be used in the natural acquisition of language by deaf children, issues discussed by Nickerson in Chapter 7 of this volume.

Reception and production of the spoken word are not the only language skills that are difficult for deaf people. Deaf people also have difficulty reading and writing English. In a study of reading comprehension, Furth (1966a,b) found that by age 11, only 1% of deaf children were functionally literate (reading scores of Grade 4.9 or better), and that even by age 16, only 12% of deaf children reached this level. Penelope Brooks reviews additional findings on deaf children's reading skills and discusses some of the possible explanations of their deficiencies in Chapter 5.

Typically, deaf people also perform poorly in the production of written English. Reviews of the kinds of errors and their prevalence may be found in Meadow (1975) and Myklebust (1960). Particularly interesting is that some of the errors made by deaf people in written English are virtually never made by hearing people of any age (Myklebust, 1960). For example, words are simply omitted, as the copula (is) in "The boy playing." Although not discussed by Myklebust, one possible explanation of many of the errors is that deaf people's writing reflects the structure of sign language. In the phrase quoted above, the sign equivalent for the word "is" probably would be omitted in American Sign Language unless the speaker (signer) were placing particular emphasis on the truth of the phrase. Findings of a study by Odom and Blanton (1970) implicate the role of sign language structure in the deaf student's abilities to process written English. Deaf (mean age: 17) and hearing (mean age: 10 : 6) subjects were given a paragraph comprehension test. One group received an

English version of the test, while a second group received a sign version (interpreters' translations of the English paragraphs). The deaf students were found to perform significantly better on the sign version than on the English version, while the same was not true for the hearing students.

It should be noted that the sign paragraphs in this study were given by English glosses of the sign translations, rather than in some written form of sign language. Stokoe, Casterline, and Croneberg (1965) have developed a notational system to represent the hand shapes, hand positions, and movements of individual signs. This system, however, is highly complex, and although appropriate for linguistic analyses (it is analogous to the International Phonetic Alphabet) it is not appropriate for normal reading and writing. There have been some recent attempts to develop idiographic representations of sign for these purposes, but none has yet progressed beyond the pilot stage. In Chapter 6, George Sperling discusses some of the issues related to designing a written representational system for sign language.

The preceding discussion implies that sign language is an important part of the linguistic environment of most deaf people. The major sign language system used by most deaf adults in the United States is American Sign Language, also known as ASL or Ameslan, differing most obviously from spoken languages by utilizing a visual–gestural mode rather than an oral–aural mode. For many decades, Ameslan was assumed to be either a loose collection of gestures, or an abbreviated form of English produced manually. More recently, however, careful linguistic analyses by William Stokoe of Gallaudet College and by Ursula Bellugi, Edward Klima, and their colleagues at the Salk Institute for Biological Studies have shown that neither of these assumptions is true. Instead, Ameslan is a language in its own right, with the full capacity for expressing both abstract and concrete thoughts and feelings. A discussion of some of the grammatical characteristics of Ameslan and of how these characteristics are particularly suited to the visual–gestual mode are discussed in Chapter 3 by Bellugi and Klima.

Several investigators also have been studying the acquisition of Ameslan by deaf children of deaf parents. In such settings, where Ameslan is the parents' primary language, the children learn Ameslan effortlessly, much the way that hearing children acquire the spoken language of their parents.

Schlesinger (Schlesinger & Meadow, 1972) studied the acquisition of sign language in two children of deaf parents and observed that the development of linguistic constructions paralleled those found in the acquisition of English. For example, children's early signs were holophrasic, with single signs being used to express complex ideas. To illustrate this stage, Schlesinger reports that when one of the children (Ann) was 15 months old, she used the sign SMELL to mean 'I want to go to the bathroom' and 'I am soiled please change me' and 'I want the pretty smelling flower' (Schlesinger & Meadow, 1972, p. 61).

By 19½ months, Ann's recorded vocabulary included 142 signs and 14 letters of the manual alphabet. This compares with the vocabulary of the typical hearing child who has been estimated to have a spoken vocabulary of about 120 words at about the same age (Smith, 1926, cited in Dale, 1972). It is notable that the vocabulary size of deaf and hearing children is not comparable in cases in which deaf children are exposed only to spoken language. The "typical" 5-year-old deaf child with hearing parents has been estimated to have a spoken vocabulary of fewer than 25 words (DiCarlo, 1964), while the "unusual" (i.e., unusually bright) 4- or 5-year-old deaf child has been estimated to have a spoken vocabulary as extensive as 200 words (Hodgson, 1953, cited in Meadow, 1975). Even the larger of these two figures is dramatically smaller than the typical hearing child's spoken vocabulary, which is estimated to exceed 2000 words by age 5 (Smith, 1926, cited in Dale, 1972).

Bellugi and Klima (1972) have also noted similarities between the milestones in the acquisition of Ameslan and of spoken English. They have found that young deaf children initially overgeneralize linguistic rules, later restricting them appropriately. They have also observed that deaf children combine signs to form phrases comparable in length and intent to those produced by hearing children and show many of the same developmental progressions (e.g., comparable increases in the mean length of utterance). Moores and his colleagues (Hoffmeister, Moores, & Best, 1974) have also been following the acquisition of sign in deaf children of deaf parents, and are examining such areas as acquisition of negation, the use of the locative, use of pointing, and question formation.

In addition to Ameslan, there are several other manual language systems commonly used with deaf children. These systems are tied directly to the structure of English, varying in how precisely the two correspond. In the forms with the most precise correspondence (Signing Exact English; Seeing Essential English, referred to as SEE), English word order and other aspects of English grammar (e.g., tense inflections) are translated directly into manual equivalents. In addition, signs are often "initialized" to match the vocabulary distinctions of English. For example, in Ameslan, "way," "road," and "street" are all signed identically, with the two palms facing one another and moving out from the body at about waist level. In SEE, all three would be signed with the same movement and at the same position, but would be distinguished by substituting letters of the manual alphabet ("w," "r," and "s," respectively) for open hands.

In more common forms of manual English (referred to as Signed English or Siglish), signs still follow English word order, but other correspondences are not maintained. For example, prepositions are often omitted, few inflections are added to signs (so that, for example, the difference between "I cry" and "I cried" would be indicated by context rather than by a past tense "ed" marker), initialization is used less extensively, and so on. It is most useful to conceptualize these forms of sign language as points along a continuum from lesser to greater correspondence to English, rather than as separate languages.

Thus, although Ameslan and the various forms of signed English share much of the same sign vocabulary, they do not share the same grammar. For those who learn Ameslan as a native language, learning English may be compared to learning a second language. Given this perspective, Cicourel and Boese (1972) and Charrow and Fletcher (1974) have suggested that English instruction for deaf children should utilize the kinds of techniques that have been developed for teaching English as a second language to other nonnative speakers of English. It should be noted that the use of two languages raises many of the same issues associated with any other bilingual population. Some of these issues are discussed by Adrienne Harris, Chapter 12 of this volume.

Whereas the combination of Ameslan and English may be interpreted as bilingualism, the combination of signed and spoken English is not true bilingualism because both share the same grammar and are simply produced in different modes. Thus it is possible to speak and sign English simultaneously, that is, to produce English in two modes at the same time. (It is not possible to sign Ameslan and speak English simultaneously as their grammars are not identical.) The use of English in two modes—bimodal English—has become increasingly common, both within the classroom and the family. Schlesinger and Meadow (1972), for example, have established a program in which hearing parents are taught signed English to use with their deaf children. Hilde Schlesinger has been studying the acquisition of English by deaf children exposed to bimodal English, and she describes some of her findings in Chapter 4 of this volume.

In contrast to those who espouse bimodal English, some educators of deaf children have suggested that the simultaneous presentation of information in two modes may be dysfunctional because processing in one mode might interfere with processing in the other. Specifically, those who endorse acoupedics, or the unisensory approach, propose that reliance on visual cues detracts from training the impaired auditory mode to function optimally (Pollack, 1964). Those who subscribe to this view, therefore, try to reduce the visual cues (e.g., lip movements) available to the child. Moores, McIntyre, and Weiss (1972), however, have collected data suggesting that the deaf child's comprehension of spoken material improves with the addition of visual information. It might be argued, of course, that this is true only because the child has come to rely upon visual cues, and that had these not been available in the past, the child would perform as well with auditory information alone. Empirical data on these issues are discussed more fully by Moores, Chapter 10 of this volume.

The issue raised earlier—what is the optimal method of communication—is central not only for parent–child communication, but for educational programs as well. The following section briefly reviews how differing positions on communication modes have affected the education of deaf children. In addition, some of the other important variables in the educational experiences of deaf children are identified.

EDUCATIONAL ENVIRONMENTS

Some historical perspective is needed to appreciate the issues affecting current educational programs for deaf children. Historically, language has played an important role in defining "humanity." As language has often been unjustly equated with speech, those without speech have sometimes been considered to be less than fully human. The Justinian legal code (A.D. 530) allowed neither legal rights nor obligations for those who were "deaf and dumb from birth" (Bender, 1960). The deaf person continued to be devoid of legal rights, including the right to inherit property, through the 1500s. This condition apparently provided the impetus for a Spanish nobleman, Pedro Ponce de León, to engage a monk to educate his deaf children. The monk attempted to teach speech to the children by associating objects with the printed word, and then by associating movements of the vocal cords to printed characters (Quigley, 1969).

Education of the deaf children of Spanish noblemen was continued in the early 1600s by Juan Martin Pablo Bonet who introduced a one-handed manual alphabet for fingerspelling words in combination with speech and writing. In the mid-eighteenth century, the gestural system already used by deaf people was expanded and refined by the Abbé de l'Epée to be used in a French public school for deaf children. While l'Epée was developing a manual program in France, Samuel Heinicke was developing an oral program in Germany, emphasizing speech and speech reading, and forbidding manual communication, which he believed would interfere with the development of oral language. A continuing and vehement controversy over this issue grew between Heinicke and l'Epée.

In the United States, the key figure in establishing public education for deaf children was Thomas Hopkins Gallaudet, whose interest had been raised through his work with a neighbor's deaf child. The neighbor, Mason Fitch Cogswell, sent Gallaudet to Europe to study the oral methods being used in England and the manual methods being used in France. However, the founder of the English oral school—Thomas Braidwood—was unreceptive to the proposed visit, and thus Gallaudet studied only the manual methods refined by l'Epée. Not surprisingly, the school Gallaudet established on his return (The American School for the Deaf, in Hartford, Connecticut) utilized manual communication in its program.

Manual communication remained the norm in the United States until 50 years later when the Clarke School in Northampton, Massachusetts was established. Here the oral methods originally developed by Heinicke were used. During the next century, the oral method became increasingly popular, and manual instruction typically was used only with children who did not progress satisfactorily with purely oral methods.

In the 1970s, use of manual communication in the schools has again increased. But, unlike the earlier method of l'Epée, manual communication today is only one part of the "Total Communication" approach in which all possible communication channels are used, so that oral–aural skills are emphasized as well.

The heated debate between Heinicke and l'Epée that began in the 1800s still continues vigorously. Those espousing the "oral only" method have had three major criticisms of using manual communication in the school. First, they suggest that its use will interfere with the child's motivation for developing oral–aural skills, as it is easier for the deaf child to master sign language than spoken language. In a related criticism, the opponents of manual communication suggest that the development of manual skills rather than of oral–aural skills will prevent the child's integration into the dominant hearing community. Third, they suggest that manual languages do not have the capacity for expressing abstract ideas, and that people using manual languages will necessarily be limited to concrete thinking.

Those supporting manual communication argue that empirical evidence refutes all three criticisms. In response to the first, several studies have shown that children who have had early exposure to manual communication do as well, or better, than children who had not had this exposure. Investigators have compared deaf children of deaf parents (i.e., children exposed to manual communication) to deaf children of hearing parents (i.e., those exposed only to spoken English). Children in the former category performed better on tests of educational achievement, reading, and writing (Meadow, 1968; Stuckless & Birch, 1966; Vernon & Koh, 1970). In addition, most studies have shown that deaf children of deaf parents are not inferior even on oral skills, despite the presumably worse oral input from their deaf parents. In speechreading measures, comparable performance by the two groups of children was reported by Meadow (1968), Quigley and Frisina (1961), and Vernon and Koh (1970), and better performance by deaf children with deaf parents was found by Stuckless and Birch (1966). In measures of speech production and intelligibility, comparable performance in the two groups was found by Meadow (1968) and Vernon and Koh (1970), whereas Quigley and Frisina (1961) reported differences favoring those with hearing parents, and Stuckless and Birch (1966) reported differences favoring those with deaf parents.

Although there are many variables other than the use of manual communication that differentiate the two groups of children, the findings reviewed here strongly suggest that manual communication need not hamper later skills, even skills specifically related to spoken language. Related findings and issues are discussed more extensively by Robert Harris, Chapter 8 of this volume.

Additional evidence that the use of early manual communication need not hamper the development of oral skills is derived from the program developed by Schlesinger and Meadow (1972) in which hearing parents use Signed English with their deaf children. Rather than exhibiting increasing reliance on manual communication to the exclusion of speech, the children in this program have shown developmental increases in their use of speech, either alone or combined with Signed English.

To respond to the issue of integration into the hearing community, those who support the use of manual communication argue that even with the traditional emphasis on oral skills, the integration of deaf people into the hearing world has had only limited success. For example, in a Canadian survey, Reich and Reich (1973) found that of the deaf adults interviewed, only 18% reported that most or all their friends were hearing, 27% reported that most or all of their dates had been with hearing people, while none of the men and 31% of the women had hearing spouses. Similarly, Rainer *et al.* (1963) found that of women who were born deaf or who had lost their hearing at an early age, less than 10%

had married hearing men. Descriptions of clubs, parties, and other social interactions (Furth, 1973; Rainer *et al.*, 1963; Reich & Reich, 1973; Vernon, 1969) lead to the conclusion that, although deaf people interact with the hearing community when necessary (at work, in stores, courts, and so on), they tend to look toward the deaf community for their nonobligatory, social interactions.

The third criticism, that manual languages are inherently concrete, has been refuted by recent linguistic work. As Bellugi and Klima discuss in Chapter 3, sign language may be used for expressing abstract thought, poetry, wit, and so on, and is not a linguistically "inferior" language.

Pragmatically, decisions regarding the use of "manual" versus "oral only" approaches should not be divorced from the characteristics of the population being served. In the early 1900s, approximately two-thirds of the students in schools for the deaf had lost their hearing postlingually through ear infections, polio, scarlet fever, and similar causes (Vernon, 1968). Modern medicine has drastically reduced the incidence of such adventitious deafness, and, at the same time, has enabled severely disabled children to survive beyond infancy. Consequently, the percentage of prelingually deaf children has risen to about 95% (Bonvillian, Charrow, & Nelson, 1973), accompanied by an increase in the number of children with additional handicapping conditions.

Prelingually and postlingually deafened children present different educational goals and problems. For postlingually deaf students, educational programs must be planned to help the individual maintain existing skills (e.g., articulation) and to develop new skills (e.g., speechreading). Instruction in language and content areas can utilize and build upon the existing language and speech base. For the prelingually deaf child, educational programs must be designed to establish language itself. For these children it seems particularly appropriate to incorporate sign language into the educational setting, with instruction on skills needed for communication with the hearing world (e.g., speech and speechreading) built upon the linguistic foundation provided by sign language. Education of deaf children would be well served if decisions about the use or omission of manual communication were determined by individual children's needs rather than by general philosophical beliefs and values.

Although the oral–manual controversy has shadowed other aspects of educational programs for the deaf, there are other important variations in educational environments that affect the child's experience profoundly. One of these is whether the child lives at home or at a school residence. Some schools serve only day or residential students. Other schools serve both, encouraging or requiring children living within commuting distance to go home daily, and those living beyond commuting distance to go home on weekends. Day classes for deaf children, held in regular public schools, are also common.

In examining the effects of day versus residential settings, it is important to recognize that the two generally draw somewhat different populations. For example, because schools for the deaf are often located in metropolitan areas, there is a tendency for city children to be day pupils and rural children to be residential students. There also tends to be an overrepresentation of deaf children of deaf parents in residential settings since deaf parents regard residential schools as a center of the deaf subculture and thus show a preference for these schools (Meadow, 1972).

In addition to initial differences between the two populations (see Meadow, 1975 for additional contrasts), the two educational settings provide different kinds of experiences. Institutionalization itself has historically been associated with an attenuation of the range of experiences available to the individual. But it should be noted that there are also positive aspects of institutionalization for deaf children. Children in residential settings are more likely to have contact with deaf adults, as counselors or house parents are often deaf themselves. Moreover, in the dormitory, deaf children are surrounded by other children who share their communicative modes and have had many of the same experiences. In contrast, deaf children who return to their parents' homes typically have few playmates and face a greater degree of isolation in general (Stokoe, 1960). Similar kinds of contrasts occur between deaf children in special programs and those who are "mainstreamed," or integrated, into regular public school classes. Some of the issues and outcomes distinguishing these different educational settings are discussed in Chapter 11 by Liben.

Any discussion of education must include some indication of how well educational goals are being met. Research findings on the educational achievements of deaf students have not been encouraging. Statistics regarding poor reading levels were reviewed earlier. Similar deficiencies have been reported for general educational attainment (Goetzinger & Rousey, 1959; Lane, 1976; Miller, 1958; Vernon, 1969). Unfortunately, these deficits do not appear to be simply developmental lags, since there is evidence that the deaf child's relative deficit grows rather than diminishes with age (Moores, 1970). Similarly, statistics on the percentage of the deaf population attending college (Schein & Bushnag, 1962) and on the percentage of deaf people holding white collar jobs (Lerman, 1976; Rainer et al., 1963) indicate lower achievement in the deaf group relative to the general population (see Vernon, 1969 for a review of relevant research).

In trying to overcome the difficulties of deaf people in achieving high levels of educational success and its correlates (high income, occupational success, etc.) many of the existing environmental deficits must be corrected. In this context, Donald Moores discusses the need for improved communication between educational researchers and practitioners in Chapter 10, while Liben (Chapter 11) suggests how the empirical and theoretical traditions of developmental psychology may be helpful in the conceptualizing and overcoming the experiential deficiencies typically faced by deaf people.

SUMMARY

It is clear from this review that "deaf children" comprise a highly heterogeneous group. Differences in degree of hearing loss, etiologies, family environments, linguistic environments, and educational programs have important effects on developmental outcomes. Moreover—as emphasized by A. Harris in Chapter 12—one cannot divorce the developing deaf child from the broader historical, social, and cultural context. Thus, it is necessary to recognize diversity and change both within the individual and within the society. Only in this way will it be possible to execute meaningful research and to devise programs that optimize developmental outcomes.

REFERENCES

Bellugi, U., & Klima, E. The roots of language in the sign talk of the deaf. *Psychology Today*, 1972, *6*, 61–64, 75–76.

Bender, R. *The conquest of deafness.* Cleveland: Western Reserve University Press, 1960.

Bonvillian, J., Charrow, V., & Nelson, K. Psycholinguistic and educational implications of deafness. *Human Development*, 1973, *16*, 321–345.

Charrow, V., & Fletcher, J. English as the second language of deaf children. *Developmental Psychology*, 1974, *10*, 463–470.

Chess, S., Korn, S., & Fernandez, P. *Psychiatric disorders of children with congenital rubella.* New York: Brunner/Mazel, 1971.

Cicourel, A., & Boese, R. Sign language acquisition and the teaching of deaf children. In C. Cazden, V. John, & D. Hymes (Eds.), *Functions of language in the classroom.* New York: Teacher's College Press, 1972.

Cornett, O. Cued speech. *American Annals of the Deaf*, 1967, *112*, 3–13.

Dale, P. *Language development.* Hinsdale, Illinois: Dryden, 1972.

DiCarlo, L. *The deaf.* Englewood Cliffs, New Jersey: Prentice-Hall, 1964.

Furth, H. A comparison of reading test norms of deaf and hearing children. *American Annals of the Deaf,* 1966, *111,* 461–462. (a)

Furth, H. *Thinking without language: Psychological implications of deafness.* New York: Free Press, 1966. (b)

Furth, H. *Deafness and learning.* Belmont, California: Wadsworth Press, 1973.

Goetzinger, C., & Rousey, C. Educational achievement of deaf children. *American Annals of the Deaf,* 1959, *104,* 221–231.

Hodgson, K. *The deaf and their problems: A study in special education.* London: Watts, 1953.

Hoffmeister, R., Moores, D., & Best, B. *The acquisition of sign language in deaf children of deaf parents: Progress report* (Research Report No. 65). Minneapolis: Research, Development, and Demonstration Center in Education of Handicapped Children, 1974.

Lane, H. Academic achievement. In B. Bolton (Ed.), *Psychology of deafness for rehabilitation counselors.* Baltimore: University Park Press, 1976.

Lerman, A. Vocational development. In B. Bolton (Ed.), *Psychology of deafness for rehabilitation counselors.* Baltimore: University Park Press, 1976.

Lowell, E. *John Tracy Clinic Research Papers* (Vols. III, V, VI, and VII). Los Angeles: John Tracy Clinic, 1957–1958.

Lowell, E. Research in speech reading: Some relationships to language development and implications for the classroom teacher. *Proceedings of the 39th Meeting of the Convention of American Instructors of the Deaf,* 1959, 68–73.

Meadow, K. P. Parental responses to the medical ambiguities of deafness. *Journal of Health and Social Behavior,* 1968, *9,* 299–309.

Meadow, K. P. Sociolinguistics, sign language, and the deaf sub-culture. In T. O'Rourke (Ed.), *Psycholinguistics and total communication: The state of the art.* Washington, D.C.: American Annals of the Deaf, 1972.

Meadow, K. P. The development of deaf children. In M. Hetherington (Ed.), *Review of child development research* (Vol. 5). Chicago: University of Chicago Press, 1975.

Miller, J. Academic achievement. *Volta Review,* 1958, *60,* 302–304.

Moores, D. Psycholinguistics and deafness. *American Annals of the Deaf,* 1970, *115,* 37–48.

Moores, D., McIntyre, C., & Weiss, K. *Evaluation of programs for hearing impaired children* (Research Report No. 39). Minneapolis: Research, Development and Demonstration Center in Education of Handicapped Children, 1972.

Myklebust, H. *The psychology of deafness.* New York: Grune and Stratton, 1960.

Nickerson, R. *Characteristics of the speech of the deaf* (Report No. 3016). Cambridge, Massachusetts: Bolt Beranek and Newman, 1975. (a)

Nickerson, R. *Speech training and speech reception aids for the deaf* (Report No. 2980). Cambridge, Massachusetts: Bolt Beranek and Newman, 1975. (b)

Nickerson, R., & Stevens, K. An experimental computer-based system of speech training aids for the deaf. *Proceedings of the Conference on Speech Communication and Processing, IEEE,* 1972, 237–241.

Nickerson, R., & Stevens, K. Teaching speech to the deaf: Can a computer help? *IEEE Transactions on Audio and Electroacoustics,* 1973, *AU-21,* 445–455.

Odom, P., & Blanton, R. Implicit and explicit grammatical factors and reading achievement in the deaf. *Journal of Reading Behavior,* 1970, *2,* 47–55.

Pickett, J. Tactual communication of speech sounds to the deaf: Comparison with lipreading. *Journal of Speech and Hearing Disorders,* 1963, *28,* 315–330.

Pollack, D. Acoupedics: A unisensory approach to auditory training. *Volta Review,* 1964, *66,* 400–409.

Quigley, S. *The influence of fingerspelling on the development of language, communication, and educational achievement in deaf children.* Urbana: Institute for Research on Exceptional Children, University of Illinois, 1969.

Quigley, S., & Frisina, D. Institutionalization and psychoeducational development of deaf children. *Council for Exceptional Children Research Monograph,* 1961, Series A, No. 3.

Rainer, J., Altshuler, K., & Kallmann, F. *Family and mental health problems in a deaf population.* New York: Columbia University, Department of Medical Genetics, 1963.

Reich, P., & Reich, C. *A follow-up study of the deaf.* Mimeographed report, University of Toronto, 1973.

Schein, J., & Bushnaq, S. Higher education for the deaf in the United States—a retrospective investigation. *American Annals of the Deaf,* 1962, *107, 416–420.*

Schlesinger, H., & Meadow, K. *Sound and sign.* Berkeley: University of California Press, 1972.

Smith, M. An investigation of the development of the sentence and the extent of vocabulary in young children. *University of Iowa Studies in Child Welfare,* 1926, *3,* 5.

Stokoe, W. *Sign language structure: An outline of the visual communication systems of the American deaf.* Buffalo, New York: University of Buffalo, 1960.

Stokoe, W., Casterline, D., & Croneberg, C. *A dictionary of American Sign Language on linguistic principles.* Washington, D.C.: Gallaudet College Press, 1965.

Stuckless, E., & Birch, J. The influence of early manual communication on the linguistic development of deaf children. *American Annals of the Deaf,* 1966, *111,* 452–460, 499–504.

Upton, H. Wearable eyeglass speechreading aid. *American Annals of the Deaf,* 1968, *113,* 222–229.

Vernon, M. Current etiological factors in deafness. *American Annals of the Deaf,* 1968, *113,* 1–12.

Vernon, M. Sociological and psychological factors associated with hearing loss. *Journal of Speech and Hearing Research,* 1969, *12,* 541–563.

Vernon, M., & Koh, S. Early manual communication and deaf children's achievement. *American Annals of the Deaf,* 1970, *115,* 527–536.

Vernon, M., & Makowsky, B. Deafness and minority group dynamics. *The Deaf American,* 1969, *21,* 3–6.

2

The "Natural History" of a Research Project: An Illustration of Methodological Issues in Research with Deaf Children

KATHRYN P. MEADOW

There has been a growing recognition by behavioral scientists that a wide range of developmental issues can be illuminated by the study of deaf children (Meadow, 1975). Unfortunately, much of the information about human development that could be gained from such studies is lost because of inadequate methodology. Important variables are often overlooked in the selection of subjects or in the statistical control of confounding variables, producing misleading conclusions about the data. The general problem lies in the belief that all deaf children are alike. In fact, variations within groups of deaf subjects are often greater than variations between deaf subjects and hearing control groups. Even when one is aware of these variations, the course of research with deaf subjects is often difficult.

In this chapter I intend to illustrate some of the methodological issues related to the selection of deaf children as research subjects by describ-

This project was supported in part by Grant MC-R-060160, awarded by the Office of Maternal and Child Health, Bureau of Community Health Services. Acknowledgement is also made to the Office of Education, Bureau for the Education of the Handicapped (Grant No. OEG-0-74-1441) and to Social and Rehabilitation Service (Grant No. 14-P-55270).

DEAF CHILDREN: DEVELOPMENTAL PERSPECTIVE

ing the "natural history" of a particular research project that was designed to collect longitudinal data on the development of 40 deaf children. It is called a natural history because the process will be described from beginning to end and will include the problems as well as the solutions, the failures as well as the successes. This chapter will reflect the real world of research workers rather than the ideal world of research textbooks.

CRITERIA AND PROCEDURES FOR RECRUITMENT OF SUBJECTS

In the fall of 1967, a research proposal was submitted to an agency of the Department of Health, Education and Welfare outlining a study of the relationship of the young deaf child's social and personal adjustment, communicative competence, and family situation. The proposal included criteria for the selection of 40 children based on (a) parental willingness to participate in observational and interview procedures; (b) degree of hearing loss; (c) parental hearing status; (d) child's physical and mental intactness in ways other than hearing; (e) age; and (f) family minority group status. It was expected that 40 children who fit all of the prescribed characteristics could be recruited from a single preschool program for the hearing impaired, located near the project office. This program is operated by a speech and hearing center in a city of 250,000, and serves a larger metropolitan area of about 1 million people. The first rude awakening regarding the difficulty of recruitment came when it was discovered that only one child from this center met all the specified criteria. Although detailed information was not tallied on the characteristics of the children who did not qualify, many children served by this center were members of racial or ethnic minority groups and were multiply handicapped.

With the recognition of the insufficiency of this source of subjects, an extended search was begun for deaf children who fit the criteria. Finally, 1 year later, the group of 40 children had been completed. By this time, eight different preschool programs had been contacted, had agreed to cooperate, and had furnished names of children. These programs were located as far as 150 miles from the project office, which meant the geographic spread of the participating families was great, even at the outset. The protracted period spent locating subjects, and the necessary time and cost for travel, increased research expenses even before the data collection began.

This "simple" matter of locating subjects illustrates a major problem of research with deaf children: The relatively low incidence of early profound deafness means that there is usually no single, inexpensive, uncomplicated way of locating homogeneous groups. The National Census of the Deaf Population showed that in 1971, only 1 person in 1000 had become deafened before age 3 (Schein & Delk, 1974). This low prevalence of early profound deafness imposes innumerable constraints on designing research with deaf subjects.

As the research subjects were recruited through preschool programs for deaf children, all had received early education. It is difficult to determine how this compares with the population of deaf children generally. We do know that there has been an increasing trend toward early training for handicapped children, partly as a result of efforts by the Bureau for the Education of the Handicapped in the U. S. Office of Education. The National Census of the Deaf noted an increasing proportion of respondents who entered school before age 5 in successively younger age cohorts: About 25% of the respondents between the ages of 25 and 34 in 1972 had entered school before they were 5 years old, whereas only about 4% between the ages of 55 and 65 had done so (Schein & Delk, 1974). A sampling of the total deaf population of New York State showed that 45% entered school before age 6 (Rainer, Altshuler, & Kallmann, 1969). Data from a survey of all deaf children receiving special education in the greater Vancouver area showed that 86% had preschool experience. Of the matched group of hearing children, 77% had attended preschool (Freeman, Malkin, & Hastings, 1975).

Thus, although all our subjects have the special advantage of preschool education, we may assume that they are more similar to future cohorts with respect to education than a randomly selected group would have been. Their early participation in an educational program probably reflects an additional important advantage: We can expect that their parents are more involved in the educational process, have had more orientation to the consequences of deafness, and have had the support that comes from contact with other parents of handicapped children than parents of children who were not enrolled in early education programs.

Parental Willingness to Participate in Research

The willingness of parents to cooperate is a requirement of developmental research too often taken for granted in the many stages of research. Human Subjects Committees, in sponsoring institutions and federal agencies awarding research contracts, have been acting to protect the interests of children and parents from overzealous investigators; informed consent, with careful explanation of procedures, has been required. In addition to safeguarding subjects, it is important for researchers planning a long-term project to explain the entire design before including a family. Especially in the case of a group as small as 40, it is of utmost importance to maintain the integrity of the sample throughout the life of the project.

Much of the important information obtained from these children and their families was available and meaningful primarily because it was collected longitudinally, a process that has particular hazards and difficulties as well as advantages and rewards. The major problem, of course, is maintaining the cooperation and participation of all the subjects. When the group is relatively small, its stability becomes more important and substitutions create further difficulties.

The group of 40 deaf children recruited by our staff was maintained throughout the 5-year period, with one exception. It soon became apparent that one family would not continue to participate, and another child was located who fit into the younger portion of the age continuum. By completing the initial research procedures with this child early in the second year of data collection, and the second procedures late in the second data collection period, we were able to have complete data on 40 children.

The continuing integrity of the research group can be attributed to the optimum combination of three factors:

1. The characteristics of the families who were initially recruited
2. The commitment of the research staff to maintain the original group throughout the project
3. The feeling of trust and friendship that developed between families and staff as the project progressed

Age

Because of the interest in learning about the very earliest experiences of deaf children and their families, we had planned to include children as young as possible, with an age range no greater than 6 months. For several reasons, this goal was not attained: The ages of the children when they were first tested ranged from 2 : 6 to 4 years. Consistently, earlier testing was not possible because deafness often is not diagnosed until the child is 3 years old or more, with hearing loss sometimes confused with other developmental disabilities such as mental retardation (Fellendorf & Harrow, 1970; Meadow, 1968; Schlesinger, 1971). Similarly, the usual age for entering an educational program is 3 years, although the trend is toward preschool education at 18 months or even birth, if the diagnosis is confirmed that early. Thus, our efforts to find very young deaf children were thwarted because of the lateness with which medical diagnosis and educational intervention typically began.

Sex

One of the more stable characteristics of the deaf population has been the overrepresentation of males. The Annual Survey of Hearing Impaired Students for 1970–1971 showed that 54% were male, slightly higher than the general hearing population (Rawlings & Ries, 1973). No attempt was made to control for the sex distribution in our sample, and the obtained distribution reversed the population trend: 23 girls and 17 boys. One possible explanation of our unrepresentative distribution may be the result of excluding multiply handicapped children from our group: The Annual Survey showed that 35% of deaf boys, but 30% of deaf girls have at least one additional handicap (Gentile & McCarthy, 1973).

Age at Onset of Deafness

The age at which a child becomes deaf is a critical research variable because the acquisition and development of language is a major concern of the behavioral scientist. The ability to respond to sound in the early months of life is important to other aspects of human development as well. The human fetus responds to sound even *in utero,* and newborn babies can discriminate speechlike signals on the basis of frequency and intensity (Hetherington & Parke, 1975).

Thus, in selecting research subjects, it is extremely important to know when children lost the ability to respond to sound. Because the medical treatment of diseases often responsible for early childhood deafness has changed over the past few decades, the picture of age at onset has changed as well. Fewer children are deafened in early childhood as a result of measles, whooping cough, pneumonia, mumps, or meningitis. Consequently, there has been a relative increase in the proportion of children who are deafened as a result of maternal rubella or genetic defects. In addition, more children who have birth injuries survive with damage to the central nervous system, including deafness. This complex picture of medical advances, etiology, and age at onset of deafness has produced many changes in the composition of the deaf population. Of deaf children attending school in 1970–1971, 78% were deaf at birth (Rawlings & Ries, 1973). The National Census of the Deaf, in which both adults and children are included, found 41% of the respondents had been born deaf and an additional 13% had been deafened before 1 year of age (Schein & Delk, 1974).

In selecting the children to participate in our research, we set 18 months as the maximum age at onset, hoping to find children with earlier onsets. Of the 40 children in the sample, 34 (85%) were known or suspected to be deaf at birth. The remaining 6 (15%) were evenly divided between those who were deaf by the age of 1 year, and those who were deafened between the ages of 1 year and 16 months.

Etiology of Deafness

The etiology of childhood deafness is important in the selection and description of research subjects because it is related to age at onset, to additional handicaps, and to parental attitudes toward the handicapped child. Rather than controlling for etiology, however, we decided to select subjects by restricting the age at onset and by excluding children with additional diagnosed handicaps. Other researchers have made the decision to exclude children in particular etiological groups, depending on the number of subjects available to them, and the nature of the research.

Table 2.1 shows the etiology of deafness for the 40 children in the project. This table illustrates the difficulties of identifying the causes of deafness: Parents had received a confirmed etiology from their doctors in only 21 of the 40 cases, with speculations available in 13 of the remaining 19 cases.

Because of difficulties in diagnosing and reporting, it is hard to compare the etiologies of our group to the total deaf population. The large proportion of our group deafened because of maternal rubella (45–55%) reflects epidemics of German measles that began to subside not long after our cohort was born. Statistics on etiology of deafness in older groups do not reflect rubella, as it was not causally identified until 1941. Of the adults responding to the National Census of the Deaf in 1972, about one-third did not specify the cause of their deafness, and approximately another third said they had become deaf as a result of illness (Schein & Delk, 1974).

Some causes of deafness may be linked to other possible damage to the central nervous system. This is particularly true for Rh-negative factors that can lead to postnatal trauma and to anoxia at the time of birth.

TABLE 2.1

Etiology of Deafness

Cause of Deafness	Percentage	N
Etiology neither known nor suspected	15.0	6
Hereditary genetic cause suspected	2.5	1
Maternal rubella suspected	10.0	4
Maternal rubella confirmed	45.0	18
Maternal viral infection suspected	5.0	2
Rh negative factor suspected	5.0	2
Birth accident suspected	2.5	1
Ear infection or allergic drug reaction suspected	7.5	3
Meningitis	5.0	2
Pneumonia	2.5	1
Total	100.0	40

Maternal rubella also may be related to other kinds of defects in deaf children. There is widespread belief among professionals who work with deaf children that rubella children are more likely to have emotional–behavioral problems, and that they are more likely to be unmanageable in the classroom because of hyperactivity. Research reports conflict about the truth of this belief (Bindon, 1957; Hicks, 1970; Vernon, 1969). The most intensive study of rubella children as a group indicates that there is no significant relationship between maternal rubella and physiological signs of brain damage (Chess, Korn, & Fernandez, 1971).

Severity of Hearing Loss

Hearing is measured in decibels (dB) or units of sound. An individual's responses to sound, introduced at varying hertz (Hz) and at different tonal frequencies, give a picture of the hearing threshold pattern, or "audiogram." The conventional summary of this audiogram is the *average* hearing threshold in the frequencies where most speech sounds are produced (500, 1000, and 2000 Hz). A person who has a hearing threshold for speech up to 30 dB may have difficulty hearing faint or distant speech. A loss that is described as being from 30 to 45 dB means that conversational speech can probably be understood if the speaker is only a short distance away. Those who have losses up to 80 dB have some useful hearing for speech, and are more likely to approach normal hearing with the help of a hearing aid. Those with average hearing losses of more than 80 dB may hear only loud sounds. (See Silverman, 1966, for further discussion.) It is usual to identify the person with a loss greater than 80 dB in the speech range as profoundly deaf. This was the criterion used in selecting children for our research group.

Figure 2.1 shows a group audiogram for the 40 children in the study. This audiogram plots the mean loss in the right and left ears at each frequency for the 40 subjects. The children as a group are shown to have almost no residual hearing. The average loss in the speech range is approximately 105 dB. Average *aided* loss in the speech range for the group is 50 dB. This is a considerable gain and probably reflects the fact that the children, on the whole, received good audiological services with optimal amplification, and good training of their residual hearing.

While aided response to sound is very meaningful information to describe individual deaf children and a group of research subjects, it was not a meaningful criterion to screen children for participation in our study. The reason is that the difference between aided and unaided thresholds may reflect precisely the conditions that we were attempting to evaluate: The efficacy of the audiological and educational treatment received by the children during the research years. There is evidence that children need training if they are to utilize their hearing aids to best advantage. There are also many different brands and types of aids on the market. Thus, children need individualized attention from a skilled audiologist and from a cooperative hearing-aid dealer if they are to function optimally for their particular levels and types of hearing losses. Parents' attitudes toward hearing loss may also contribute to the chil-

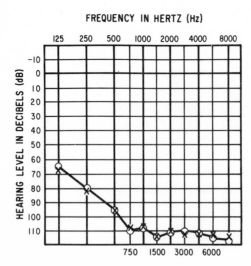

Figure 2.1 Group audiogram: Unaided hearing scores, pure tone (1974). (O) Right ear, (×) left ear.

dren's efforts and eventual ability to use the aid. These factors indicated to us that the unaided, rather than the aided, hearing loss should be the basis for defining the sample.

Figure 2.1 is based on data collected in 1974 as part of the longitudinal study. The audiograms on which the selection of the children was based were done in 1969–1970. In working with the children from 1969 to 1973, we began to feel uneasy because our only audiological information for them had been gathered when they were still very young. At preschool ages, deaf children are difficult to test, and the reliability and validity of the results are often questionable because of the children's variable cooperation. Also, the audiological testing had been completed by many different audiologists in a variety of centers. For these reasons, it was decided to test each of the children in 1974 by the same pediatric audiologist with a test assistant. The assistant was proficient in sign language, and would use it to supplement speech when appropriate.

The correlations of the mean unaided scores collected in 1970 and in 1974 are uniformly low, ranging from .30 to .66, albeit statistically significant. This indicates that for one or a combination of the reasons already suggested, the audiograms collected when the children were ages 2 : 6–4 were different from those collected 4 years later. Whereas the early audiograms were necessarily relied on in selecting the research subjects, the later scores were used to analyse the data.

Handicaps in Addition to Deafness

A sizable number of deaf children have secondary handicaps, usually stemming from the same condition that created the hearing loss. Therefore it is important to consider the existence and the influence of additional handicapping conditions in selecting research subjects.

The Annual Survey of Hearing Impaired Children shows that nearly one-third have at least one additional handicap. These conditions include brain damage (8%); cerebral palsy (7%); heart disorders (6%); perceptual–motor disorders (10%); emotional or behavioral problems (19%); visual defects (16%); and miscellaneous others (9%) (Gentile & McCarthy, 1973). It is apparent that these additional handicapping conditions can create further disabilities for the deaf child in areas related to language, cognition, and socioemotional development. We decided to eliminate from our research group all children who had additional handicaps severe enough to interfere with their development.

Several of the children had mild impairments, however. Two had congenital visual impairments in one eye at the time of recruitment, and two others were found to need glasses later. One of the children with a visual impairment had corrective heart surgery in 1975. One child had a cleft palate repaired in 1974 and one other child was diagnosed as having a "learning disorder." Two of the children had been referred for psychiatric treatment in 1970; a third was referred in 1971. These three were later withdrawn from treatment. However, in 1975, six other children were receiving psychiatric treatment and two others had been recommended for treatment. Thus, the incidence of behavior disorders in 1975 was 20%. The prevalence figure for the entire 5-year period was 27.5%. These figures are quite close to rates reported in other studies (Schlesinger & Meadow, 1972; Freeman, Malkin, & Hastings, 1975). However, it is surprising that such a large proportion of this group were so defined, as it is an advantaged group compared to the children included in other surveys. (See also Schein, 1975.)

Children with "Normal Intellectual Potential"

The research was visualized as a study of normal, not of mentally impaired, deaf children. There were several difficulties in arriving at a definition that could be used for selection purposes, and it was decided to rely on teachers' judgments. If the teacher felt that a child's intelligence was within the normal range—if the child did not seem to be retarded or unusually slow—the child was not excluded from the research group.

As with several of our other selection criteria, it is difficult to differentiate between selection criteria and outcome criteria. If children are selected on the basis of some kind of intelligence test during the initial phase of an investigation and researchers are interested in evaluating cognitive performance at a later stage of the project, selection and outcome become confused. Another problem is that intelligence tests for preschool children are not very reliable, even for children with normal hearing. When the children are deaf, the meaning of any test score is even more questionable.

Intelligence tests administered to the 40 children as part of the research battery in 1970 and 1972 indicated that teachers' judgments were relatively adequate. The mean score on a 1970 administration of portions of the Stanford–Binet, prorated on nonverbal items, was 103.85 (*SD,* 17.39). In 1972, portions of the Wechsler Preschool and Primary Scale of Intelligence and of the Snijders–Oomen were administered.

Mean scores were 106.07 (*SD*, 13.34) on the former, and 105.35 (*SD*, 11.27) on the latter.

Characteristics of Participating Families

Two constraints related to family characteristics were placed on the selection of children. One was that no children of deaf parents should be included in the group, the other that no children from racial, ethnic, or linguistic minorities were to be included.

A number of studies have shown differences in the performance and adjustment of groups of deaf children with deaf and with hearing parents (Meadow, 1969, Schlesinger & Meadow, 1972; Stuckless & Birch, 1966; Vernon & Koh, 1970). Differences have usually favored the children with deaf parents. Two broad reasons for these results have been suggested: First, deaf parents are more likely to use manual communication with their children from infancy onward; and second the response of deaf families to the diagnosis of deafness in their child is likely to be less traumatic. For these reasons, it was decided to eliminate the children of deaf parents from consideration for participation. Moreover, because the children of deaf parents represent no more than 10% of the deaf population, children of hearing parents are more representative. (See Chapter 1 by Liben and Chapter 8 by R. Harris for additional discussion of related issues.)

As a major focus of the research was to be on the family's use of language and style of interaction with the deaf child, it seemed wise to limit participation to a homogeneous group of white, English-speaking families to prevent the confounding influences of cultural differences. Although one child was included whose mother's native language was French, both parents used English in communicating with the deaf child.

SELECTION OF MATCHING OR COMPARISON GROUPS

Depending on the focus of the research, it may or may not be necessary to select a matching or a control group to evaluate the data collected from deaf children. Matching individual children has some advantages in terms of precision. However, this procedure requires a large pool of subjects, and places constraints on the statistical techniques appropriate for analysis of the data. The more usual, and ordinarily more convenient, method of selecting a control group is to obtain a group that meets criteria that will allow comparative evaluation of the eventual results. That is, when test scores or other data from deaf and hearing children are compared, the investigator needs to have some assurance that differences, or lack of differences, are due to factors related to deafness and not to some other social or developmental variation. The larger the number of variables on which experimental and control groups are matched, the greater the assurance that this is true. However, each variable added to the definition for inclusion in the control group increases the cost in terms of time, money, and effort. Again, reality usually dictates a balance between the possible and the desirable.

The decision to recruit a group of hearing children that could be compared with the 40 deaf children was made after the research process had already begun. Initially, the plan had been to compare the linguistic and social development of the deaf children with norms already available and to report family interview data descriptively and qualitatively. However, as the data collection progressed, it appeared that the home observations of family interaction were inadequate. A plan was therefore devised to videotape the deaf children with their mothers in the project office using a semistructured format. This new format necessitated collection of similar data with normal-hearing children and their mothers.

As all the deaf children were receiving preschool education, it was logical to recruit hearing children who were enrolled in nurseries. In addition to ensuring educational comparability, this approach offered a reasonable way to contact families with children of appropriate ages; added to the likelihood of finding families who would be interested in participating in the research; and allowed for group contacts, thus reducing the time and expense of recruitment. Another decision was made in the interest of economy: the size of the hearing sample was set at 20 rather than 40.

Several preschools were contacted and the recruitment process began. Problems appeared again, however, concerning dimensions related to deafness. There is state and federal support for the development of public preschool education for handicapped children. Preschool education for nonhandicapped children is of three general types: (*a*) private, with tuition at parents' expense; (*b*) Headstart, for children who are presumed to be "disadvantaged" in some way; and (*c*) daycare nurseries, predominantly serving children of working mothers. By contacting private nursery schools, we found that we were recruiting children whose mothers and fathers were more likely to be highly educated, upper-middle-class professionals. This could influence styles of childrearing and mother–child interaction, thus introducing a spurious element to our comparisons of the groups of deaf and hearing children. To achieve a better cross section of families in our control group, we therefore shifted our recruitment from private nursery school to publicly sponsored facilities.

Because past research has demonstrated differential family and child-rearing attitudes to boys and to girls, the sex distribution of the group of hearing children was matched to that in the group of deaf children. Similarly, the ages of the hearing children were within the same limits as those of the deaf subjects. Hearing children with known physical or mental handicaps were excluded.

Ten of the original 20 hearing children participated in all three rounds of data collection (1970, 1972, and 1975), a poor record when compared with the 100% participation of the 40 deaf children at each stage of the data collection process. All of the hearing children who did not complete testing were from families who had moved out of the area or who could not be located, rather than from families who simply refused to continue in the project. New hearing children were chosen to replace these geographically mobile hearing children, rather than spending the time and money to visit them in their new homes (as had been done with the mobile deaf children).

OTHER POTENTIAL VARIABLES FOR
THE SELECTION OF SUBJECTS

Other variables that were not important or that could not be taken into account in selecting our group of 40 children may be critical for other investigators. These will be described briefly in the remainder of this chapter.

Linguistic Mode and Ability

Too often, it is assumed that the linguistic abilities of the members of any given group of deaf children will be comparable. This assumption is frequently erroneous and can lead to inaccurate interpretation of research data. A common mistake is to ignore the possibility that deaf children who are almost without spoken English may be quite proficient in American Sign Language. Investigators who select research groups on the basis of the hearing status of parents are attempting to summarize this linguistic and psychological variable by selecting on the basis of a demographic variable. Most deaf parents use sign language with their young deaf children from infancy. If this is the case, we can assume that the children develop sign language in the same manner as hearing children develop spoken English (Schlesinger & Meadow, 1972). However, not every deaf couple uses sign language, and not all those who use it communicate with their young children in this mode (Stuckless & Birch, 1966). There may even be regional variations in proportions of deaf parents who are comfortable with manual communication within the home (Meadow, 1972).

With increasing acceptance of the use of some forms of manual communication with young deaf children, and increasing use of Total Communication[1] by school systems, a new dimension is added to the consideration of the evaluation of the language of deaf research subjects.

The history of the linguistic input of the 40 research children is instructive in terms of the kinds of changes that are occurring in school systems. In 1970, when the children were preschoolers, 5 of the 40 were receiving some combination of signed and spoken language at home and at school. In each case, the decision regarding language input was initiated by the parents and then used by teachers in the classroom. In 1975, 21 of the 40 children were receiving some combination of signed and spoken language. In some cases, parents had instigated the change, but most of the changes represent changes within the school of communication systems, which parents accepted—sometimes reluctantly and sometimes enthusiastically. The formal sign language to which these children are exposed is quite different from the sign language known to deaf children in earlier groups (Bornstein, 1973). The early use of sign language, and its use by teachers rather than by peers only, are also major changes.

One gap in available research tools is the lack of an instrument to measure sign language proficiency. There are a number of tests for reading, arithmetic, and general academic achievement that have been used with deaf children, and several that can be utilized for assessing generalized language abilities. However, there is no screening tool available to the behavioral scientist who might wish to equate groups with proficiency in sign language. With the renewed interest in sign language of the past 5 years, it is likely that this deficiency may soon be remedied.

---

[1] Total Communication (TC) refers to the combined use of all available means of communication, including oral–aural language, some form of sign language, fingerspelling, visual aids, etc. More extensive discussions of TC are found in the chapters by Liben and Moores in this volume.

Type of School Program

There are several different types of school programs available for deaf children, including residential and day programs in public and private schools. In addition to differences in living style, the various types of programs are tied to additional and more subtle differences in philosophy that are critical to the experience of the deaf child. It may, therefore, be important for the researcher to consider this factor when planning to select a research group.

The most obvious difference in the residential and the day school experience is the contrast between dormitory life, with its restrictions and freedoms, and home life, with family attention or lack of concern. In recent years, administrators of residential schools have become more insistent on children returning to their homes for weekends and holidays, regardless of distance.

The two types of school settings also differ demographically. Residential schools for the deaf exist in most states. Generally, these programs admit children after age 5, and allow them to continue until age 21, if desired. These schools typically have several hundred students, drawn from most parts of the state, and emphasize educational services for children whose home school districts have no program appropriate to their needs. Thus, there are fewer students from metropolitan areas and more from rural areas.

For many years, state residential schools have been viewed by the deaf community as representing its subculture, and as the locus of the preservation of American Sign Language. Residential schools have provided employment for deaf adults as dormitory counselors and occasionally as teachers in upper grades. Day programs, on the other hand, have consistently discriminated against deaf teachers at every grade level. This pattern is changing, as residential schools begin to emphasize oral skills and day schools begin to employ deaf teachers and use signed communication.

A major difference between public and private schools lies in the fees charged and, thus, in the income levels of families served. In addition, private schools are free to be selective and to refuse to admit or retain children who do not progress in their programs. Private schools, have, almost without exception, traditionally been devoted to oral-only programs, and staff and students aligned with a somewhat "militant" advocacy of exclusively oral–aural methods of education.

In addition to the contrast between day and residential schools, programs also vary in the extent to which deaf children are 'mainstreamed', or 'integrated', into classrooms with normally hearing children. The increasing trend toward mainstreaming reflects both educational philosophy and administrative economics. For many years, the efforts of parents and educators were devoted to the provision of small classes with high teacher–pupil ratios for children with some kind of handicap. The recognized ratio for deaf education was usually six or eight children to one teacher. There has been a growing feeling that the isolation of deaf children from hearing children is bad in and of itself.

These considerations are critical in selecting and describing groups of deaf children of school age. However, since we were selecting younger children—all of whom were attending preschool—the type of educational program was not a relevant variable. We did, however, use school attendance as an outcome measure. Our 40 deaf subjects were found in a wide variety of programs by 1975: 15 children were attending public day school programs utilizing Total Communication, 11 were integrated, full time, in neighborhood schools; 10 were enrolled in public day programs for deaf children using oral-only communication; 1 was in a private day program for deaf children using oral-only methods; 1 was in a private church-related program, integrated with a full-time sign language interpreter; 1 was a day pupil in a state residential school using Total Communication; and 1 was a dormitory student in a state residential school using Total Communication.

Family Position

The child's position within the family can significantly influence some variables that are likely to interest developmental scientists (Clausen, 1966). Parents' treatment of the child, and their response to the diagnosis of a handicap may be related to the child's ordinal position and/or adoptive status.

In the Vancouver survey, it was found that 12% of deaf children were living with foster parents, whereas none of the hearing control group was a foster child, "due to the matching procedures that were carried out [Freeman *et al.,* 1975, p. 392]." To the best of our knowledge, no one has studied adopted handicapped children and their families. Kirk (1964) has suggested that adoptive parents suffer from "role handicap" because they believe that adoptive parenthood is an inferior status. Parents of handicapped children also experience difficulties perceiving themselves positively (Meadow & Meadow, 1971). Thus, the adoptive status of deaf children would seem to be an important variable for the description of research groups. However, this is information that is difficult to obtain from records, and may not be a practical selection criterion. In our group of 40 children, 5 were adopted. One was adopted because the parents were interested in adding a handicapped child to their family; the other parents learned about the child's deafness after the placement had been made.

Ordinal position within the family is possibly also important to understanding the development of handicapped children. Farber (1960) found that the handicapped child in a family was treated "as if" he were the youngest, regardless of his true ordinal position. Freeman *et al.* (1975) reported that mothers of deaf, only children rated their children's behaviors as much worse than did the mothers of hearing, only children, even though actual ratings of their school behavior did not differ from those of other deaf children. In our own research group, 15 of the 40 children were first-born, and 22 were the last-born. Distribution of ordinal position in the group of hearing children is approximately the same, with 10 first-born and 9 last-born.

Social Characteristics of the Families

The social and economic resources of families are of special importance in considering the development of handicapped children, particularly because these families have extra financial burdens that can become a constant source of concern and frustration. The investment that parents of deaf children make in their children's hearing aids is considerable. Ear molds, batteries, repairs, and audiological examinations all drain the family budget. Thus, the economic aspects of the handicap can become enmeshed in the emotional response and create tension, particularly within families whose financial resources are limited in the first place.

Parents' education can also be an important factor in relation to a handicapped child. A major requirement for parents of handicapped children is that they be able to deal with various professionals who are an important part of their child's life. Often, parents with less formal education feel, or are made to feel, that they are less able to provide the optimum environment and special help for their handicapped child. Thus, level of parental education is an important factor in assessing the total developmental environment of a deaf child.

As the focus of selection for our research group was the preschool child, and because we eliminated children from ethnic and racial minority groups where socioeconomic status is likely to be lower than average, it is not surprising that most of our children are from middle-class homes. This is yet another example of how initial decisions about the recruitment of research subjects have wide-ranging effects, and of the need for caution in generalizing results from a particular study.

SUMMARY AND CONCLUSIONS

Selecting deaf children as subjects for behavioral–developmental research is a complex and difficult task. Deafness is a biological–medical phenomenon that has social–psychological concomitants, all of which interact to create a very complicated picture of interrelated variables. The researcher is often faced with the difficult choice of selecting a random sample that can be viewed as representative of a much larger population, or of selecting a homogeneous group based on rigid and limiting criteria. One basis for determining which path to follow is the number of subjects that can be tested or observed within existing economic or logistic constraints. Another is the size of the pool from which subjects may be drawn, as this may limit the criteria that can be met.

A basic requirement in establishing guidelines for selecting deaf research subjects is broad familiarity with the world of the deaf child. This means that the researcher must have a basic understanding of audiological definitions of hearing loss, know what can and cannot be expected from the use of hearing aids, know both the medical and the psychological implications of various etiologies of deafness and of the age at onset of deafness. The researcher must understand the social and educational dimensions of the world of the deaf child, and the alternatives that exist for that child as an adult. The demands of the research process are great when deaf children are involved, but the rewards for the behavioral scientist are great as well.

REFERENCES

Bindon, D. M. Personality characteristics of rubella deaf children: Implications for teaching of the deaf in general. *American Annals of the Deaf,* 1957, *102,* 264–270.

Bornstein, H. A description of some current sign systems designed to represent English. *American Annals of the Deaf,* 1973, *118,* 454–463.

Chess, S., Korn, S. J., & Fernandez, P. B. *Psychiatric disorders of children with congenital rubella.* New York: Brunner/Mazel, 1971.

Clausen, J. A. Family structure, socialization and personality. In M. Hoffman, & L. Hoffman (Eds.), *Review of child development research* (Vol. 2). New York: Russell Sage Foundation, 1966.

Farber, B. Family organization and crisis: Maintenance of integration in families with a severely mentally retarded child. *Monographs of the Society for Research in Child Development,* 1960, *25*(1) (Serial No. 75).

Fellendorf, G., & Harrow, I. Parent counseling 1961–1968. *Volta Review,* 1970, *72,* 51–57.

Freeman, R. D., Malkin, S. F., & Hastings, J. O. Psychosocial problems of deaf children and their families: A comparative study. *American Annals of the Deaf,* 1975, *120,* 391–405.

Gentile, A., & McCarthy, B. *Additional handicapping conditions among hearing impaired students, United States: 1971–72.* Washington, D.C.: Office of Demographic Studies, Gallaudet College, 1973.

Hetherington, E. M., & Parke, R. D. *Child psychology.* New York: McGraw-Hill, 1975.

Hicks, D. E. Comparison profiles of rubella and non-rubella deaf children. *American Annals of the Deaf,* 1970, *115,* 86–92.

Kirk, H. D. *Shared fate: A theory of adoption and mental health.* New York: Free Press, 1964.

Meadow, K. P. Early manual communication in relation to the deaf child's intellectual, social, and communicative functioning. *American Annals of the Deaf,* 1968, *113,* 29–41.

Meadow, K. P. Parental responses to the medical ambiguities of deafness. *Journal of Health and Social Behavior,* 1969, *9,* 299–309.

Meadow, K. P. Sociolinguistics, sign language and the deaf sub-culture. In T. J. O'Rourke (Ed.), *Psycholinguistics and total communication: The state of the art.* Washington, D.C.: American Annals of the Deaf, 1972.

Meadow, K. P. The development of deaf children. In E. M. Hetherington (Ed.), *Review of child development research* (Vol. 5). Chicago: University of Chicago Press, 1975.

Meadow, K. P., & Meadow, L. Changing role perceptions for parents of handicapped children. *Exceptional Children,* 1971, *38,* 21–27.

Rainer, J. D., Altshuler, K. Z., & Kallmann, F. J. (Eds.), *Family and mental health problems in a deaf population* (2nd ed.). Springfield, Illinois: Thomas, 1969.

Rawlings, B., & Ries, P. W. *Characteristics of hearing impaired students by hearing status, United States: 1970–71.* Washington, D.C.: Office of Demographic Studies, Gallaudet College, 1973.

Schein, J. D. Deaf students with other disabilities. *American Annals of the Deaf,* 1975, *120,* 92–99.

Schein, J. D., & Delk, M. T., Jr. *The deaf population of the United States.* Silver Spring, Maryland: National Association of the Deaf, 1974.

Schlesinger, H. S. Prevention, diagnosis, and habilitation of deafness: A critical look. In D. Hicks (Ed.), *Medical aspects of deafness,* Atlantic City, New Jersey: Council of Organizations Serving the Deaf, 1971.

Schlesinger, H. S., & Meadow, K. P. *Sound and sign: Childhood deafness and mental health.* Berkeley: University of California Press, 1972.

Silverman, S. R. Rehabilitation for irreversible deafness. *Journal of the American Medical Association,* 1966, *196,* 843–846.

Stuckless, E. R., & Birch, J. W. The influence of early manual communication on the linguistic development of deaf children. *American Annals of the Deaf,* 1966, *111,* 452–460, 499–504.

Vernon, M. *Multiply handicapped deaf children: Medical, educational, and psychological considerations.* Washington, D.C.: Council for Exceptional Children, 1969.

Vernon, M., & Koh, S. D. Early manual communication and deaf children's achievement. *American Annals of the Deaf,* 1970, *115,* 527–536.

II

LINGUISTIC ISSUES

3

Structural Properties of American Sign Language[1]

URSULA BELLUGI
EDWARD S. KLIMA

What is American Sign Language? What is the form of the visual–gestural communication used by the deaf? It might seem, at first glance, that the basic units, that is, the signs of the language used by the deaf in America, differ uniquely and holistically from each other. It has been said, presumably by those lacking close acquaintance with American Sign Language, that the language *is* just such a loose collection of gestures—gestures that have no systematic internal structure and that are strung together without hierarchical syntactic organization. We claim that this is *not* the case—that what may have begun at one time as a loose collection of pantomimes or gestures, has become, over time and generations, a *language,* with a considerable degree of the systematicity and hierarchical organization we have come to expect of human languages. The question becomes even more intriguing when sign language is viewed as a language that has arisen apart from the mainstream of human evolutionary

[1] This research was supported by National Institutes of Health Grant No. NS09811, and National Science Foundation Grant No. BNS 76-12866 to The Salk Institute for Biological Studies. Portions of this chapter appear in J. Kavanagh and J. Cutting (Eds.), *The role of speech in language.* Cambridge: MIT Press, 1975. Illustrations for this chapter by Frank A. Paul.

development. After all, there can be little doubt that modern man is well designed for learning, processing, and using spoken language analyzed by the ear. However, when we examine the special situation in which hearing is blocked from birth and in which a primary language composed of articulated gestures is learned by eye, we may be able to isolate the special effects of the particular transmission system.

In this chapter we will describe some of our research related to such questions. Our basic concern is with the structure and acquisition of a language in another mode, specifically, the visual–gestural language used by the deaf. We are attempting to determine, on the one hand, the degree to which the "linguistic" function puts its distinctive stamp on the form of expression regardless of the particular mode of communication, and on the other hand, the extent to which differences in the mode "predispose" essential differences in the form of expression. Our studies are concerned with

1. How signs of American Sign Language (ASL) differ from "nonlinguistic" pantomimic gestures and from words in spoken language
2. The degree to which the formational aspects of ASL constitute a tightly constrained system
3. The nature of this system from the point of view of its internal structure
4. The nature of the grammatical processes (if any) that modulate the meaning of signs

We have been engaged in these studies for only a few years now, and it must be clearly understood that studies of the structure and organization of sign languages are very much in their infancy. This chapter will attempt to draw together some initial thoughts on the organization of ASL, and should be considered exploratory research. We will touch on results of controlled experiments and observational data. Our working group has included Susan Fischer, Scott Liddell, Patricia Siple, Robbin Battison, Nancy Frishberg, Don Newkirk, Carlene Canady Pedersen, Ted Supalla, Bonnie Gough, and Shanny Mow.[2] Thus far, the research has been a collaboration among linguists, psychologists, and articulate deaf people.[3]

[2] A book, *The signs of language*, Edward S. Klima and Ursula Bellugi, Harvard University Press, is now in press. This discusses and includes research by several members of the group.

[3] We are grateful to the more than 100 deaf people and hearing people of deaf parents who have worked with us in aspects of the research on sign language. In particular, we should like to thank Bernard Bragg, Dorothy Miles, Jane Wilk, Henry Chen, Lou Fant, Lawrence Fleischer, Elizabeth Lay, David McKee, and Steve Turner, and the many students at Gallaudet College and California State University at Northridge who participated in our studies.

BASIC ISSUES IN THE STUDY OF SIGN LANGUAGE

Earlier Studies of Sign Language

Serious linguistic interest in sign languages is relatively recent, starting from the original work in the 1960s of William Stokoe—in *Sign Language Structure* (1960) and the *Dictionary of American Sign Language* (1965), published with Casterline and Croneberg. The *Dictionary* was the first attempt to make a phonemic-like analysis of ASL; that is, to catalogue signs according to some of the gestural characteristics that differentiate one sign from another. Recently, I. M. Schlesinger and his colleagues in Israel have developed a notation system, based on dance notation, that corresponds more closely to a "phonetic" description (Cohen, Namir & Schlesinger, 1977).

There has been considerable research in the past on memory and cognitive functions in the deaf with respect to written English (e.g., Furth, 1971), but almost none, until recently, with respect to the system of communication used among the deaf themselves. To our knowledge, with few exceptions, there had been little linguistic or psychological research on the properties of the communication system that develops in the absence of hearing and in a visual–gestural mode.[4] The original objective in our research was to understand better the human capacity for language through research into the child's acquisition of a language in a different mode and to compare this process with the acquisition of spoken language. To pursue the investigation of the language learning process, it is of course, necessary to understand the structure of what is being learned: the target language. While studies in first-language acquisition of English abound, these studies rest upon an extremely sophisticated knowledge of the structure of English and of speech perception and production.

Faced with a form of communication in a different mode, we were confronted with a new and essentially different set of problems. Not only was there very little research on the language (with the exception of Stokoe's work), there was considerable question about whether this form of communication had the status of a "language" in the sense that English, for example, is a "language." We decided to limit the scope of our inquiry, wherever possible, to the acquisition of sign language as a natural language; that is, as acquired by deaf children of deaf parents. We located three local deaf families with young deaf children, and have nearly completed collecting longitudinal data consisting of monthly vid-

---

[4] At the time this chapter was originally written, little research on visual–gestural systems was available. In the past few years, the linguistic investigation of sign language has been undertaken in several laboratories and has now generated a substantial body of research.

eotapes of these children with their parents, in our studio and in their homes. We also have embarked on an intensive investigation of the grammatical aspects of sign language. During our investigations, we discovered fertile areas of exploration regarding other facets of the language and its use.

Sign Language in America

A few words are in order about the subjects of our experiments and about the varieties of sign languages. The 1971 census reported about 1,700,000 profoundly deaf people in the United States, including people who have become deaf later in life. The number of deaf people who have been deaf either from birth or since the first 3 years of life is far smaller (closer to 200,000) and of these "prelingually" deaf, most were born to hearing parents. Less than 10% of deaf children are born to deaf parents, and in our studies, we work primarily with this small group of deaf people who have learned to communicate by gesture from their parents as a natural language (see Chapter 1 of this volume).

As with spoken languages, there are different sign languages just as there are different spoken languages—differing from one another most obviously in the form of the signs they use. British Sign Language, for example, is quite unrelated to ASL. Within the American deaf, there are several varieties of gestural communication currently used. As discussed elsewhere in this volume (see Chapter 1 by Liben and Chapter 10 by Moores), there are various methods of rendering English on the hands often used in educational settings; (a) by fingerspelling each letter of the words of English sentences; (b) by one of a number of sign systems developed in an effort to approximate English word order, morphology, and syntax; or (c) by speaking English and signing simultaneously. Our studies, however, are of ASL rather than of a gestural form of English. American Sign Language is the communication form typically used by prelingually deaf people among themselves, by deaf families, and is a language totally different from English.

Because there is very little general knowledge about ASL, we find that there are frequent misunderstandings about its status:

1. American Sign Language is not a derivative or degenerate form of written or spoken English. It has a lexicon that does not correspond to English, but must be considered a different language. The grammatical principles governing the modification of meaning of signs are different, in form and content, from the grammatical processes in English and in spoken languages in general.

2. American Sign Language is in no way limited to "concrete ideas." It is a full-fledged language with the possibility for expression at any level of abstraction. There is vocabulary dealing with religion, politics, ethics, history, and other realms of mental abstraction and fantasy (see Klima, 1975; Bellugi & Newkirk, in press).
3. American Sign Language is not a universal form of pantomime. For example, as noted, it differs from British Sign, and, for all but the most rudimentary purposes, the two sign languages are mutually incomprehensible.

The General Linguistic Approach

When we consider the full range of possible speech sounds across spoken languages, it becomes clear that each language constrains itself to a small subset of this staggering variety. Each selects those sounds that will count as the same in that language; each further selects, from the various physically possible sequences of these sounds, the particular combinations that will be permitted to occur in sequence in the structure of its words. All languages do not select the same sounds. Moreover, the sounds that an individual language selects as its language sounds need not coincide with sounds that are used within the same culture for non-linguistic vocal communication. (Speakers of English, for example, use sounds in such interjections as "phew!" and "tsk! tsk!" etc. which, although they count as language sounds in certain languages, do not count as language sounds in English.)

Modern linguistics has done more than catalogue the sounds that individual languages select to form their words; it has shown that in an individual language there will be regularly recurring relationships between the particular sounds chosen; rather than a helter-skelter, arbitrary selection from the possible speech sounds, there tends to be symmetry in each particular system. Modern linguistics has also argued that there are certain universal constraints that hold across languages—constraints whereby the existence, in one language, of a given type of sound implies the existence of another type of sound in the same language. At every level we find a system—and a highly constrained one at that.

Modern linguistics has also shown the complexity of the coding between the *continuum,* which is the acoustic signal, and the discrete phonetic *segments* we perceive when we hear the signal but to which no individual isolable segments of the acoustic signal need correspond. A stretch of acoustic signal often simultaneously contains information about more than one segment. This parallel transmission of information is, according to Liberman (1970), the most basic formal resemblance between speech and the higher levels of language.

One central notion within recent linguistic theorizing, at least along generative–transformational lines, is that in the description of a particular spoken language the domain of the phonological rules is not restricted to the finite set of morphemes of that language, but includes also those strings of sounds that are phonologically regular in the language but happen not to have a meaning. Thus, within a system, there are stretches of sound that actually *are* morphemes, and stretches of sound that *might be* morphemes were it not for certain accidents of history. In current American English, [brik] ('brick') is an actual word, whereas [bik] is a possible word, but not an actual one, an accidental gap in the system. In contrast, [bnik], with its initial [bn-], is extrasystemic (impossible in the English system), although this sequence is permissible, and occurs, in other languages. It is assumed that a native speaker of English has appropriate linguistic intuitions along these lines. The rules formulated by the linguist are, according to this view, not just a tidy way of cataloguing the "facts"; rather they are supposed to represent what the speaker–hearer has internalized regarding the structure of his language.

There is no reason, a priori, to assume that these characteristics of spoken language should also appear in a primary language based on gestures. In fact, sign languages differ in at least one obvious respect from spoken languages: The individual signs in sign languages are not analyzable as linear sequences of segments (see Klima, 1975). Still open, however, is the question of whether there is a system in the form of signs and, if so, what is the nature of this system.

Before we consider the evidence with respect to the internal structure of ASL signs, let us compare pantomime and signs.

ON PANTOMIME AND SIGNS

There are aspects of "deaf communication" that we believe present real problems when one attempts to analyze the signs of sign language. In particular, when deaf people communicate with one another in colloquial or everyday narrative style, the signing is often interspersed with elements of pantomime. The amount of such pantomime varies with the individual and the situation, but it far exceeds that generally found in communication by hearing speakers of standard American English. What is significant is that in deaf communication the sign-symbolic (i.e., the "linguistic") and the pantomimic are in the same mode. In fact, the signs themselves occasionally may undergo clearly mimetic modification.

From the perspective of signers, however, there seems to be a perceived difference between the extremes of what is clearly signing and what is clearly pantomiming. (We are currently attempting to develop criteria for differentiating the less clear area between the extremes.) In a preliminary study we asked 12 people to convey in pantomime objects and actions for which there are common English words and corresponding ASL signs. One of the words was "egg." Most people did a pantomime something like the following:

1.   They gestured picking up a small oval-shaped object.
2.   They hit it on the edge of an imaginary surface.
3.   They gently gestured breaking it open and emptying the contents.
4.   They gave the impression of having a part of the shell in either hand.
5.   Most feigned putting the two parts in one hand and throwing them away (Figure 3.1a).

Let us consider now what happens in making the sign EGG in ASL. The sign EGG is clearly related to a part of the pantomimed act: breaking the shell and emptying its contents. The sign EGG in ASL is shown in Figure 3.1b.[5]

Correctly made, EGG in ASL requires a particular handshape *and that handshape only*. We have seen mothers correct their children, if they signed it with the hands in other shapes, as shown in Figure 3.1c. The handshape used in signing EGG in ASL is also used in signing NAME, TRAIN, CHAIR, SHORT, and in many other signs that differ from the sign EGG in movement and orientation (see Figure 3.1d).

When a nonsigner sees the sign EGG and is given its meaning, the relationship between the sign and a part of the pantomimed version we have described is certainly not entirely opaque. The critical issue, how-

---

[5] We use a special notation in this chapter. Words in capital letters represent English translation equivalents (glosses) of ASL signs, as in NAME. The gloss is chosen on the basis of common usage among deaf informants in giving an English translation for the sign. The gloss represents the meaning of the basic unmarked and unmodulated form of a sign. In this chapter, some gestures are pictorially represented.

In discussing our experiments in short-term memory, the spoken word is represented as "name." The written form of a response to an item in the memory experiment is represented as *name*. The concept which the sign or word represents is indicated as 'name'.

Glosses joined by ⌢ indicate compound signs in ASL; for example, BLUE⌢SPOT is a compound. When a sign is followed by a bracketed superscript [+], this indicates that the sign is made with some change in form associated with a change in meaning from its basic, unmodulated form. Superscript symbols thus indicate grammatical changes on signs. NAME[+] indicates that the sign referred to is not made in its root (uninflected) form, but does not specify precisely what change the sign has undergone.

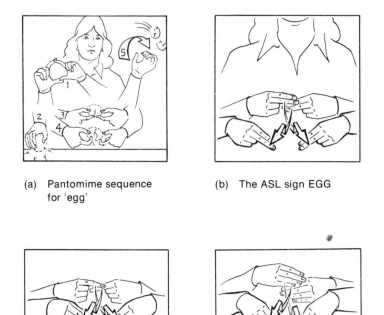

(a) Pantomime sequence   (b) The ASL sign EGG
    for 'egg'

(c) Mispronunciations of the ASL sign EGG

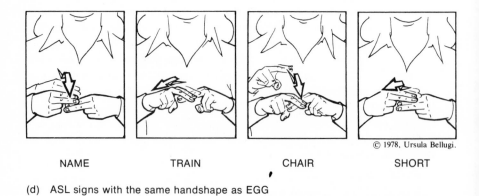

© 1978, Ursula Bellugi.

NAME   TRAIN   CHAIR   SHORT

(d) ASL signs with the same handshape as EGG

Figure 3.1 Distinctions between pantomime and ASL sign.

ever, is the relationship of this sign to other ASL signs for a deaf native signer. That there is a recognizably adequate way to form the sign and that there are conditions of well-formedness in sign are already indicated by the mother's correction of the child's "mispronunciations." Certainly there are individual differences, differences between children's and adults' formations of the sign (because of the development of the hands), and differences from one rendition to the next in the same signer. Yet, it seems that certain elements must remain constant if the gesture is to count as a recognizable rendition of *that* sign. In fact, if the handshape is otherwise the same, but with the two fingers spread, this would constitute a mispronunciation for an American signer. We have tried this, and native signers either look puzzled, or nod encouragingly and make the sign correctly, or openly show us our "error." And if, instead of making the motion as shown in Figure 3.1b, we stop at the point of contact of the two hands, the sign would be understood, not as EGG, but as NAME.

In contrast, there are no conditions of well-formedness in the pantomimed versions. The only restriction on the hands for Steps 1 through 4 of the pantomime in Figure 3.1a seem to be that the hand be shaped *as if* holding an egg. With each person, in each version, and in each step, the hands could and did vary in configuration. Each person 'held' the imaginary egg and cracked it in a different way; the only constant was the imagined shape of the egg.

We have asked some deaf people to communicate very complex information in pantomime, without using signs. The complexity of the information that can be successfully expressed seems to be limited primarily by the ingenuity and imagination of the individual. A language-like system is obviously not necessary for communicating some kinds of cognitive information. (We are disregarding relative economy of means of communication.) Although there may be some conventional gestures in pantomime, there is no sense in which the gestures of pantomime overall are limited or restricted in form, or composed of a much smaller set of recurring shared features. With pantomime, the issue of well-formedness does not arise, only the issue of effectiveness. (See also Bellugi & Klima, 1976.)

HISTORICAL CHANGE IN AMERICAN SIGN LANGUAGE

It seems plausible to us that at least certain aspects of what is now ASL originated from some form of pantomime or iconic representation. The language has, by now, lost a great deal of its transparency. Some aspects

of the process by which this occurs can be traced by investigating historical change.

There is evidence that some ASL signs have changed during the last
50 years. We have been fortunate enough to see films, courtesy of the
Gallaudet Archives Library (Gallaudet College, Washington, D.C.),
made in 1913 of some elderly and very eloquent signers. With these as a
starting point, we have noted the changes in the formation of some signs.
As another source, we have located a book describing signs that was
published around the same date (Long, 1918). We also located some
elderly deaf couples who are a rich source of information on change in
formation of signs over time.

In the few examples we have already considered, the change is often
from what seems more "iconic" toward somewhat more "systematic"
aspects of the language. For example, in one 1913 film, the sign BODY
was made by moving both hands parallel from the shoulders down to the
hips. The current sign is made with the flat hands in the same orientation
but, instead of outlining the contours of the body from the shoulders to
the hips, the sign is made with a touch at the chest, a slight movement
away and downward, and another touch above the waist. There are
many signs which involve two contacts in an area, such as HOME, YES-
TERDAY, WE, QUEEN, BACHELOR, etc. It seems possible that the
older sign has become modified so that it is more like other ASL signs in
movement.

Another example is the sign SWEETHEART, which, according to our

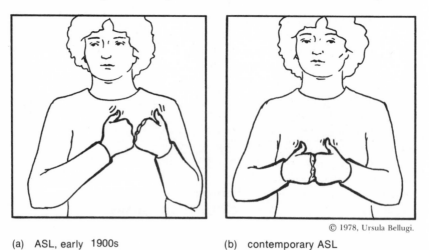

© 1978, Ursula Bellugi.

(a)   ASL, early 1900s   (b)   contemporary ASL

Figure 3.2 Historical change in ASL sign SWEETHEART.

elderly informants, was made over the region of the heart, touching the body, with the two hands together at the edge of the little fingers (Figure 3.2a). The sign is now made without touching the body, centered, with the two hands in contact in the same orientation as several other ASL signs (see Figure 3.2b).

To investigate further what may be systematic pressures in ASL, we are conducting more intensive studies of such historical changes in signs. We note that the direction of change is often toward some recurring element or aspect that occurs in existing signs of the language. That is, we begin to see that there are recurring shared aspects of signs to which new and old signs come to conform. (See Frishberg, 1975, 1976, for other examples of historical change.)

ON THE INTERNAL STRUCTURE OF SIGNS: EVIDENCE FROM THE EXPERIMENTAL STUDY OF SHORT-TERM MEMORY

Studies of short-term memory have been useful in determining whether various aspects of language have psychological reality for the language-user. Studies in which printed letters are presented visually to hearing subjects show that the intrusion errors that are made typically are auditorily—rather than visually—confusable with the target letters (e.g., Conrad, 1962). For example, when the printed letter "C" is given as a stimulus, errors are generally not the visually similar closed "O," but rather the phonologically similar voiced "Z."

We have completed several studies of short-term memory in deaf subjects to discover what parameters of sign have psychological reality for the signer. In the study of immediate memory, described below, we asked deaf subjects whose native language is ASL to remember lists of signs (presented on videotape by a native signer) and asked hearing subjects whose native language is English to remember lists of spoken English words (presented on audiotape). All responses required immediate ordered recall. Among the questions asked in this study was whether deaf subjects' intrusion errors would reflect formational properties of signs, thus paralleling hearing subjects' intrusion errors that were expected to reflect phonological properties of spoken words.

Procedure

For this experiment there were eight deaf subjects (students at Gallaudet College) who had deaf parents and had learned sign language as a primary natural language, and eight hearing subjects (students at the University of California, San Diego) who had no knowledge of sign language. For the deaf subjects, the lists were presented on videotape. Lists containing three to seven ASL signs, were presented on videotape by a native signer at the rate of one sign a second. The signs were given in the equivalent of "list intonation", without facial expression. Although rather unnatural for ASL, as facial expression is usually concurrent with signing, the absence of facial expression allowed us to study the processing of ASL signs without other confounding factors. Hearing subjects were given lists of the same length, order, and rate, except that the items were spoken word–equivalents of the signs presented on audiotape. Recall was immediate, ordered, and written. Thus, the deaf subjects responded by writing down what is for them the English translation-equivalent of the sign, while the hearing subjects responded by writing the alphabetic representation of the spoken word. In other words, an extra step— giving the translation-equivalent in English for the signs—was required for the deaf subjects. The details and results of this experiment have been presented elsewhere (Bellugi, Klima, & Siple, 1975). Here we shall be concerned only with the intrusion errors made by the deaf subjects.

Intrusion Errors

We have said that intrusion errors are often used to investigate the nature of encoding in short-term memory with hearing subjects. Similarly, the intrusion errors in short-term memory for signs by deaf native signers will give clues to the nature of processing in sign. In this study, an intrusion error was defined as any incorrect response at any particular serial position, excluding repetitions or intrusions from a previous list.

Data from this study showed that in no case did the same item elicit an identical intrusion error from deaf and hearing subjects. This finding was consistent with an earlier study (Bellugi & Siple, 1974) in which intrusion errors made by deaf subjects had little or no overlap with the intrusion errors made by hearing subjects. Moreover, in the earlier study we had compared deaf subjects' responses in ASL signs with their responses in translations into written English words. Very significantly, we found that the intrusion errors made by deaf subjects when responding in *signs* had considerable overlap with the errors made by deaf subjects responding in written English translation–equivalents of signs. These results suggest that deaf subjects use the same strategies for encoding and remembering signs regardless of whether the required response is in ASL signs or is in a different language (English) and a different mode (writing). Overall, results from both studies indicate that deaf subjects use different strategies for encoding than do hearing subjects.

Let us consider some specific examples of intrusion errors for hearing and for deaf subjects in this experiment. For a word "horse" presented to a hearing person, the intrusion error *house* was given in the written response. For the ASL gesture that would be translated as HORSE, the intrusion error was the written response *uncle*. There is similarity in phonological form between the spoken words "horse" and "house": they differ only in the medial segments. Similarly, there is a close relationship in form between the signs glossed as the English words HORSE and UNCLE: that is, the signs are highly similar visually. In another example, the written response *tree* was given by more than one hearing subject as an intrusion error for the word "tea." The written translation *tree* was given as an intrusion error by more than one deaf subject for the sign which they named NOON. In both cases, the errors bear a resemblance to the original item; "tree" and "tea" are auditorily similar and the signs TREE and NOON are visually similar (Figure 3.3). As we began analyzing the data we were struck by several cases in which there was clearly a relationship of visual similarity between the ASL sign presented on the test and the sign represented by the translation-equivalent that deaf subjects wrote as an intrusion error response.

SIGN ON TEST   INTRUSION ERROR

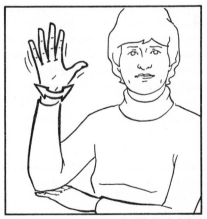

NOON   TREE

Figure 3.3 NOON and TREE are visually similar.

Deaf subjects seemed *not* to be using a phonological form of the spoken word as a basis for remembering signs. If they had, we would expect some overlap between the errors made by hearing and by deaf subjects. But what kinds of codes could they be using? There are many other possibilities: a visual code based on the printed or written form of English word responses; a semantic code based on the *meaning* of the gestures; or a visual code based on the *form* of the original signs, on specific formational parameters. It was the frequency of the latter type of errors that impressed us.

Ratings of Visual and Auditory Similarity

We wanted to measure the degree to which the errors made by deaf subjects were *visually* based (i.e., the signed translation–equivalent of the written word response was visually similar to the original sign presented), compared with auditorily based intrusion errors made by hearing subjects. We paired original items and the intrusion errors made by hearing and by deaf subjects, presented them once signed for ratings on visual similarity and again spoken for ratings on auditory similarity.

We selected all the intrusion errors which were made more than once to a single stimulus item. There were 26 of these multiple errors for the deaf, and 8 for the hearing subjects with auditory presentation. In order to have lists of equal length, from the deaf and hearing subjects, 18 additional errors were randomly selected from those made once by hearing subjects. The printed form of the item–intrusion pairs made by both the deaf and the hearing subjects were combined into one list and randomized. These 52 pairs were again prepared in the two different modes: on audiotape in spoken form by a hearing person, and in signs of ASL on videotape by a native signer.

Ten hearing subjects with no knowledge of sign language were asked to rate the 52 pairs of signs for visual similarity. The raters were not told the source of the pairs nor the meaning of the signs. A scale of 1 to 5 was used with a 1 rating meaning "highly similar" and a 5 rating meaning "highly dissimilar." Ten other hearing subjects were asked to rate the set of items from the audiotape presentation in terms of acoustic similarity with the same scale. For the pairs derived from the hearing subjects, the mean rating for auditory similarity (spoken words) was 2.58, and for visual similarity (signs) it was 4.19; for the pairs derived from the deaf subjects, the auditory similarity (spoken words) was 4.20 and the visual similarity (signs) was 2.64.

Findings on mean ratings suggest that the errors made by deaf subjects are visually similar to the original item presented to the same degree that the errors made by the hearing subjects were auditorily similar to the original item presented. Not only was there no overlap in terms of actual intrusion responses made by the deaf and by the hearing, but there is also evidence of fundamental differences in the nature of the errors made by hearing and deaf subjects. The intrusion errors made by the deaf subjects to ASL signs are demonstrably signs that are visually similar to the sign presented.

Intrusion Errors and Linguistic Shared Parameters

Again, hearing subjects' intrusion errors to spoken words were, as in previous experiments, words that resembled the original word presented. Thus hearing subjects wrote *coat* for "coke," differing only in the final segment; *bother* for "father," differing only in the initial segment, or *cover* for "color," differing only in a medial segment. These findings imply that storage and retrieval are based on sequential phonological segmentation of words.

When we examined the intrusion errors made by deaf subjects to signs, we found a totally different pattern of responses. We have established that the signs represented by the written word response are *visually similar* to the signs originally presented. Now let us define more precisely the nature of the visual similarity. We shall see that it may be based on an internal analysis of signs into simultaneously occurring parameters. Let us consider some typical examples of signs–and–error pairs, presented in Figure 3.4.

For the sign HOME, a common intrusion error was *yesterday*. The two signs have many similarities: HOME and YESTERDAY are both made on the cheek with one hand, and with a movement involving a touch near the mouth, movement away, and another touch on the upper cheek (what we have called "two-touch" signs). The two signs *differ only in hand configuration,* one using a tapered /O/ hand, and the other a closed hand with thumb and little finger extended, a /Y/ hand (Figure 3.4a). For the sign BIRD, a multiple intrusion error was *print*. The signs BIRD and PRINT both have the same handshape and orientation, and the same closing movement. They *differ only in place of articulation:* BIRD is made on the mouth and PRINT is made on the palm of the hand (Figure 3.4b). For the sign SOCKS on the test, more than one deaf subject responded *star*. The signs SOCKS and STAR are both made with two hands in the same configuration, in the space in front of the body, and with a brushing motion backward and forward along the side of the

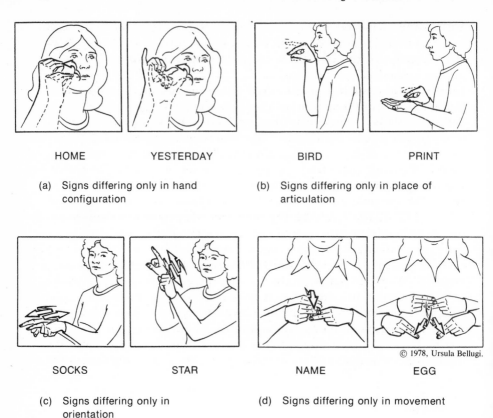

HOME	YESTERDAY	BIRD	PRINT

(a) Signs differing only in hand configuration

(b) Signs differing only in place of articulation

© 1978, Ursula Bellugi.

SOCKS	STAR	NAME	EGG

(c) Signs differing only in orientation

(d) Signs differing only in movement

Figure 3.4 Sign-and-error pairs from immediate memory task.

index fingers. The two signs *differ only in the orientation of the hands* (Figure 3.4c). Finally, for the sign NAME presented on the test, more than one deaf person wrote *egg.* The signs NAME and EGG have the same hand-shape and the same orientation, and both are made with two hands, in the same place of articulation. Both signs, in fact, *differ only in movement* (Figure 3.4d). These examples give us a clearer notion of the dimensions along which signs are stored in short-term memory.

We note that in each case the intrusion error was similar to the original sign presented in some formational aspects, but was not the same. We have discussed several aspects of signs, which we have called parameters: (*a*) the Configuration of the Hands in making the sign; (*b*) the Place of Articulation of the sign, which may be a contact with the body, contact with another hand, or the space in front of the body; (c) the Movement involved in making the sign, and (d) the Orientation of the hands. With the exception of the last, these are the aspects of signs presented by Stokoe in the *Dictionary of American Sign Language* (see Friedman, 1977, for further discussion of orientation). The results of the experiments we have described are consistent with the hypothesis that deaf subjects code and store signs in immediate memory not as holistic gestures, but in terms of formational parameters. Note that these are *simultaneously occurring aspects* of a sign, and not sequentially occurring segments as in speech. For each parameter, we could list a set of elements or *primes*. Among the hand configurations used in ASL, for example, are the closed fist, the pointing index hand, /V/ hand, etc. Among the places of articulation are the forehead, the nose, the chin, the wrist, etc. Among the movement types are opening of the fingers, movement away from the signer, circling movement, contact, and so forth.

How strong is the evidence for the nature of the storage in short-term memory? We have completed three experiments in short-term memory for signs. Examining the ordered responses, we can list the intrusion errors which occurred more than once within each test. From this listing, for each experiment, more than two-thirds of the sign–error pairs differed in one parameter only. Thus, most of the sign–error pairs are highly similar formationally and form minimally contrasting sign pairs.

Summary

The general question that interested us in these studies was how signs are coded in memory. Our findings indicate that there is no reason to suppose that signs—in contrast to spoken words—are processed more in terms of meaning, because of their "representational character," or as "unitary wholes without internal analysis." Evidence against holistic processing is found in the types of errors deaf subjects made in ordered recall of lists of signs (in particular, the intrusion errors made by more than one subject). Our results support a model of short-term memory in which signs are coded in terms of primes of the major formational parameters including hand configuration, place of articulation, movement, and orientation. The task of the subject in remembering a list of signs and their order of presentation would involve, according to this model, the storage and recall of the particular primes of the major parameters. The simplest error, according to this model, would be to recall an inappropriate prime for a single major parameter.

SLIPS OF THE HAND

As another source of information on the organization of signs, we have
made a collection of signing errors that are equivalent to slips of the
tongue. We have gathered more than 100 such "slips of the hand," all
made by deaf people in sign language, and most of them on videotape.
This work is reported in Newkirk, Klima, Pederson and Bellugi (in
press).

What units of organization are affected by slips of the hand? Occasionally entire signs are switched. More frequently, a prime of one sign in an
utterance is erroneously realized in another sign: Hand configurations of
two signs may be switched; the movement of one sign may persevere and
replace movement of a latter sign, or the location of a sign may be
anticipated. This is striking evidence for the independence and reality of
the parameters of ASL.

We have found that sometimes the error results in something that is an
actual ASL sign, although it was not the one intended by the signer. For
example, one person intended to sign CAN'T SLEEP. Instead of using
the correct hand configuration of the sign CAN'T, she anticipated the
hand configuration of the sign SLEEP, resulting in what looks like the
ASL sign THAN instead of CAN'T.

More commonly, however, slips of the hand result in gestures that are
not actual ASL signs but that seem to be "possible" ASL signs. That is, the
slip represents a lexical gap in ASL. Similarly, Fromkin (1971, 1973) has
shown that slips of the tongue generally result in actual or possible sound
sequences of spoken language.

In intending to sign DEAF WOMAN, a deaf person made an anticipatory slip. She used the handshape for WOMAN with the movement and
place of articulation of DEAF, resulting in a gesture that is not a citation
form sign of ASL. The resulting slip is not, but could be, an ASL sign
(see Figure 3.5a). That is, there are many signs with that particular
handshape, as in TREE, FATHER, and DEER. There are many two-
touch signs, as in HOME, FLOWER, BODY, and BACHELOR. And
there are many signs using the cheek as a place of articulation, such as
GIRL, TOMORROW, APPLE, and TELEPHONE. Thus, the slip that
was made is not an ASL sign, but has recurring shared elements with
ASL signs, and in that sense counts as a possible sign in ASL.

Most frequently, it is the handshape of two signs that is switched,
although we have found instances of errors involving movement only
and of slips involving place of articulation only. A slip of the hand in
which movement persevered is shown in Figure 3.5b. A deaf person
intended to sign PLEASE HELP. PLEASE is signed with a circular mo-

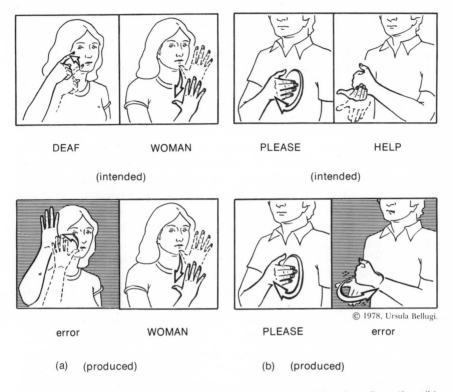

DEAF   WOMAN   PLEASE   HELP

(intended)   (intended)

© 1978, Ursula Bellugi.

error   WOMAN   PLEASE   error

(a)   (produced)   (b)   (produced)

Figure 3.5 Slips of the hand in signing: (a) anticipation of hand configuration; (b) perseveration of movement.

tion and that motion persevered to the sign HELP. Thus, we can identify and locate "possible" signs in ASL with reference to a limited set of recurring shared elements of the language, giving us further evidence for some kind of underlying system to the formation of ASL signs.

GRAMMATICAL PROCESSES

But the internal structure of basic units reflects only one aspect of a language-like system. Language is characterized by complex internal organization at several levels, as sound segments are arranged in sequences to form morphemes, morphemes are arranged in sequences to build up words, and words are arranged in sequences to build phrases and sentences. When we began our studies of the special nature of a visual–gestural system, there was no evidence that ASL had grammatical devices of any sort.

Contrary to this view, however, we have found a variety of mechanisms whereby American Sign Language elaborates and modulates its signs. Two of these devices will be examined here (*a*) processes of compounding, which form new lexical units from existing signs; and (*b*) a variety of inflectional devices, which modulate the meaning of lexical units.

Compounding

There are numerous ways in which the lexicon òf ASL is expanded from within. One such device makes use of two lexical items joined together as a compound to create a new lexical unit. For example, the sign unit commonly used for 'streaker' is a composite of the signs NUDE and ZOOM-OFF, an appropriate way of designating one who dashes away nude. A sign for 'genetic engineering' which was coined recently is a combination of the sign HEREDITY and a modulated sign for CHANGE. Other recent ad hoc inventions include PREVENT CAVITY for 'fluoride' and HOT SWIRL for 'Jacuzzi'.

There are numerous lexicalized compounds within ASL. We have collected hundreds of such instances that should be listed in a dictionary of the language. For example, TIME SAME meaning 'simultaneous', GOOD ENOUGH means 'just barely adequate', TIME BLINK meaning alarm clocks for the deaf which blink instead of buzz, WRONG HAPPEN meaning 'unexpectedly' or 'accidentally', and THRILL INFORM meaning 'news' or 'entertainment'.

Such composites not only have the specialized idiomatic meaning characteristic of compounds in general, they also function within sentences of ASL in the same way that single lexical units do. Moreover, there are regular clues to their identification in the signing stream. If we contrast the same two signs as a phrase and as a compound, the distinction becomes clear. The signs BLUE and SPOT can form a phrase meaning 'a spot that is painted blue'. As a compound sign, BLUE SPOT means 'a bruise'. The sign BLUE is ordinarily made with a back and forth repeated movement of the wrist, which appears in the phrase; in the compound, the movement of BLUE is reduced to a brief half-turn of the wrist. The compound is distinguished from the phrase by rhythmic differences: an overall temporal compression, and in particular a temporal reduction and weakening of the sign in the first position of the compound. (Processes of compounding are further described in Klima & Bellugi, Chapter 9, in press.)

In addition to such lexicalized compounds, there are syntactically-based compounding processes available within ASL. One such productive process of compounding combines a noun object with a modulated verb form. The signs MEASURE and SOIL can form a phrase in which MEASURE refers to a single event, as in "I will measure that soil for you tomorrow." As part of a compound, SOIL⌢MEASURE, the sign no longer refers to a single event but rather to an ongoing activity of measuring, as in the occupation meaning 'surveying' or 'the general activity of measuring soil'. The sign form MEASURE as a single event is made with the tips of the thumb contacting several times as in Figure 3.6a. Under the syntactically based compounding process, the sign form MEASURE[+] must be modulated, that is, made with the thumb tips in continued contact with the hands alternately moving up and down, meaning the activity of measuring (Figure 3.6b).

By a similar process, the signs COUNT and MONEY can form a compound MONEY⌢COUNT[+] meaning 'auditing'; the signs BURN and BODY can form a compound BODY⌢BURN[+] meaning 'cremating'. In each case, there is an order reversal, the verbs (COUNT[+], BURN[+]) have undergone a change in form that specifies the meaning of ongoing activity, and the sign in first position is temporally reduced.

Compounding is thus a way of creating new names from existing lexical roots, combining them into a special meaning. Note that the compound then can take on its own natural extensions, so that the component signs need not retain the meaning they have as single signs. Thus the signed phrase BLUE SPOT means a spot that is blue in color, but the

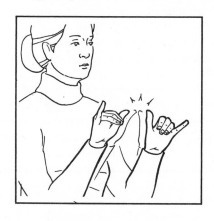

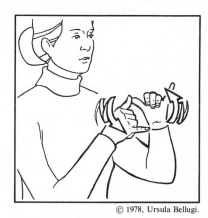

© 1978, Ursula Bellugi.

(a) MEASURE   (b) MEASURE (derived form)

Figure 3.6 The uninflected sign MEASURE (a) and its form under a derivational process (b). The derived form means 'the general activity of measuring'.

compound sign BLUE⌢SPOT, which means 'bruise', may refer to a bruise that is purplish, or even yellowish in color, and is in no way restricted to bruises that are blue. The compound TIME⌢BLINK was coined for the clocks used by deaf people which emit flashes of light rather than sound, but it is also used for any alarm clock, whatever its method of signaling. Thus compounding operates as a grammatical process, submerging the iconicity of signs.

Clearly this marks ASL as a language separate from English, for the instances of compounds in the two languages—as well as the meanings they express—are distinct. Moreover, the process of compounding has different realizations in English and in ASL: in English the phrase *a dark room*, a room which is poorly lit, is distinguished from the compound *a darkroom*, a room for developing photographs, by a difference in stress. In the compound, there is heavy stress on the first element. In contrast, compounds in ASL exhibit a reduction and weakening of the first element. Such indications suggest that English and ASL are separate languages with distinct grammatical patterning.

Inflectional Devices

That ASL is a separate language is brought out more clearly when we consider how ASL and English inflect their lexical items and what meanings are expressed by inflectional processes. Languages differ widely in the degree to which they employ inflectional processes, as well as in the meanings expressed by those processes. In languages like Chinese, the individual lexical items are more or less immutable. English shows some variation of its lexical items for such distinctions as progressive aspect, as in "he walks" and "he is walking"; tense, as in "walk" and "walked," and number as in "boy" and "boys." But English has relatively few inflectional devices compared with languages like Latin or Greek. American Sign Language, we are discovering, has regular ways of varying its words to reflect a wide variety of distinctions. Verbs in ASL, for example, are varied to distinguish number (singular, dual, multiple); distinctions of distributional aspect (action distributed with respect to each, certain ones, any one); distinctions of temporal aspect ('regularly', 'characteristically', 'for a long time', 'from time to time', 'incessantly'); distinctions of temporal focus ('starting to', 'progressively', 'resulting in'); distinctions of manner ('with ease', 'uncontrollably', 'readily'), as well as distinctions for indexic reference. Each inflectional process has a distinct overall form that it imposes on classes of signs. For example, the inflectional device whereby signs referring to transitory states change to refer to permanent characteristics or dispositions (e.g., 'wrong' to 'error-prone'; 'quiet' to 'reserved by nature') and actions into characteristics (e.g., 'command' to 'bossy'; 'give' to 'generous') is made in the following way: The sign is doubled (that is, made with two hands), the inflectional movement imposed is a smooth circular repetition, and the hands alternate as they move. Thus, the general meaning of 'prone to _____' or 'tends to _____' is added to signs by making them with two hands alternating in repeated smooth circular movements. Figure 3.7 shows the signs WRONG, DIRTY, and QUIET in the uninflected forms and after modulation for characteristic aspect. This is only one instance of the kind of patterning used in inflectional devices in ASL.

This is not just an optional expressive change in the sign; it is a required inflectional process in linguistic contexts that call for a characteristic state or disposition. We have discovered numerous linguistic contexts in which uninflected signs may not be used and in which a particular inflected form is required. For example, the sentences "BOY REGULARLY _____" or "SEE[+] BOY TEND͡ HIS ALL-HIS-LIFE _____" may be completed with signs such as SICK, CARELESS, INSULT. But in so doing, the signs added may not appear in uninflected form. The sentence "BOY TEND͡ HIS ALL-HIS-LIFE CARELESS (uninflected)" is considered awkward, poor ASL, that is, ungrammatical, but the sentence "BOY TEND͡ HIS ALL-HIS-LIFE CARELESS (two hands alternating in smooth circular movements)" is considered correct in ASL. In the linguistic contexts we have specified, deaf native signers complete the sentences with signs which have automatically undergone inflectional processes.

Clearly such inflectional processes (inflection for characteristic aspect and the others that we have studied) are not derived from English but are endemic to ASL. In their form they are radically different from the devices used to represent English, such as the signlike markers used as affixes which are added to signs (-ING, -ED). The inflectional devices that have developed within ASL use spatial dimensions and modulations of movement, as well as patterning with the hands.

From our recent studies it appears that ASL employs a wide variety of regular inflectional devices, varying its words in regular ways to reflect many different distinctions. Thus, American Sign Language may turn out, unlike English but like Latin, to be an inflecting language, with inflection as a favored form of patterning. A single sign form GIVE can be varied to mean 'giving different things at different times to unspecified recipients' or 'give to each member of a group regularly'. The form of the inflectional devices used appears to be entirely different from the form of devices used in spoken languages: making patterned

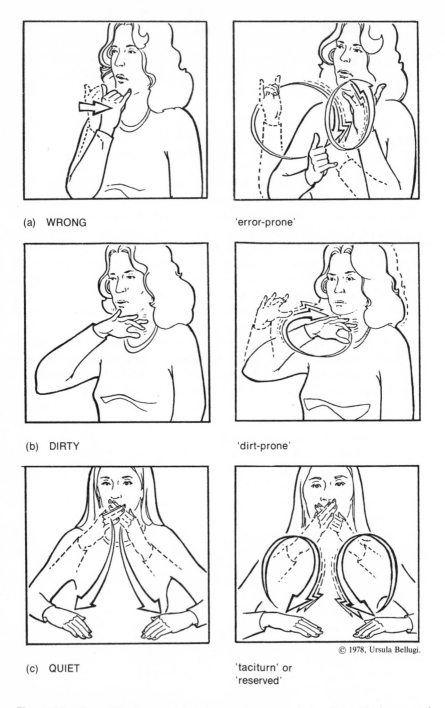

(a) WRONG   'error-prone'

(b) DIRTY   'dirt-prone'

© 1978, Ursula Bellugi.

(c) QUIET   'taciturn' or
'reserved'

Figure 3.7 Three ASL signs and their form under a modulation that adds the general meaning of 'prone to be' or 'tends to be' to the sign.

use of the hands and different contours of movement in space. These and other grammatical devices are described in more detail in Klima and Bellugi (in press, Chapters 11 and 12).

SUMMARY

We have been concerned with new avenues of inquiry regarding visual symbols in general, and the sign language of the deaf in particular. We have focused on the internal nature of the signs of American Sign Language and their behavior under grammatical processes such as compounding and inflection. Data on historical change in signs and from experimental and behavioral observations suggest that ASL signs are not simply signals that differ uniquely and holistically from one another, but rather suggest that signs are composed of and are decomposable into recurring shared sublexical elements. These elements appear concurrently in a unit of time in constituting the sign.

Furthermore such signs regularly undergo a variety of grammatical processes—regular ways by which the lexicon is expanded and the meaning of its units is modulated. Whereas compounding involves concatenation of lexical units, signs are inflected not by adding signlike affixes, but by manipulating dimensions of the visual–spatial mode—changing the contour of movement, the rate, the tension, manipulating the two hands in alternating movement, and so forth.

Thus, despite the transparent relation of sign language to pantomime—nonlinguistic forms of communication—in ASL we find a great deal of restructuring. The particular form that this restructuring has taken seems to be largely dependent on the modality: from the ear to the eye and from the vocal apparatus to the hands. It does seem that our research presents evidence that grammatical processes indeed bear the marks of the particular transmission system in which the language developed.

REFERENCES

Bellugi, U., & Newkirk, D. Formal devices for creating new signs in ASL. In W. Stokoe (Ed.), *Proceedings of the National Symposium on Sign Language Research and Teaching*, Chicago, in press.

Bellugi, U., & Klima, E. S. Two faces of sign: Iconic and abstract. In S. Harnad (Ed.), *The origins and evolution of language and speech*. New York: New York Academy of Sciences, 1976, *280*, 514–538.

Bellugi, U., Klima, E., & Siple, P. Remembering in signs. *Cognition,* 1975, *3,* 93–125.

Bellugi, U., & Siple, P. Remembering with and without words. In F. Bresson (Ed.), *Current problems in psycholinguistics.* Paris: Centre National de la Recherche Scientifique, 1974.

Cohen, E., Namir, L., & Schlesinger, I. M. *A new dictionary of sign language.* The Hague: Mouton, 1977.

Conrad, R. An association between memory errors and errors due to acoustic masking of speech. *Nature,* 1962, *193,* 1314–1315.

Friedman, L. Formational properties of American Sign Language. In L. Friedman (Ed.), *On the other hand.* New York: Academic Press, 1977.

Frishberg, N. Arbitrariness and iconicity: Historical change in American Sign Language. *Language,* 1975, *51,* 696–719.

Frishberg, N. *Some aspects of historical change in American Sign Language.* Unpublished doctoral dissertation, University of California, San Diego, 1976.

Fromkin, V. A. The non-anomalous nature of anomalous utterances. *Language,* 1971, *47,* 27–52.

Fromkin, V. A. Slips of the tongue. *Scientific American,* 1973, *229,* 109–117.

Furth, H. G. Linguistic deficiency and thinking: Research with deaf subjects, 1964–69. *Psychological Bulletin,* 1971, *76,* 58–72.

Gallaudet Archives Library, Gallaudet College, Washington D.C. 1913 films made by the National Association of the Deaf.

Klima, E. S. Sound and its absence in the linguistic symbol. In J. Kavanagh & H. Cutting (Eds.), *The role of speech in language.* Cambridge, Massachusetts: M.I.T. Press, 1975.

Klima, E., & Bellugi, U. *The signs of language.* Cambridge, Massachusetts: Harvard University Press, in press.

Liberman, A. M. The grammars of speech and language. *Cognitive Psychology,* 1970, *1,* 301–323.

Long, J. S. *The Sign Language: A manual of signs.* Washington, D.C.: Gallaudet College Press, 1918.

Newkirk, D., Klima, E. S., Pedersen, C. C. & Bellugi, U. Linguistic evidence from slips of the hand. In V. Fromkin (Ed.), *Slips of the tongue and hand,* Proceedings of the 12th International Congress of Linguists, Vienna, in press.

Stokoe, W. C. *Sign language structure.* Buffalo: University of Buffalo, 1960.

Stokoe, W. C., Casterline, D., & Croneberg, C. *A dictionary of American Sign Language on linguistic principles.* Washington, D.C.: Gallaudet College Press, 1965.

4

The Acquisition of Signed and Spoken Language[1,2]

HILDE S. SCHLESINGER

Deaf children occupy a unique place in research on cognitive and linguistic development. Deaf youngsters, although not totally deprived of sound (as is frequently assumed), perceive it in such a diminished or distorted form as to make spoken language immensely difficult to encode, to process, and therefore to reproduce. Although school starts early for deaf children and the elements of spoken language are drilled unceasingly, many deaf youngsters do not acquire even the rudiments of their maternal language—spoken English—and even larger numbers never acquire the finer modulations of spoken language. Educational achievement studies indicate that there is a 3- to 4-year language gap; the average deaf person reads at a fifth-grade level or below; only 12% achieve linguistic competence; and a mere 4% are proficient speech readers or speakers (see chapters by Liben, Brooks, Nickerson, and Moores, this volume). In summary, most deaf children born to hearing

[1] An earlier version of this chapter was published in I. M. Schlessinger & L. Namir (Eds.), *Sign language of the deaf.* New York: Academic Press, 1978.

[2] An expanded version of this chapter will appear in K. Meadow & H. Schlesinger, *Deaf children in the first decade of life,* University of California Press. The longer version further describes the first sign utterance, the growth of sign vocabulary, and gives additional examples of word–sign order. Support from Maternal and Child Health and Crippled Children's Services, Department of Health, Education and Welfare, and from the Powrie V. Doctor Chair of Deaf Studies at Gallaudet College, as well as editorial assistance from Paula Mathieson, are gratefully acknowledged.

parents do not become proficient in the phonology, semantics, or syntax of English.

Most deaf adults do, however, acquire mastery of language. But it is a language in the visual–motor mode rather than in the auditory–vocal mode of spoken language. Others before us have demonstrated that American Sign Language (Ameslan), the sign system used by most deaf American adults, is a language with its own morphology, semantics, and syntax (Bellugi & Klima, Chapter 3 of this volume; Stokoe, Casterline, & Croneberg, 1965). Although adults usually use Ameslan, most deaf children do not learn it at an early, propitious age, nor, as already mentioned, do they learn their maternal (spoken) language successfully.

TRADITIONAL TRANSMISSION OF AMESLAN:
DEAF CHILDREN OF DEAF PARENTS

Although most deaf children do not acquire Ameslan as a native language, there is a group of deaf youngsters for whom traditional transmission of maternal language is possible. This group is the 10% of deaf children who have deaf parents. In these families, children are exposed to sign language early and, thus, they are able to acquire it effortlessly. In our work with deaf children and adults, we have noted— as have other investigators—that deaf children of deaf parents perform better than deaf children of hearing parents, both academically and psychologically (Brill, 1960, 1970; Meadow, 1968, 1969; Quigley & Frisina, 1961; Vernon & Koh, 1970). One reason postulated for this superiority is that deaf parents have a greater acceptance of deafness, a greater and more realistic expectation of a deaf individual, and consequently a greater acceptance of the children as they are. A second reason postulated is the early use of sign language between parent and child. We have been involved in research investigating these issues.

Our initial interest in the communication patterns of deaf youngsters and their parents was primarily psychiatric in focus. Having noted repeatedly that "normal" deaf youngsters in our longitudinal study (Schlesinger & Meadow, 1972), as well as our young psychiatric patients and their parents, were beset with linguistic retardation and "disturbed communication," we were curious if early, reciprocal, meaningful, and joyful communication between parents and their deaf youngsters could alleviate linguistic retardation and provide more access to successful communication in terms of feedback, appropriateness, efficiency, and flexibility (Ruesch, 1957). Also having noted that deaf children of deaf parents do approximate successful communication more frequently, we wanted to know if a pioneer group of hearing parents and their deaf youngsters could give us further clues to early linguistic events and their influence on cognitive, affective, and linguistic development. Thus, we have examined the development of deaf children in families in which hearing parents have learned and used both manual and spoken representations of English, that is, bimodal English (Schlesinger & Meadow, 1972). This chapter focuses on aspects of language acquisition in deaf children who have been reared in such families.

CONNIE'S CHILDREN[3]

The pioneer parents in our linguistic study differ in hearing status and educational level; they live in bustling cities, on army posts, and on isolated ranches. They are all young and intelligent and appear to place deafness in a realistic perspective, not needing the rose-colored glasses of denial, nor the dark-colored glasses of despair. They are all vitally interested in the traditional transmission of their culture to their children. Transmission of culture invariably entails transmission of language. As most of our parents are hearing, the vehicle of expressing the maternal language is spoken English. However, they were all willing to learn a new language modality in order to enhance the development of their children. We had postulated from the inception of our studies that bimodal imput would favor accelerated language acquisition and the production of speech. Early in our work we provided an operational definition of optimal input which stated: "Sign language is generally considered helpful in the development of deaf children when it is used with positive affect, without conflict, is accompanied by speech and auditory training and is used early before a feeling of communicative impotence occurs between mother and child [Schlesinger & Meadow, 1972, p. 216]."

THE PROCESS OF LEARNING BIMODAL LANGUAGE

As we shall see more fully later, perceptual salience plays a role in the acquisition of formal linguistic markers. In terms of the more or less bimodal language acquisition of our deaf infants, we must consider both

[3] Most groups of children studied for their language acquisition have been identified by the city of their respective studies. Our children live in many cities, but many of them have had some contact with Connie Yannacone, one of the pioneer teachers of bimodal, or total communication. Her skill and sensitivity have contributed greatly to the ability of parents and children to use bimodal language competently and joyfully.

the auditory and visual perceptual systems. The input language must be accessible to the infant perceptually, environmentally, psychologically, and for a sufficiently long time to become encoded. The encoded symbols must be reproducible by the infant. There must be some feedback mechanism, and the expressive language of the infant must be met with some minimal acceptance. These factors are summarized in Table 4.1. Thus, in order to optimize language acquisition we attempted to influence perceptual, environmental, and psychological factors to increase the accessibility of the auditory and visual linguistic building blocks.

Acoustically, we tried to use optimal, modern auditory techniques. Visually, we attempted to provide the parents with a system of communication that they could use comfortably and competently. This was not easily done; the parents had to choose among innumerable proponents of innumerable sign language systems. Was it to be Ameslan or one of the new sign systems? (See Chapters 1 and 11 by Liben and Chapter 10 by Moores, this volume, for discussion of these systems.) Most of the

TABLE 4.1

Effect of Deafness on the Accessibility, Processing Mechanism, and Reproduction of Bimodal Language

Accessibility (Input)	Processing	Reproduction (output)
Accessibility of *acoustic* signals	Processing mechanism intact	*decreased* by lack of auditory feedback
decreased by severity of loss shape of loss early onset of loss		*decreased* by felt prejudice against deaf speech
increased by optimal auditory intervention hearing aids auditory training		*decreased* because of low communicative value to child
Accessibility of *visual* signals–signs		
decreased by taboo mechanisms	Processing mechanism intact	*increased* by kinesthetic proprioceptive feedback system
increased by maternal acceptance competence frequency of use		

parents elected to use one of the newer versions of sign language, that is, one more closely resembling English in word order, prefixes, suffixes, tenses, etc. Their choice appears to have been influenced by a strong desire for English language and speech acquisition, which is more easily accomplished by simultaneous bimodal input and by a greater ease in their own acquisition of a new modality of English, rather than of a sign language (e.g., Ameslan) with its own syntax. However, all the parents have expressed acceptance of Ameslan, and most expect their children to learn it from their peers and deaf adults.

After deciding to use a particular variety of sign language, the parents were further burdened by accepting the fact that the new signs created by different groups varied from teacher to teacher, and from time to time. The children were not similarly distressed; they quite easily incorporated the changes and occasionally used two different signs in the same sentence. The parents' decision to use sign language created problems in educational settings. Some schools frowned on the choice, thereby precipitating the parents into a conflict. An additional crisis was precipitated by the achievements of the youngsters exposed early to bimodal language: Existing school placements were not adequate in view of the linguistic superiority of the children. When feasible, we worked with the teachers to diminish conflict or to help change the curriculum.

We postulated that youngsters with varying degrees of hearing loss—but with the optimal linguistic input already described—would be able to function linguistically, able to assert, deny, request, order, and so on, in the same sequence, and at almost the same rate, as children learning any other language. We further postulated that the youngsters could learn language with a high level of complexity and could do so joyfully and confidently.

We proceeded to observe a series of youngsters by monthly videotape sessions in several natural settings: home, school, zoo, market. We recorded the visual and the auditory components—the modalities—of the language systems used by the children and parents. The sounds range from vague approximations of adult signs, through adult signs, to strings of signs.

FIRST SIGNS

Deaf youngsters exposed to sign language had an earlier appearance of the first sign than the first spoken word even for hearing youngsters, and their vocabulary growth was accelerated. Later sequences of language acquisition paralleled that of hearing youngsters.

The early signs were combined meaningfully to express certain semantic notions. Semantic notions depend on cognitive development, but cognitive development and linguistic development do not necessarily occur in unison. The child must find linguistic means to express his intentions. Slobin (1973) notes that "the rate and order of development of the semantic notions expressed by language are fairly constant across languages, regardless of the formal means of expression employed [p. 183]." The formal means of any language, however, can be easily accessible as, for example, the Hungarian locative, or quite inaccessible as the Finnish yes–no questions or the Arabic noun plurals. These last two linguistic markers are apparently so difficult that young Finnish children simply do not ask yes–no questions, and Arabic youngsters up to 15 do not use noun plurals. What makes a given linguistic means of expression in a language more or less accessible to the child? It probably varies from language to language as a function of the psycholinguistic complexity of the mechanisms used to express particular semantic intents (Slobin, 1973). Slobin has organized his framework of linguistic universals in terms of self-instructing mottos, in which the child gives himself advice about the task of organizing and storing language. We shall attempt to follow his framework by utilizing examples of utterances analyzed from the output of our youngsters and to emphasize crucial similarities and differences to spoken languages.

WORD–SIGN ORDER

Slobin's (1973) operating word-order principle reads, "Pay attention to the order of words and morphemes [p. 197]." We would like to add, "and transmit to each sender the word order that you receive from that sender."

How well did our youngsters follow that basic instruction? There is one major difference observable in the modality of sign representation. Although two spoken words cannot be said at the same time, two distinct signs can be produced at the same time with both left and right hands (Bellugi, 1972; Hoffmeister & Moores, 1973). Such dual production has been observed in our youngsters. Jessica, at 2 : 6, while wanting something of both her parents, signed FATHER and MOTHER simultaneously. Roberto, at 20 months, signed CANDY and DONKEY simultaneously.[4]

---

[4] Our bimodal transcripts are coded as follows: WORD = sign alone; "word" = spoken word alone; "WORD" = sign and spoken word produced simultaneously; A-B-C = fingerspelling.

END OF WORDS–SIGNS

One of Slobin's (1973) important and richly documented operating principles is: "Pay attention to the ends of words [p. 189]." There is evidence from studies in acoustic phonetics (i.e., final syllable lengthening) that gives additional support for the argument that word endings attract the child's attention. Studies of cross-cultural acquisition of spoken languages indicate that the child learns to express his semantic intentions more quickly in inflectional systems that follow, rather than precede, the content words. Bulgarian articles are suffixes and appear early. German and English articles precede nouns and appear relatively late. Hungarian locatives, which are expressed inflectionally, were in advance of Serbo-Croatian prepositional locatives in a bilingual child. The example from English that best corroborates this principle occurs in the acquisition of the English present progressive tense, which the child represents in its earliest forms by the verbal inflection *ing*, without a preverbal auxiliary.

We have some tentative data that seem to indicate that this universal principle may be directly related to the acoustic properties of the language and may show important differences when the main channel is visual. Our data can be subdivided into two main observational studies.

The *ing* Phenomenon: The Present Progressive

The present progressive, as acquired by English-speaking children, is a fascinating phenomenon. As already noted, grammatically it first occurs as the *ing* in the absense of a preverbal auxiliary. It is acquired as the first of a series of morphemes that modulate early English grammar. Its order of acquisition is not related to parental frequency of usage (Brown, 1973). Its semanticity is principled (in contradistinction to most other English grammatical markers, which are purely arbitrary). It refers to a process, named by a verb, that is temporarily in progress at the time of speaking. It is further subdivided semantically in that action verbs can always take the progressive state, while state verbs need the further distinction of volition. Thus, state verbs declared to be involuntary (such as *want, need, know, like, see,* and *hear*) never take the progressive, while state verbs (like *look, listen,* and *sleep*), which have a large voluntary component, do take the progressive. Children appear to learn this principle early. It is noted that children who frequently use these involuntary state verbs never use them incorrectly. Children learning spoken English thus follow Slobin's principle of "pay attention to the ends of words" and pick up the inflection before they pick up the auxiliary.

What can the study of our deaf youngsters add to the *ing* phenomenon? The *ing* suffix in sign is a new invention, and does not exist in Ameslan. It is represented by the *I* hand twisting slightly downward and to the right. In addition to being used in the present progressive with the copula, the *ing* is also used in the gerundive, such as *stop crying,* and in noun modifiers, such as *sleeping bag.* The *ing* form is generally considered important by parents and is soon incorporated in their signing; it can be represented motorically by very young children.

Although the gerundive and present participle forms of *ing* are not usually coded as part of the acquisition of the present progressive, we shall combine the two features because of our focus on perceptual salience. We have noted that the perceptual salience to any one individual youngster seems to depend on at least two variables: the youngsters' residual hearing, which permits them to perceive some phonetic component of the inflection, and the mothers' precision in its use. Brown (1973) refers to the fact that some spoken inflections are likely to be touched very lightly in moving from one word to another (i.e., *mommy's girl* and may partially contribute to the relatively late acquisition of the spoken possessive. Motorically, *ing* is attached to a verb sign and may perceptually fuse into the main sign. The light vocal touch of the possessive may be found again in the light touch of a plural inflection. On the other hand, the motoric auxiliaries such as *is* and *are* (with the *I* or *R* hand touching the chin and moving outward and upward) are perceptually very distinct and probably do not fuse for the child.

Ruth's acquisition of *ing* was first noted

2:10   SWIMMING
2:11   KITTY CAT RUNNING
3:1   CRYING CRYING GOING HOME, YES.

The next transcript, at 3:8, contains some complicated grammatical transformation but no form of progressives. The example

"C-I" IS "DROPPED HER SLIPPER"

seems to be an occurrence of a past regular and is seen as a semantic correction on Ruth's part rather than as a new acquisition of the auxiliary. Ruth's approximation toward adult syntax at

4:4   "WE ARE GOING TO THE TREE FARM."
4:6   "I'M GOING TO HELP ROGER SAY THAT TAPE."
       "SHE SAID, SHE SAID YES, SHE IS SAYING TO ME THAT
       SHE IS ON THE TELEPHONE."
       "WHEN I WAS SWIMMING WITH MY SUNGLASSES WITH
       MY OLD BOOK."

> "she is talking to her teacher, she is coming home from school."
> "I'm putting on my boots."
> "BECAUSE, BECAUSE WE ARE COMING BACK TO
>   AMERICA."
> "WHEN WE WERE IN HAWAII THEN I AM GOING TO
>   HAVE A NEW FRIEND."
> "what are you doing?" "where are you going?"
> "WHAT IS DOING?"
> "CONNIE IS PEEKING A CAR AND SHE WAS IN A
>   ACCIDENT."
> "NO, JACKIE IS GOING TO BE IN THE HOSPITAL FOR
>   TEN WEEKS. C-A-S-A-R WILL BE HERE IN TWO WEEKS.
>   HE STAYS IN THE . . ."

There are only two examples, at ages 2:11 and 3:1, where the auxiliary is missing, followed by another transcript in which it was not used at all. This was immediately followed by the consistent use of the adult form of the present progressive. The adult forms exist both in the spoken and the sign version. It is to be noted that Ruth probably has sufficient hearing to perceive some portion of the *ing* inflection. Furthermore, Ruth's mother tends to be quite precise in both her spoken and sign inflections.

End of Words-Signs and Perceptual Salience

One of our other youngsters, Josette, is particularly fascinating. Just as Brown (1973) describes Eve as a "harried executive" because of her frequent usage of *hafta* (have to), Josette appears to approach the world as if all actions were taking place at the exact moment of utterance and at her volition. She appears to be incessantly and voluntarily in action. Let us look at some examples of her *ing*. We first see Josette at 4:1, following 1 year and 3 months of sign language with her parents and in the school system:

> "WRITE R-U [Ruth] IS WRITE."
> "WASH, WASH YOU IS WASH."
> "MAMA. DOLL ARE RUN AWAY."
> "YOU DON'T. OH, DOLL ARE DROP. BAD."
> "HE SLEEPING AND O.K."

One month later:

> "THE TREE IS FALL THERE."
> "NO, DADDY IS JUMP OVER THE WOOD FOR THE TREE. THE
>   YELLOW HORSE IS EAT."

Josette points to the barn and says, "SLEEPING" in response to questions of where the horse sleeps, but continues:

"THE YELLOW HORSE IS SLEEP IN GROUND."
"YELLOW HORSE SLEEPING THERE."
"NO, THE YELLOW HORSE IS EAT BROWN HAY."
"MAMA IS RUN."
"YELLOW HORSE IS WENT SLEEPING IN HAY."
"YELLOW HORSE IS RUNNING AWAY."
"YELLOW HORSE IS JUMP. YELLOW HORSE IS FALL DOWN
   ON THE SAND."

A month later, she is excitedly describing an accident:

"THE MAN CRASHED HER THE RED CAR IN THE OTHER.
   FIRE MAN IS HOSE HER WATER IN THE OTHER. A SICK,
   YES. MAMA'S HOUSE."
"DADDY IS HELP HER YELLOW CAR SAFE."
"DADDY IS PULL IN THE WHITE CAR."
"POLICEMAN IS H-I ME."
"YELLOW HORSE IS WAIT NOW AND RUN."
"J-O-S-E-T-T-E IS RIDE, RIDE THE HORSE. YELLOW HORSE."
"MANY, MANY PEOPLE ARE WATCH THE MANY COW
   HORSE."
"NO, I AM COWBOY. RIDE THE YELLOW HORSE AND ROPE
   THE COW."

At 4:8 we still find occasional:

"SHE IS RUN AWAY."

or

"THE GHOST WENT TO SLEEPING AND THE SANTA
   CLAUS WILL DO COME HERE?"

Also,

"I'M GO TO BE TEACHER. WAIT AND ME TO GO WAIT
   FOR TEACHER."

At 4:8, she overgeneralizes interestingly;

"T-S-Y IS HEARING ME CALLING. YES. CALLING. YOU WANT
   SOME CHOCOLATE? HOT CHOCOLATE? OKAY NOW?"

As Brown (1973) has indicated that involuntary verbs such as *seeing* and *hearing* are not used in the present progressive, and that children tend not to overgeneralize on that inflection, we shall postulate that *hearing* for Josette is not an involuntary activity due to the state of deafness. Furthermore, it might appear that she is correcting herself and changes it to *calling* which is, of course, a voluntary action verb. At 5 years many examples switch back and forth:

> "RIDE YELLOW HORSE." (In response to "WHAT HAVE YOU
>   BEEN DOING?")
> "SHE IS STAYING A NO. DOLL IS STAY. A-T GRAMMA
>   B-A-R-B-A HOUSE."
> "SHE IS SEEING MAMA AGAIN."
> "HE IS CRY."
> "SHE IS LAUGH. SHE IS LAUGHING A CONNIE."
> "SHE IS SLEEPING. HE IS FEELING SO HOT, HOT, HOT."
> "SHE IS CRY. BECAUSE MAMA IS SWIM AGAIN. CAR
>   DRIVING AWAY."
> "I NOT GOING TO WAIT ANYMORE. YOU HAVE TO GO
>   BY YOURSELF.
> YOU WILL PUT ON YOUR HEARING AID AND YOU WILL
>   BE SWIM WITH YOU."
> "BABY IS SLEEPING. HE NOT EAT. DADDY IS CUT BY
>   THE TURKEY AGAIN."

And in answer to "HOW ARE YOU?"

> "FEELING FINE."

In most of her examples, especially the early ones, the present progressive includes the auxiliary and omits the inflection. Auditorily, this youngster is less likely to perceive the *ing* than Ruth. Visually we need further analysis of the maternal input for the present progressive. One of our staff members believes that Josette's mother is quite precise and consistent in making the sign, although I would imagine that she does it with somewhat less than military precision.

Having noted this potentially significant difference, we were anxious to videotape Serjei, a youngster with considerably more hearing than either Josette or Ruth and with a relatively precisely speaking and signing mother. Audiograms for each of these three children are given in Figure 4.1. We theorized that both the inflection and the auxiliary would be clearly accessible to Serjei and that he would produce both early. Another interesting feature was noted in his utterances. The maternal linguistic input is relatively identical in both modes; however, there are instances where the mother modulates her spoken language, while her sign modality leaves out articles, prepositions, auxiliaries and the copula,

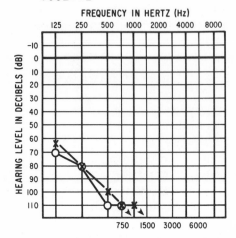

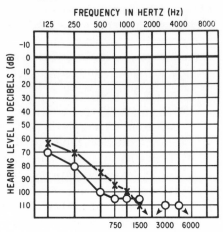

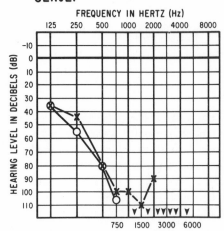

Figure 4.1 Audiograms of Josette, Ruth, and Serjei. (O) Right ear, (×) left ear.

as well as inflections. The bimodal linguistic examples will be represented by two lines when the simultaneous versions of grammatical modulations differ:

Serjei's mother:

"SHAWN"	PLAY	"IN THE SNOW YESTERDAY"
	"played"	

DO E-R-I-C   "SLEEP IN THE SNOW?"
"Did Eric"

"OH ELSBETH" SLEEP   "in a"   SLEEP   "BAG ON VACATION"
              "slept"   "sleeping"

"IS CONNIE"   HAVE   "GIRL OR BOY BABY?"
              "having"

"ARE YOU"   FEEL   "SICK?" YOU "NOT" TALK
              "feeling"   "You're"   "talking"

Although these are exceptions rather than the rule, it does appear that
Serjei's linguistic modulations in sign and spoken English are most
consistent with his input and its accessibility to him. Serjei himself uses
a simultaneous bimodal output. He regularly omits the *ing* morpheme
and auxiliaries when signing, but uses them in his spoken utterances.
Serjei, age 4:6, produced the following:

> "SERJEI   GO   "LAKE TAHOE"
>   "going"
> "Daddy working FOR PEOPLE over THERE."
> "SERJEI'S (pronounced z) GOING FAR AWAY."
> "GOING TO THE HAMBURGER STORE."
> "ME and YOU"   PLAY
>   "playing"
> DREAM   "CANDY"
> "Dreaming of"
> "No, no Daddy"   WORK   "ON the FIREHOUSE."
>   "working"

Although an exact phonetic transcription of his utterances has not yet
been completed, there are instances that indicate that there are similar
differences between his sign and spoken modulations in other tenses:

> "I"   FORGET   "the pie."
>   "forgot"

In the third person singular:

> "SERJEI" WANT   "CHOCOLATE MILKSHAKE."
>   "wants"

In the contracted copula:

> WHERE   "ANOTHER CHAIR?"
> "Where's"

His possessive, which hopefully will immortalize Connie's baby, was
noted in speech only:

> "Connie's tummy's fat."

A careful examination of his linguistic utterances reveals that there are no instances of signing alone and frequent instances of both bimodal utterances or purely spoken utterances. Bimodal ones continue to rivet our interest.

Another feature of interest must be noted. Serjei's mother decided when he was 2:6 to use bimodal total communication. Serjei had received early, consistent, and relatively successful amplification, and the degree and shape of the hearing loss was such that his initial vocalizations were relatively intelligible. Indeed, his imitations of individual vowel sounds at the age of 2 were excellent. (Serjei represents the type of hearing loss in which deafness is frequently missed in the early stages.) However, when consonants occurred, his hearing was frequently inadequate. Moreover, when individual sounds became combined into words, the intelligibility of his speech decreased further. Since the outset of bimodal communication, Serjei's intelligibility has increased, and his receptive understanding has considerably increased.

PERCEPTUAL SALIENCE AND OTHER MORPHEMES

Another of Slobin's operating principles reads: "Underlying semantic relations should be marked overtly and clearly." Hearing children scan adult spoken utterances for clues to meaning and are aided by overt, morphological markers that are regular and perceptually salient. Such markers probably play a similar role in production, helping the child keep track of where he is in the transition from thought to utterance. Children apparently prefer grammatical functors to be present not only whenever possible but also to be marked clearly acoustically or, in our cases, visually. Brown (1973) summarized the acquisition of 14 morphemes and found that a detailed study of the grammar and semantics of the morphemes suggested that the order of acquisition depends on relative complexity—grammatical or semantic—but was not related to the frequency of morphemes in parental speech. Perceptual salience, broken down into such variables as amount of phonetic substance, stress level, and usual serial position in the sentence, is probably a more important variable for the acquisition of spoken languages.

How are deaf children helped to scan adult spoken and signed utterances? Which morphological markers are for them regular and perceptually salient? The new English morpheme markers in signs may vary in interesting ways in their perceptibility for deaf children. Although we have not scored the 14 morphemes with Brown's criterion, we have observed the order and frequency of their initial occurrence, noting their position (TAB), hand configuration (DEZ), and motion (SIG) (Stokoe et al., 1965). Some observations suggest that visual perceptual salience plays an important role in the acquisition of sign grammatical modulations. Two of our youngsters, for example, use articles *a, the,* and *some* long before they acquired plurals and possessives. Some of the grammatical, motoric morphemes are in such close proximity to the content words that they might fuse into the content word. Others differ and have a greater visual lag either in terms of distance, time, or location in space between the content word and any of the motoric morphemes.

The articles *a* and *the* are produced in the neutral zone (somewhere in front of the body) with the *A* or *T* hand moving to the right. All the nouns modified by the articles require very distinct movements, either in front of the body, as in THE BOX, or to the midzone (at the chin), as in A GIRL and SOME JUICE. The article *some* is represented by the left hand lying palm up in front of the body with the right hand open and perpendicular to it and moving towards the body. We saw that sign preceding JUICE, which is made near the chin, some distance from the neutral zone of the body.

Plurals and possessives are both represented by an *S* hand at the shoulder. The plural marking is stationary, whereas the possessive marking moves toward the body with a twist. Although the position and movement of the hand have been observed as described, the usual shoulder position is changed to somewhere in front of the body, usually in close conjunction to the content sign. Either *S* thus may become imperceptible to the child even while watching attentively.

The past regular, as well as early past irregulars already noted, have two features that might contribute to early acquisition. The sign is clearly visible, the palm of the open hand facing the body at the right shoulder and flipping backwards; a more sophisticated version suggests a *D* hand flipping backwards. Both versions are some distance from the action verbs most frequently used by the youngsters, verbs that are usually signed in front of and away from the trunk, such as DROP and PUSH. The tense marker itself contains a semantic marker in that the hand indicates visually something behind me as the WILL indicates something in front of me. We thus postulate that some of the visual representations of the morphemes are more likely to be perceived at earlier stages than others. Some of the bimodal examples also suggest that perceptual salience plays an important role and varies for different children. Thus we have Ruth saying:

> "J-S"   FOUGHT   "with Ruth yesterday;"
>   ⟵"fight"

or Josette:

"I"   HAD   "a new hat;"
"have"

or Serjei:

GO
"going"
DREAM   CANDY
"dreaming of"

Ruth and Josette, with their greater hearing losses, clearly first note the more adult morphemes in sign rather than in speech. Serjei, having more hearing combined with a maternal input that occasionally omits the sign modality, also uses the more adult morphemes in the modality (speech) that is more frequently and more clearly accessible to him.

SUMMARY

We have presented fragments of linguistic bimodal utterances to illustrate some language universals. Bimodal language acquisition appears to share many of the known facts of spoken language acquisition. This chapter suggests that the bimodal perceptual salience affects the order of morpheme acquisition and notes some special features of bimodalism and bilingualism. We have also been delighted by the psychological concomitants of early meaningful communication. Our children differ from one another in many ways, but they are all acquiring the languages of their mothers. Our hearing parents have demonstrated that language in another modality can be learned in adulthood. Our deaf youngsters have demonstrated that they have the capacity to learn one language in two modalities or even two languages in two modalities.

REFERENCES

Bellugi, U. Studies in sign language. In O'Rourke, T. J. (Ed.), *Psycholinguistics and total communication: The state of the art*. Washington, D.C.: American Annals of the Deaf, 1972, 68–74.

Brill, R. G. A study in adjustment of three groups of deaf children. *Exceptional Children*, 1960, *26*, 464–466.

Brill, R. G. The superior I.Q.'s of deaf children of deaf parents. *Maryland Bulletin*, 1970, *90*, 97–111.

Brown, R. *A first language: The early stages.* Cambridge, Massachusetts: Harvard University Press, 1973.

Hoffmeister, R. J., & Moores, D. F. *The acquisition of specific reference in the linguistic system of a deaf child of deaf parents* (Research Report No. 53, Project No. 332189, Grant No. 01-09-332189-4533 [032]). Washington, D.C.: Department of Health, Education and Welfare, U. S. Office of Education, Bureau of Education for the Handicapped, 1973.

Meadow, K. P. Early manual communication in relation to the deaf child's intellectual, social, and communicative functioning. *American Annals of the Deaf,* 1968, *113,* 29–41.

Meadow, K. P. Self-image, family climate, and deafness. *Social Forces,* 1969, *47,* 428–438.

Quigley, S. P., & Frisina, D. R. Institutionalization and psycho–educational development of deaf children. *Council for Exceptional Children Research Monograph,* 1961, *3.*

Ruesch, J. *Disturbed communication.* New York: Norton, 1957.

Schlesinger, H. S., & Meadow, K. P. *Sound and sign: Childhood deafness and mental health.* Berkeley: University of California Press, 1972.

Slobin, D. J. Cognitive prerequisites for the development of grammar. In C. Ferguson, & D. J. Slobin (Eds.), *Studies of child language development.* New York: Holt, Rinehart and Winston, 1973.

Stokoe, W. C., Jr., Casterline, D. C., & Croneberg, C. G. *A dictionary of American Sign Language on linguistic principles.* Washington, D.C.: Gallaudet College Press, 1965.

Vernon, M., & Koh, S. D. Early manual communication and deaf children's achievement. *American Annals of the Deaf,* 1970, *115,* 527–536.

5

Some Speculations Concerning Deafness and Learning To Read[1]

PENELOPE H. BROOKS

Despite dedicated and tireless efforts by educators of the deaf, early severe hearing loss persists as a promissory for reading failure. Not only do deaf students not progress in reading achievement according to grade level expectations, but the deficiency is cumulative. Cross-sectional data collected in the 1969 Annual Survey of Hearing Impaired Children and Youth indicated that by 15:6–16:6 years of age the mean reading achievement grade equivalent is 3.5—1 year's advancement over the mean grade equivalent of 10:6–11:6-year-old deaf students, which was 2.5 (Primary II battery, SAT). Data compiled 10 years earlier, cited by Furth (1966), are quite similar. In a later study, Balow, Fulton, and Peploe (1971) assessed reading comprehension skills in 157 deaf adolescents (14 to 21 years of age) in Minnesota, and found mean equivalence scores ranging from 4.5 to 6.1, depending on the test and what was measured. Hammermeister (1971) examined the reading achievement

[1] This work was supported in part by NICHHD Grant No. HD-00973 to the Institute on Mental Retardation and Intellectual Development, which is a component of the John F. Kennedy Center for Research on Education and Human Development, and also by NIE Grant No. NE-G-3-0089.

DEAF CHILDREN: DEVELOPMENTAL PERSPECTIVES

of 60 deaf adults 7–13 years after leaving school, and found that, although the deaf adults had made significant gains in word meaning, they
had made no gains in paragraph meaning. Thus, the results of these
reading assessments concur in their conclusion that deafness from an
early age is universally associated with serious reading problems.
Moreover, this problem appears not to be just a matter of delayed
development, but appears to represent a cessation in the usual progression through the various stages of reading skills.

LOCUS OF THE PROBLEM

This conclusion of relative inevitability of reading failure depends on
what one means by "reading." Reading is a complex skill consisting of the
coordination of many subskills (see Singer, 1970; Venezky & Calfee,
1970, for theories that enumerate subskills). Surely some of these
skills—such as word identification—must be unrelated to deafness. It
should be possible, for example, for a visually represented pattern to be a
symbol for something without being mediated by the sound system.
Chomsky (1970) refers to such representation as lexical representation,
which in turn, has complex rules of correspondence with the sound
system of the language (but not necessarily). Most research has located
the source of the deaf person's difficulties within the vague construct of
reading comprehension (paragraph comprehension, paragraph meaning, etc.). Although this designation is intuitively sound, we still do not
know why or how this deficit develops, or what to do about it, or even
what processes are involved.
One way to investigate such an issue would be to look at
developmental changes in reading ability. Is there critical perceptual–
cognitive structuring occurring at the onset of adolescence that would
significantly affect measures of reading power? Singer (1965) and his
associates have devised a factorial account of reading that includes a
large test battery assessing progress along several substrata reading skills.
Their analysis indicates that some factors accounting for reading power
at lower grades no longer play a major role in the variability at higher
grades. They assume that development of reading power consists of
advanced processes that integrate the basic processes. At Grade 6, for
example, "visual–verbal" meaning accounts for 36% of the variance,
compared with 16–19% in earlier grades. "Word recognition in context"
decreases from about 26% in Grade 3 to 14% in Grade 5. A comparison
of high school readers with sixth-grade readers shows 75% of the variance among the former to be contributed by several factors: vocabulary

in context and isolation; visual–verbal meaning; verbal analogies; auding; and three other minor factors. At Grade 6, 73% of the variance is contributed by visual–verbal meaning, meaning of affixes, and matching sounds to words. Among his many conclusions, Singer (1970) suggests that "at the advanced levels of reading, individual differences in power of reading are primarily attributable to factors other than word recognition [p. 167]." Word reading and word meaning measures are also not included in the advanced batteries of the SAT; paragraph meaning and language scales are the only reading-related measures remaining in the battery at that level.

What happens in the reading process beyond sixth grade is not known. Whatever typically happens, apparently it does not happen in deaf persons. Adolescent readers are undergoing dramatic cognitive changes as they enter formal operations (Inhelder & Piaget, 1958). However, something peculiar to reading occurs, as there are deaf adults who show evidence of formal operational thinking (see Furth & Youniss, 1971, for evidence of the age and generality of this achievement) but who do not show correlated changes in reading skill.

One view of the reading problem is that the cognitive wherewithal to understand experience is delayed in the deaf because much information is sought and conveyed via spoken language (perhaps Blank, 1974, would represent this position). The other view is that the deaf are cognitively intact except for the knowledge of linguistic structure itself that is necessary to decode the occasion for expressed relationships (Furth, 1966).

COGNITIVE FACTORS

According to Bever (Kavanagh, 1968, p. 27), most researchers view reading as a constructive process. That this idea has been around for years is shown by a quote from Horn (1937): "The author, moreover, does not really convey ideas to the reader; he merely stimulates him to construct them out of his own experience. If the concept is already in the reader's mind, the task is relatively easy, but if, as is usually the case in school, it is new to the reader, its construction more nearly approaches problem-solving than simple association [p. 154]." The idea of construction could be seen as the reader's assembling of a puzzle for which he already has the pieces, according to a set of directions. These directions, conveyed linguistically, prescribe relations between entities, or between other relational terms. The possible relations describe classes of experience, that is, they are derived from nonlinguistic events, at least in the early years of life. Thus, the deaf child should possess the cognitive structures underlying these relations, as there is considerable overlap in the kinds of experiences young hearing and deaf children have; that is, similarities in play, exploration, motor development, etc. Furth's work (1971) would indicate that deaf people have relatively little deficit in the cognitive abilities that do not depend on language comprehension for their assessment. The assumption that these underlying abilities are prerequisite to language comprehension, and isomorphic with relations expressed in language, is an assumption usually made by theorists in cognitive development, because, to understand some expression, one must already know how to interpret it (see Weimer, 1973) or how to integrate its components. That knowledge is not derived from linguistic sources.

According to Boothroyd (see Stark, 1974, p. 138), deaf people are extremely good at constructing possible interpretations from some of the reading tests, a strategy he believes is debilitating. However, if Horn and Bever are to be believed, this is a strategy that we all use extensively. Either people with normal hearing are better constructors than the deaf by virtue of knowing more about the possible relationships in the world (see Chapter 7 by Nickerson for a further discussion of this possibility), or hearing people are better scanners in that they know ahead of time the role each designated referent will play in a relationship, for example, subject, object. It is assumed that overall reading rate is a self-regulated phenomenon, regulated by one's awareness of one's comprehension state. Comprehension of a passage is a unique function of the state of a person's knowledge and the density of information in the passage. Thus, in a very gross sense, reading comprehension in a timed situation can be directly related to one's constructive abilities. The latter aspect of linguistic information—structural determinants of relationships in reading—is the topic of most of the remainder of this chapter. The thesis is this: Deaf people have difficulty reading, not because their constructive processes are deficient, but primarily because they integrate information from a different basis, that is, without the data provided from knowledge of particular aspects of linguistic structure.

SOME ASPECTS OF LINGUISTIC STRUCTURE
RELEVANT TO READING

The grammatical code could be very roughly described as a set of events distributed in time. These events—whether phonemes, syllables, or larger units—have identities that can be discriminated by listeners. That is, these classes of events have a finite number of dimensions and features that we can use to identify and distinguish one member of a class from another.

Much of the work in grammar has been concerned with the rules of ordering these events in sequence. Developmental psycholinguists have spent much effort collecting and characterizing the grammar of young children (Braine, 1963; Brown & Fraser, 1963; McNeill, 1972; Slobin, 1971). The results of these and other related linguistic endeavors have been sets of rules describing regularities in sequences of classes of events, for example, sentence frame grammars, phase structure grammars, transformational grammars.

There are also values along sound-related dimensions common to several different speech events that give us more information about a particular event. These are the suprasegmental features of speech, for example, stress and accent. The interpretation of a speaker's intent depends on the listener's accurate reading of both of these aspects of the speech segment. Much of the rest of this chapter will discuss accent and its role in comprehension, as it is one of the abstract properties of language that is not directly represented in our orthography.

J. G. Martin (1972) argues that accent—defined as any kind of marking of an element, for example, loud, high relative to another element— is organized into temporal patterns or rhythms. He reminds us that the source of rhythm lies in motor movements. Speech production has rhythmic aspects because the size, speech, inertia, etc. of the vocal apparatus put constraints on what we say when. These constraints are reflected in the temporal distribution of events in time.

The concept of rhythm further specifies that relative timing is the significant invariant. Tempo of a sequence of events may vary (as in different styles and arrangements of a musical composition), but onsets, durations, and intervals maintain the same ratios. The locus of each event in a temporal dimension, or time-line, is determined by every other event in the rhythm pattern—both adjacent and nonadjacent. Martin has outlined a hierarchical plan for the generation of any natural rhythm pattern. Details of his model are not important for this discussion and are omitted here (the interested reader is referred directly to Martin's paper). What is of extreme interest here is one point he makes concerning the relationship between rhythm and grammatical elements; he suggests that the rhythm patterns in speech production determine the locus of important, informational content. That is, speakers are constrained in the sequencing of sounds by rhythmic patterns such that important content is inserted as maximally accented events. One implication of this conception is that many events are irrelevant from an information standpoint and serve a marking or pacing function.

Several other implications have a great deal of importance for those researching the difficulties deaf people have learning to read, write, and speechread. One implication is that input to the ear—the perceptual aspect of speech—is also rhythmically patterned. This may be more than a trivial observation, as it could be that one of the things people learn in the process of language reception is to tune in on patterns and consequently to predict when important events are going to occur. J. Martin (1972) suggests that this anticipation of accents in real time would allow "attention focusing on accented syllables [p. 153]" and "attention cycling such that previous inputs could be processed during the low-information intervals between accented syllables [p. 153]." A similar idea has been advocated by McNeill (1971) in trying to explain why speech mechanisms operate at a particular speed (1 to 2 sec). He suggests that as a new sentence is processed, it must be encoded into some semantic form, which requires a shift of attention—something that occurs every 1 to 2 sec according to Broadbent (1954) and Treisman (1960). McNeill goes on to conclude that, in language production, the "brain processes for constructing underlying sentences operate in such a manner as to produce new foci of attention at this natural rate [p. 24]."

There seems to be, then, a very subtle, intricate relationship between speech comprehension (processing) and speech production. Liberman (1974) alludes to this delicate nature of the speech–ear relationship, suggests that it is a product of biological evolution, and maintains that the "capacity for grammatical processing evolved as a kind of interface, matching the output of the intellect to the vocal tract and the ear. Thus, the biological development of those grammatical processes should have been limited by possibilities and limitations of the mismatched structures they connect [p. 156]." In the present account, the comprehension process is governed partly by a relative-time and order code and, in turn, the language production process is also guided by a program that has rhythmic, relative-time determinants. Such a symbiotic association between two anatomically and physiologically disparate processes represents a significant species adaptation. This relationship gives experienced listeners expected "timeouts" from attending to more physical aspects of incoming speech so that they can expend effort at assimilating the information. The scientist's discovery of such a relationship is a definite gain as noted by Bruner (1970):

> Psychology has always been bedeviled by separation in its theories of action on the one hand and sensing–knowing on the other. Tolman was accused by Guthrie of leaving his organism locked in thought, and Hull surely could be perceptually innocent as the day he was born, save for a little afferent neural interaction. There is a structure in knowing (whether we are speaking of perception or imaging or thought). Any conscientious contem-

porary theorist recognizes some deep relationship between the two forms
of structure—that action must be affected by the nature of perceptual organization and, in turn, that perception must be programmed by the requirements of action [p. 83.].

In addition to his work, J. Martin marshalls a convincing array of other
studies to support his theory. They range from a finding that temporal
distortions in segment durations are most likely to go unnoticed when
the original timing relationships between accented syllables in the
sentences remain intact (Huggins, 1972); Boomer and Laver's (1968)
finding that when slips of the tongue are made, the reversals most often
involved accented syllables, less often nonaccented syllables, but rarely
an accented and unaccented syllable; Blesser's (see Stark, 1974, p. 138)
noting that when pairs of subjects had to converse through spectrally
rotated speech (which does not distort temporal patterning) they often
reported hearing sentences that were syntactically identical but semantically incorrect to the input, for example, "Hoist the load to your left
shoulder" was reported as "Turn the page to the next lesson." Dooling
(1974) read to subjects in a monotone a list of sentences from which they
were to recall the key words. The sentences had the same rhythmic
structure, for example, *"They are: heavy smokers, pretty flowers, older women,
sneaky foxes, ugly muscles, etc."* After 10 such study–test sequences, the next
sentence may have violated the accent pattern, as in, *"They are severe de-
feats."* A significant decrement in performance when accent pattern was
changed led Dooling to conclude that subjects do indeed use the very
abstract temporal structure in speech perception and that they can use
this structure to predict the characteristics of an incoming message and
to impose a structure on it. Other approaches such as Goodglass and
Blumstein's (1973) stress-saliency hypothesis are certainly congruent
with J. Martin's thesis.

This aspect of linguistic structure—rhythmic patterning of accent—
may be very important in reading development. Once the student has
mastered some of the grapheme–phoneme correspondences and refers
the visual symbols to a phonologically based reference system, his reading may begin to map into some of the other functional aspects of the
speech perception apparatus.

A PROSPECTUS FOR ONE STAGE IN READING DEVELOPMENT

At some point in development, a child ceases to rely on a syllable-by-
syllable sounding of the orthography. Reading then changes in nature in
such a way that the reader skips, scans, and actively searches for some-

thing in the text. This search process appears to be a product of increasing knowledge of linguistic structure. Levin and Turner (1968) suggest it begins as early as the second grade in some readers. How the mapping between spoken and written language comes about is still an open question. According to E. Gibson (1972), "Finding the supraordinate structure in written language is a crucial problem for the reader. How does it happen? The answer must include knowledge of how already learned rule structures in speech are put to use or activated in reading [p. 17]." Levin (see Kavanagh, 1968) agrees that skilled reading is a search process guided by some aspect of meaning, that it is not a random process but is governed by some packaging or structural account of meaning in the language.

The resources marshalled by the reader in mapping what is written (in conventional orthography) onto a speech and hearing system are interesting in their ingenuity. The first operation the reader performs on the written text is that of dispersing the visual display along a time dimension. This is done in two ways: using a motor mechanism—programmed eye movements, and using a perceptual mechanism—guided attentional processes.

The most peripheral aspect of reading that we control is eye movements. They appear to be jerks consisting of scan–fixate–scan–fixate, usually in left-to-right direction, but sometimes nonsequentially, according to Morton (see Kavanagh, 1968, p. 154). Eye fixations during reading change dramatically in the elementary grades (Singer, 1965). In the first grade, there are an average of two fixations per word lasting .7 sec each and an average of one regression every two words. By college age, eye movements are more rhythmic with an average of 1½ words per fixation, an average fixation length of .25 sec and one regression every two lines of print. Span and pause duration both change quickly in Grades 1–4 and level off from Grades 5–10.

There are a couple of problems associated with rate measures of eye movements. The first is that rate indices ignore qualitative aspects of eye movements. The developmental changes shown in rate measures may also reflect changes in the structuring of direction, sequencing, and relative timing of eye movements. The second difficulty concerning fixation times and rate changes is that we do not know what is happening during scanning or during a fixation. In one of the reports of conferences I surveyed in the process of writing this chapter, Bever (see Kavanagh, 1968, p. 151) asked the cogent question: "Has it ever been demonstrated that you actually are 'looking' at the point where you fixate? Or are you thinking about what you were just looking at?" G. Kaplan (see Kavanagh, 1968, p. 151) noted that "eye movements are complicated business. The exact linkage, the exact articulation between whatever the motivation for the eye movements are and the actual eye movements is not known." Researchers are beginning to suspect, however, that linguistic structure has much influence on the way we move our eyes. E. Gibson (1972) believes that the reader's "knowledge of the rules tells him where and how far to look and this assists him to chunk the material in higher-order units [p. 15]."

The other way we group and disperse the visual display is with attentional processes. Venezky and Calfee (1970) recognize cycles of forward scanning and subsequent integration as descriptive of the course of reading. Eye–voice span is an index of at least one aspect of these perceptual processes. The eye–voice span is the amount of material one can "read" after print is removed from visual accessibility (usually by turning off a light). Eye–voice span is related to sentence structure, that is, it is longer for sentences than word lists. The eye–voice span is very large at the "by" of passive sentences and at highly constrained parts of sentences (Levin & Turner, 1968). It also undergoes developmental change in that it is greater in length for older readers than younger readers above second grade. Again, then, there is evidence that one of the tasks of learning to read is to bring our knowledge of structure, however, it is coded, to govern not only the motor movements of our eyes but also what we attend to as the eyes move.

Moreover, the assignment of an attentional switching pattern early in a written segment may allow one to have expectations about later events. J. Martin (1972) notes that in listening, rather than "following" the speaker, a programmed anticipation allows the listener—given initial cues—to enter actively into the speaker's tempo. The same basic idea could operate in the process of reading; the reader projects the important elements to occur in the remainder of a sentence based on some sort of initial assessment of the text. As Hochberg (1970) says, "because eye movements are fully programmed in advance of their execution, any efficient sampling of the peripheral vision also tells him roughly where his present fixation falls in the overall pattern [p. 221]," and "when he looks at text with an intention to read it, he fits speech fragments to the letters glimpsed with each fixation; the speech fragments then afford a meaningful linguistic structure by which successive glimpses may be stored and repeated [p. 224]."

How is what we look at programmed in advance? How do we know what to expect? What cues on the printed page do we learn to detect and use as indices of structure or as indices of where we should look next for information? There are many clues on the printed page—spacing, capitalization, punctuation, and spelling patterns—all of which give us data about where we are in a pattern. Hochberg, Levin, and Frail (1966, also cited in Hochberg, 1970) conducted a study on the usefulness of spaces and punctuation and found that young children were more disrupted by the absence of spaces. There are many other cues that might signal importance or nonimportance in the reading process. Word length, or length of letter group, is somewhat correlated with content. Several short words together, for example, *will be in the,* as in *he will be in the third grade next year,* signal function words and auxiliary verbs, often redundant and preceding important content words. What I would like to suggest here is that, more than content, they also signal timing aspects of the text, perhaps acting as fillers in a cadence, pacing the beats or fixations.

There is intuitive appeal in a comment of Levin's (see Kavanagh, 1968, p. 91): "But would you buy the assumption that there are some things you look at hard and some things you look at lightly and some things you don't look at at all."[2] This description is congruent with the idea that attentional processes are tightly controlled during reading. Because reading appears to be mediated by reference to the phonological system of the language, it can also benefit from the kinds of factors that operate in speech perception and comprehension. One of these may be a time-patterning of attention, with the result that the more important elements are detected and processed to a greater degree than the less important elements. Such a program may have rhythmic properties. In addition, there are cues in the printed text that could help us know when to process deeper ("to look at hard," in Levin's terms). A study by Birch and Belmont (1964) is indirectly related to this idea. They gave 200 9- and 10-year-old students, 150 of whom showed retarded reading achievement, one of their sensory-integration tests. The students were asked to identify dot patterns, for example, ... , that were identical to a sequence of pencil taps they had just heard. The poor readers (independent of IQ) performed significantly less ably on this task than normal readers. Where children learn that dots are beats and spaces are unfilled intervals is not known, but spatial–temporal coordination is necessary to detect words, sentences, and idea boundaries.

If this or a similar account is reasonable, where deaf people lose in the reading process is a complicated but intriguing issue. They lose, in the first place, because English orthography is so beautifully designed to

---

[2] "Hard," "light," and "not at all" are metaphoric of course, but sound as if they might fit into a depth of processing framework such as the one proposed by Craik and Lockhart (1972). In this context what is proposed in reading is a programmed differential depth of processing at various times in the scanning process.

map into the English phonological (morphophonological?) system. According to Chomsky (1970), the task of contemporary linguistics to the study of literacy is in "clarifying the relation between conventional orthography to the structure of spoken language. The relation is much closer than ordinarily supposed . . . conventional English orthography is a near optimal system for representing the spoken language [p. 4]."

There are alternative orthographic systems that do not necessarily project on a phonological system. S. Martin (1972) has catalogued five major categories of Chinese characters: pictographs, which are iconic representations, for example, *sun,* should be represented by a picture; ideographs, which represent a logical idea like three lines depicting the number *3;* compound ideographs, for example, two trees equal *grove,* three trees equal *forest;* phonetic loans, which are characters that are borrowed for another idea because the name sounds the same (homonyms); and phonetic compounds, which contain parts that give clues to the meaning.[3] An orthography such as this, one not so closely tied to the properties and demands of the vocal tract, might be beneficial to deaf people.

In fact, it would be theoretically possible to design the ultimate in an efficient orthography—efficient spatially and temporally such that the maximum amount of information is compressed into a minimum amount of space or time. Although this might bypass the cumbersome phonological system for deaf people, reading rate is not determined or limited by the capacities of the modalities involved, but by the rate that the ideas can be assimilated into the knowledge system. Learning to coordinate eye movements and attentional processes may impede increases in overall reading rate for a while, but not permanently. If one can comprehend the material faster than it can be read under usual conditions, one simply adjusts the motor and attentional processes, as in scanning and rapid reading. If this assertion is true, then a whole paragraph could be compressed into a single symbol or kinesthetic pattern, and the time to "read" it should be the same as the original paragraph, printed in the customary orthography. (See Chapter 6 by Sperling for a discussion of alternative orthographic systems.)

What we really mean when we talk about teaching deaf people to read, however, is that we want them to learn to read the text in the ortho-

---

[3] Such an orthographic system appears suspiciously like what a representation for a nonkinesic transcription of American Sign Language (ASL) could also look like. Comprehension of ASL is a real form of reading, just as speechreading is. Although the time and order characteristics of ASL have different determinants, the information rate (idea per second) is the same as in spoken English (Bellugi & Fischer, 1972).

graphy of the hearing world. Liberman (see Kavanagh, 1968, p. 201) has implied that such a feat is impossible; that the reading of conventional orthography depends on phonological-based projections. Furth (see Kavanagh, 1968, p. 197) feels that people could learn English through visual means, that linguistic competence is independent of sensory channel. Although Furth may be correct, competence in English has not yet been mastered through the visual channel on any large scale (see Chapter 7 by Nickerson for additional discussion of this issue). Perhaps we have been trying to do this by using the wrong techniques (obviously we have not been using the right ones). In the past we have treated linguistic structure as either a serial sequence—as in sentence frame grammars—or, we have taught students about grammar by defining transformations and giving exercises in transforming sentences. In both attempts our goal has been to get students to arrange properly certain orthographic or linguistic events in time. Until now, our definition of "arrange" has been an ordinal scale—what element comes after what other element, a ranked position or order in time. Maybe we should try to think of arranging events along an interval scale of time; speech does this and, given the intimate relation between speaking, comprehension, and conventional orthography, perhaps reading does as well.

J. Gibson's (1966) position that development consists of the education of attention is appropriate when the learning of reading is considered. Whether the reader learns to notice lines and curves or whether he learns to detect and integrate more complex patterns like sentences, he is modifying his attentional processes. Whether there is a change in spatial orientation of the senses or temporal organization of perception, attentional processes are being altered. Perhaps what we should be considering is how to go about controlling these changes. When teaching reading to most children we present textual material in sentences and paragraphs with all parts of a page simultaneously available to their visual field. What we *hope* will happen is that they learn to control their own internal scanning and attentional processes as a function of practice at oral reading. We actually take no active part in training those processes.[4] It might be reasonable to propose that, instead of praying that young readers automatically modify attentional processes and parcel the text, we arrange the text in time according to some rules or patterns that seem to have psychological reality. J. Martin and D. Meltzer (personal com-

---

[4] Tinker (1958) reports and dismisses some attempts at training eye movements to occur rhythmically. Rhythm in these studies, however, was established as when readers used the same eye-movement pattern from line to line. Fortunately, Dixon (1951) in his studies of eye movements of professors and graduate students found only a few records of the good readers whose eye movements had these properties.

munication), for example, have worked out a program that will determine the temporal properties of text (using the syllable as a unit) and will present the printed syllables on a television monitor according to their prescribed temporal (rhythmic) characteristics. They have suggested that this might be useful in training deaf students in appropriate reading habits.

SUMMARY

As deaf people seem to reach a ceiling in reading achievement at about fifth grade equivalency, several advanced reading skills were examined in an attempt to account for this failure to develop further. The evidence would suggest that advanced levels of reading speed and comprehension are closely tied to the structural constraints of language, that is, there are data demonstrating that both eye movements and attentional processes in reading develop a correspondence with the phrasal units and informational content of speech. Reading becomes a seemingly irregular process of searching, expecting, integrating. The old paradox of how the reader knows what to attend to and look at until he has already "read" something is an important issue. Some investigators believe that attentional processes in reading are programmed before their execution. Because reading, like speech, occurs in time, such a program must stipulate when to stop, when to scan, and when to attend. Timing specifications may very well be its basis. J. Martin's account of the rhythmic structure of speech is one possible blueprint for this type of control.

Deaf people suffer in the development of reading proficiency relative to hearing individuals for whom the orthographic system (of English) affords the application of the principal strategies of speech perception to reading comprehension. The reading problem manifested by deaf people may not necessarily reflect their inability to exploit structural linguistic constraints in learning to read, however. A more basic source of the problem may be the lack of guidelines by which to regulate the processing of the information.

REFERENCES

Annual survey of hearing impaired children and youth: Academic performance of hearing impaired students. Washington, D.C.: Office of Demographic Studies, Gallaudet College, 1969.

Balow, B., Fulton, H., & Peploe, E. Reading comprehension skills among hearing impaired adolescents. *The Volta Review*, 1971, *73*, 113–119.

Bellugi, U., & Fischer, S. A comparison of sign language and spoken language. *Cognition*, 1972, *1*, 173–200.

Birch, H. G., & Belmont, L. Auditory–visual integration in normal and retarded readers. *American Journal of Orthopsychiatry*, 1964, *34*, 852–861.

Blank, M. Cognitive functions of language in the preschool years. *Developmental Psychology*, 1974, *10*, 229–245.

Boomer, D. S., & Laver, J. D. M. Slips of the tongue. *The British Journal of Disorders of Communication*, 1968, *3*, 2–12.

Braine, M. D. S. The ontogeny of English phrase structure: The first phase. *Language*, 1963, *39*, 1–13.

Broadbent, D. E. The role of auditory localization and attention in memory span. *Journal of Experimental Psychology*, 1954, *47*, 191–196.

Brown, R., & Fraser, C. The acquisition of syntax. In C. N. Cofer & B. S. Musgrave (Eds.), *Verbal behavior and learning: Problems and processes*. New York: McGraw-Hill, 1963.

Bruner, J. Constructive cognitions. *Contemporary Psychology*, 1970, *15*, 81–83.

Chomsky, N. Phonology and reading. In H. Levin & J. Williams (Eds.), *Basic studies on reading*. New York: Basic Books, 1970.

Craik, F., & Lockhart, R. Levels of processing: A framework for memory research. *Journal of Verbal Learning and Verbal Behavior*, 1972, *11*, 671–684.

Dixon, W. R. Studies on the eye-movements in reading of university professors and graduate students. In *Studies in the psychology of reading, University of Michigan Monograph in Education, No. 4*. Ann Arbor: University of Michigan Press, 1951. Pp. 113–178.

Dooling, D. J. Rhythm and syntax in sentence perception. *Journal of Verbal Learning and Verbal Behavior*, 1974, *13*, 255–264.

Furth, H. *Thinking without language: Psychological implications of deafness*. New York: Free Press, 1966.

Furth, H. Linguistic deficiency and thinking: Research with deaf subjects 1964–1969. *Psychological Bulletin*, 1971, *6*, 49–64.

Furth, H., & Youniss, J. Formal operations and language: A comparison of deaf and hearing adolescents. *International Journal of Psychology*, 1971, *6*, 49–64.

Gibson, E. Reading for some purpose. In J. Kavanagh & I. Mattingly (Eds.), *Language by ear and by eye: The relationships between speech and reading*. Cambridge, Massachusetts: M.I.T. Press, 1972.

Gibson, J. *The senses considered as perceptual systems*. Boston: Houghton Mifflin, 1966.

Goodglass, H., & Blumstein, S. (Eds.), *Psycholinguistics and aphasia*. Baltimore, Maryland: Johns Hopkins University Press, 1973.

Hammermeister, F. Reading achievement in deaf adults. *American Annals of the Deaf*, 1971, *116*, 25–28.

Hochberg, J. Attention in perception and reading. In F. Young & D. Lindsley (Eds.), *Early experience and visual information processing in perceptual and reading disorders*. Washington, D.C.: National Academy of Sciences, 1970.

Hochberg, J., Levin, H., & Frail, C. *Studies of oral reading: VII: How interword spaces affect reading*. Mimeographed paper, Cornell University, 1966.

Horn, E. V. *Methods of instruction in the social studies.* New York: Scribner, 1937.

Huggins, A. W. F. On the perception of temporal phenomena in speech. *Journal of the Acoustical Society of America,* 1972, *51,* 1279–1290.

Inhelder, B., & Piaget, J. *The growth of logical thinking from childhood to adolescence.* New York: Basic Books, 1958.

Kavanagh, J. (Ed.). *The reading process.* Washington, D.C.: U.S. Government Printing Office, 1968.

Levin, H., & Turner, A. Sentence structure and the eye-voice span. In H. Levin (Ed.), *The Analysis of reading skill: A program of basic and applied research* (Final Report, Project 5-1213). Ithaca, New York: Cornell University and U.S. Office of Education, 1968.

Liberman, A. M. Language processing: State-of-the-art report. In R. Stark (Ed.), *Sensory capabilities of hearing-impaired children.* Baltimore, Maryland: University Park Press, 1974.

Martin, J. G. Rhythmic (hierarchical) versus serial structure in speech and other behavior. *Psychological Review,* 1972, *79,* 487–509.

Martin, S. E. Nonalphabetic writing systems: Some observations. In J. Kavanagh & I. Mattingly (Eds.), *Language by ear and by eye: The relationships between speech and reading.* Cambridge, Massachusetts: M.I.T. Press, 1972.

McNeill, D. *Sentences as biological processes.* Paper presented at the Conseil National des Recherches Scientifiques Conference on Psycholinguistics, Paris, 1971.

McNeill, D. *The two-fold way for speech.* Unpublished manuscript, University of Chicago, 1972.

Singer, H. A. developmental model of speed of reading in grades three through six. *Reading Research Quarterly,* 1965, *1,* 29–49.

Singer, H. Theoretical models of reading: Implications for teaching and research. In H. Singer & R. Ruddell (Eds.), *Theoretical models and processes of reading.* Newark, Delaware: International Reading Association, 1970.

Slobin, D. *Psycholinguistics.* Glenview, Illinois: Scott, Foresman, 1971.

Stark, R. (Ed.). *Sensory capabilities of hearing-impaired children.* Baltimore, Maryland: University Park Press, 1974.

Tinker, M. A. Recent studies of eye-movements in reading. *Psychological Bulletin,* 1958, *55,* 215–231.

Treisman, A. M. Contextual cues and selective listening. *Quarterly Journal of Experimental Psychology,* 1960, *4,* 242–248.

Venezky, R., & Calfee, R. The reading competency model. In H. Singer & R. Ruddell (Eds.), *Theoretical models and processes of reading.* Newark, Delaware: International Reading Association, 1970.

Weimer, W. Psycholinguistics and Plato's paradoxes of the *meno. American Psychologist,* 1973, *28,* 15–33.

6

Future Prospects in Language and Communication for the Congenitally Deaf

GEORGE SPERLING

This chapter deals with four major issues concerning the improvement of the language and communication of congenitally deaf people. First, it is hypothesized that the more language people know, the easier it is for them to learn still more language. Based on this conjecture, it is argued that early acquisition of a manual sign language would enhance later development of other language skills—including those of oral–aural languages such as English. Second, it is hypothesized that the deaf child's language skills would be further aided by early acquisition of a written form of sign language. As there is not yet a written form of sign language (other than notational systems for linguistic analysis, see Liben, Chapter 1, and Bellugi & Klima, Chapter 3, this volume), some criteria for its development are discussed in this chapter. It is suggested here that it would be possible to create an ideal written language combining the good features of an ideographic language (such as Chinese) and of a phonetic language (such as English).

Two additional aspects of communication are considered briefly in this chapter. One concerns the development of a technology that would

DEAF CHILDREN: DEVELOPMENTAL PERSPECTIVES

provide an interpretable visual or tactual representation of speech. Despite extensive research with visual representations of speech, particularly for speech teaching, a visual representation of speech feasible for normal communication has not yet been developed. (See Nickerson, 1975, for a review of this area.) The last issue concerns developing inexpensive and widely available video communication services that would have particular utility for deaf people.

THE EARLY ACQUISITION OF LANGUAGE

—The more language a person knows, the easier it is to learn still more language.

This conjecture is really a slogan. Although it might be possible to create artificial situations where it fails, it is argued here that in practical situations the conjecture is so likely to be true, and is so important, that it should be taken as an operative principle. What the conjecture means is that there is negligible negative forward transfer in language learning. Whatever language task a person confronts now, and whatever language experiences he may have had in the past, he is better off for having had each of those experiences; conversely, having omitted any one of them would be disadvantageous. This kind of conjecture is also plausible in other domains involving highly practiced skills, such as performing on musical instruments. The more instruments one has learned to play, the easier any new instrument will be to learn. The greatest positive transfer occurs between similar instruments: piano–harpsichord; violin–viola; trumpet–French horn. But there are so many different subordinate skills in musical performance that there is positive transfer even between diverse pairs, especially from the first instrument studied to the second. The same applies to language.

The conjecture applies to forward transfer of skills. Backward transfer is frequently negative, particularly in early stages of learning. Thus, learning to play the viola may impair previously acquired skills on the violin (negative backward transfer) even though the violin skill enormously facilitates learning the viola (positive forward transfer). Knowing Spanish facilitates learning Portuguese or Italian, even though learning the new languages may interfere with retention of Spanish. But in language learning the net effect of new learning generally is positive—it does not produce more task-relevant forgetting than learning—and this is really the main point of the conjecture.

There is an a priori *theoretical basis for expecting that "language knowledge facilitates language learning," namely, the classical and well established observation that associative learning is faster and more enduring per unit of effort than is rote learning. Each language learned after the first can benefit from associations to prior languages, and from the previously acquired concepts and skills.*

Associative learning and rote learning refer to pure cases—ends of a continuum on which is ordered the number of associations of a new item with items already in memory. In rote learning, associations are formed primarily among the materials being learned; in associative learning these are also formed, but the predominant associations are with material already in memory. We are all familiar with the methods of the stage mnemonicists who retain in their memory an ordered list of items, such as 1-chair, 2-clock, 3-table, 4-bookshelf, etc. and then "instantly" memorize new lists, such as the names of people in the audience, by inventing associations of the new names to the list items. By contrast, "rote learning" would consist of associating each new name only to the previous name. To state it more quantitatively: the greater the number of associations of new material to previously learned material, the easier it is to learn the new material.

Of course, facilitation is not the only effect in learning. In the laboratory, where we emphasize the learning (often rote) of small, unconnected units of relatively meaningless material, interference effects are often quite large. There is proactive (forward) interference of materials learned-early upon later learning, and retroactive (backward) interference of materials learned-later upon earlier memories. But in natural language learning, the assertion here is that proactive interference is small relative to proactive facilitation.

The associative argument is an argument for the later utility of rich and varied early experience. But there is a unique role played by initial language learning that is more crucial than merely providing associations for later learning. Experience and observation can provide us with many facts about the world, even without language. To build intelligence—that is, intelligent behavior—we need concepts, not merely facts. In modern theories of memory, concepts function as nodes—organizing principles—in the memory structure; but it is not necessary to subscribe to a particular formal theory to appreciate the importance of concepts for new learning.

Some concepts are formed readily and naturally prior to language, such as the concept of "the same person" seen, heard, and touched in various places. However, language facilitates even this kind of learning by assigning a name to the person. Other concepts, such as weight, volume, and spatial relationships, may, at first, have only minor linguistic components. While the language-deficient deaf child may acquire these elementary concepts as readily as normal-hearing children (Furth, 1966), the child with language—spoken or signed—has an irresistibly useful structure for organizing the facts of experience into concepts. The essence of human intellectual development is not merely the acquisition of elementary concepts, but also the acquisition of increasingly complex conceptual structures in which elementary concepts are used in increasingly complex combinations. Perhaps a child genius without language (or with a private language) could organize the elementary facts of his or her experience into a structure of concepts even more useful than that which the language of the community would have provided. I doubt it. But the competence as an adult in contemporary Western civilization requires substantially more. For the ordinary child, the possibility of ever achieving adult intellectual performance without language is absurdly small.

It is crucial here to distinguish the role of language as an interpersonal communicative medium from its role in organizing thought, even in the absence of interpersonal communications. Language communication may or may not be necessary for normal emotional development; the absence of language would certainly be a handicap. But full human intellectual development is impossible without language. This primacy of language (as opposed to speech) has been argued by some authors (e.g., Lenneberg, 1967; Moores, 1970) and taken for granted by others, but on the whole it simply has not received the weight it deserves in practical decisions regarding what is to be taught and when.

The conclusion we are led to by accepting the first conjecture is that children—all children—should learn as much language as possible, as early as possible, to facilitate their intellectual (and emotional) development. For deaf (and perhaps even for hearing) children, this means learning a manual sign language at about age 1:6. Even if the linguistic concepts of their early (sign) language are not isomorphic to those of their later (oral–aural) language, it will be easier to map the new concepts onto the old than to start from scratch with the new concepts. The communicative power of Ameslan—in terms of information rate and precision of expression—is quite comparable to that of spoken English (Bellugi, 1972; Bellugi & Fischer, 1972), and thus can serve deaf children and adults as adequately as a spoken language serves hearing children and adults.

Given that children have acquired one language, they may not wish to acquire new ones, no matter how easy the learning process may be. For example, deaf children with a manual sign language may not wish to acquire spoken English, nor for that matter, may French Canadian children desire to learn English. These are important motivational problems. The attempt of the hearing community to prevent a later motivational problem by depriving the deaf child of early language, reminds me of the false mother who would have let King Solomon cleave the disputed child in two so that she would be sure to get her share. The ideal solution, of course, would be to give the deaf child such great language facility that bilingualism (signs and English) does not require overwhelming effort and motivation.

AN IDEAL WRITTEN LANGUAGE

As already noted, it is hypothesized that the deaf child would benefit from the early use of a written form of sign language. This section contains a discussion of what criteria should be used in developing such a written system. In discussing this problem, we consider some of the good and bad features of two classes of written languages: written Chinese or Japanese (Kanji) and written English or German. First, relating this to the previous discussion, some Chinese ideographs and Japanese Kanji are acquired at an earlier age than written English words (Sakamoto & Makita, 1973).

Any early advantage there may be to reading ideographs is quickly lost when schooling begins. In languages such as English or German, once the rules for phonetic or syllabic spelling are acquired—complicated though they may be—the child can bring his reading (and writing) vocabulary to within range of his spoken vocabulary in a relatively short time. On the other hand, Chinese and Japanese children spend a major portion of their education simply learning how to read and write ideographs. The Japanese educational system provides a beautiful example of both kinds of language learning. Children initially are taught to read Hiragana, letters that represent syllables, and then each year a certain number of Hiragana words must be learned as Kanji (e.g., 46 Kanji in first grade, 105 in second, 187, 205, 194, and 144 in successive years of elementary school). In Chinese schools the rate of learning ideographs is much greater, presumably because there is no phonetic or syllabic transcription of Chinese to fall back on (Leong, 1973).

The most interesting feature of a pure ideographic language is that it has no special relation to any particular spoken language. The various dialects of Chinese use the same written language. A literate Chinese person in Japan who has no knowledge of Japanese can communicate reasonably well by writing (Wang, 1973). Insofar as ideographs represent concepts, they could be pronounced in any language—Japanese, Chinese, or even English. An American could learn to read Chinese without knowing a single word of spoken Chinese. One could imagine a world in which everyone used a universal written or signed language; it would merely be spoken differently in each of the different languages. If there were a universal manual sign language, the same sequence of signs would be translated into spoken English or French by a bilingual speaker of each respective language.

This most interesting feature of ideographic language also reflects its greatest problems. That is, the main trouble with the ideographic languages is that the written form has no relation to the spoken form, and thus it must be learned essentially as a new language. There also are other problems, too, with the Chinese–Japanese ideographs. The amount of effort that is required to master a substantial vocabulary suggests that Kanji are visually confusable. Perhaps this is a consequence of their being difficult to parse. Moreover, the parsing difficulty means it is difficult to order Kanji into a dictionary or to find an unfamiliar Kanji in such a dictionary. (Kanji are listed simply according to the number of strokes used in writing them.) For the same reason, Kanji are difficult to produce by typing or printing processes. There is, as yet, no convenient set of elementary strokes that can be efficiently typed to construct a Kanji in a way that is comparable to typing letters to construct a word. On the other hand, computers can be programmed to construct Kanji (Fujimura & Kagaya, 1972; Nagao, 1972), and the advent of cheap microprocessors may stimulate the development of a Kanjiwriter that would be comparable to a typewriter in cost and size.

The Japanese defend their Kanji transcription system by saying that they can code a given message into Kanji quicker than into a phonetic or syllabic transcription because fewer strokes are used in a Kanji than in writing the one or several words needed to express the same concept in a phonetic transcription. And Japanese bilinguals claim that reading a novel written in Kanji is much faster than reading the same book in a phonetically or syllabically transcribed language.

We should remark that the good features of ideographs do not depend on their being accurate—or even recognizable—pictorial representations of the concepts they represent. Some ideographs were pictorial at an early stage in the development of the language, but the ideographs have long since become stylized and standardized. To help students learn Kanji, stories are invented to explain how various features of a Kanji have been derived from a picture. Similar stories are invented for manual signs to account for their origin (as noted by Bellugi during the discussions of this study group). This is an excellent illustration of the use of association to facilitate language learning, but most stories have little validity as history.

The advantage of phonetic written language is that the written and the spoken language can be translated from one form to the other by a manageable set of rules. Given familiarity with the rules, a speaker of the language can learn to read and to write in short order. Parsing and ordering are implied because there is only a limited set of symbols and because the order of transcription follows from the order of pronouncing. The written language can be typed, and dictionaries are easy to use because there is at least one unambiguous ordering of the words of the language and even unfamiliar words can be located. Before the age of printing and of dictionaries, the advantages of ideographic languages might have been balanced against these of phonetic languages; since that time, however, the pendulum has swung to phonetic languages.

I assert that it is possible, in principle, to produce a written language that combines the best features of phonetic and ideographic languages, a parsable ideographic language that is superior to either pure kind. Consider, for example, the set of strokes illustrated in Figure 6.1a, which can be combined to produce "ideographs" (6.1b) or "words" (6.1c). The ideographs can be treated as ideographs per se, but in fact rules can be made to guarantee a unique parsing. For example, the rule in Figure 6.1 is to read a character from top to bottom and then from left to right. Thus, these characters can be produced by a typewriter and they can be ordered just as the letter-by-letter word representations of Figure 6.1c can be ordered. Comparison of Figures 6.1b and 6.1c illustrates the enormous perceptual salience of ideographs relative to letter sequences.

The ability of subjects to learn to read texts composed of characters joined either as ideographs (Figure 6.1b) or as letter-by-letter words (as in Figure 6.1c) has been investigated in a restricted context by Brooks (1976). He found that after several hundred practice trials there was a reading advantage of the ideographic over the letter-by-letter word forms. He also studied the effect of parsing and found that the existence of a consistent parsing scheme was advantageous for both forms. This experimental demonstration of the superiority of parsable ideographs is encouraging, but it does not enable us a priori to predict the possible advantages of a cleverly designed set of parsable ideographs for a full vocabulary. Contending systems of orthography must be tested against each other to determine the best one.

Theoretically, the basis of the salience of ideographs can be understood in terms of *feature detectors,* postulated units of visual analysis. Al-

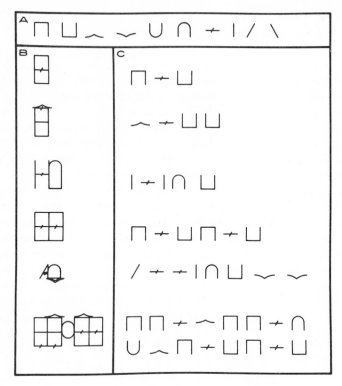

Figure 6.1 (a) An alphabet of 10 characters; (b) Some ideographs produced with the alphabet; (c) Letter-by-letter words. Parsings of the ideographs in (b).

though we do not know what the characteristics of the human sets of feature detectors are, we can think of them heuristically as detectors of straight lines (vertical, horizontal, diagonal, etc.), curved lines, intersections, angles, etc. When strokes are combined ideographically, they excite different classes of feature detectors from those excited by any of the individual parts. Thus, a richer assortment of new detectors is brought into play by arraying the strokes as an ideograph rather than linearly as a letter-by-letter word. The differences between the two alternative representations of words, ideographic and letter-by-letter, are analogous to the differences between decimal (0–9) and binary (0,1) representations of numbers. In most applications, people find binary representations of numbers so difficult to deal with that they translate them into octal or hexadecimal equivalents. The human visual system appears to deal more successfully with collections of many different features in one place (ideographs, decimal numbers) than with collections of similar features in different places (letter-by-letter words, binary numbers).

The main advantages of a parsable ideographic language for deaf children are: (a) cleverly-designed ideographs probably can be learned at an earlier age than a wordlike written language; and (b) at a later age, when the parsing scheme is learned, new words can be added at the advantageous rates characteristic of phonetic and syllabic transcriptions.

But what language is to be represented by ideographs? The answer is obvious: a manual sign language such as Ameslan. "Phonetic," wordlike transcriptions of signs have been proposed by Stokoe, Casterline, and Croneberg (1965), but this system is cumbersome and does not have the appeal of ideographs. The goal is to produce a transcription of signs that is at least as descriptive of the signs themselves as, say, written English is descriptive of spoken English. The problem of inventing and obtaining acceptance of a suitable code for the ideographic, parsable transcription of signs is challenging. It simply has not received an amount of attention commensurate with the potential rewards of success.

CROSS-MODALITY TRANSFORMATION RULES AND SUPPLEMENTARY COMMUNICATION DEVICES

Supposing that the transcription problem is solved, and that a good written system related to sign language is developed, what are the consequences for educating the deaf child? We assume that the child is exposed intensively to the signed and the written language. As we have read in this volume, deaf infants apparently acquire manual signs as early as hearing children acquire speech, and perhaps even earlier because the motor control of the hands matures before motor control of the voice. We know we can design ideographs that can be learned earlier than letter-by-letter words so that a child with an ideographic language can have a headstart in reading. If the ideographs can be parsed, and if the parsing rules can be learned, then there is no reason for this reading advantage ever to be lost. With a superior written language, the reading advantage, and thus language development, of deaf children over hearing children, is more likely to grow than to diminish.

From this position of advanced rather than retarded development, the deaf child can hope to succeed in the problems of second and third language learning—that is, in learning to communicate with hearing people in their own vernacular. The normal, literate, hearing person knows his language in four modes: hearing, speaking, reading, and writing. In phonetic languages, the various modes are connected so that there is basically only one language to be learned, plus three sets of rules. The first two sets of rules are actually skills: the transformations that enable us to go from hearing to speaking (imitation), and the transformations from reading to writing (copying). The third set consists of the phonetic transcription rules to connect the written and spoken forms. Of these three sets of rules, the deaf person has normal access to only one set: the rules connecting reading and writing (copying). The connection between lip reading and speaking is much more tenuous for the deaf person than is the connection between hearing and speaking for the hearing person (not to mention the extraordinary intrinsic difficulty of both of these language forms for the deaf person).

Similarly, phonetic transcription rules are of much less utility for a person who cannot hear speech than for one who can. Thus the deaf person who is attempting to communicate in the vernacular is faced with the task of acquiring, in effect, three new vocabularies instead of just one. The deaf person would certainly benefit from being advanced linguistically in sign language, as the more language he knew the easier it would be to acquire still more, but the difficulty remains formidable. Thus, it is important to consider other systems that could facilitate the communication process.

If a visually or tactually interpretable kind of sound spectrogram of speech could be developed—one of the sort being investigated by Nickerson (e.g., Nickerson & Stevens, 1973; see brief discussion by Liben, Chapter 1 of this volume)—it would go far toward facilitating the acquisition of spoken language by deaf people. A visual representation of speech could function analogously to the auditory information available to hearing people, with the remaining language forms derivable by rules analogous to those used by hearing people. Communicating in the vernacular would require acquisition of just one new language and two sets of rules, one connecting visual representations to speaking, and the other, the phonetic transcriptions connecting visual representations to written forms.

Finally, another mechanism that would be enormously useful for deaf people is the development of low-cost devices for visual communication. Such devices do exist, but currently the cost is prohibitive. For example, the National Technical Institute for the Deaf in Rochester, New York uses a Stromberg–Carlson system for internal video communication. However, when the Bell System offered a similar videotelephone (PIC-TUREPHONE®) service to the central Chicago business community on a trial basis, there was so little demand that full-scale introduction of such service was indefinitely postponed. The interest in the system was not sufficient to meet the offering cost, which in Chicago was $87.25 a month for a PICTUREPHONE® station with 30 min of video connection time.

At a reasonable price, videomonitors located within individual homes and offices, and videotelephones located in homes and businesses throughout the country, would do much to ameliorate the communication handicap of deafness. Such visual communication would also provide an impetus for further development of manual sign languages. Person-to-person communication by video might require more language redundancy than direct face-to-face communication. But sign language might replace many of the functions that writing serves, and might make other functions more efficient, such as shopping by telephone at stores that offer "sign language spoken here."

In the development of video communication devices, it is notable that basic studies of the bandwidth (channel capacity) requirements for manual–visual communication have not yet been conducted. Comparable studies of spoken language provided useful insights into the nature of spoken language, and there may yet be much of interest to be learned about manual–visual communication from studies of the channel capacity needed to transmit this kind of communication. For example, it may be that by judicious choice of such factors as the number of pictures transmitted per second, the quality of each picture, the arrangement of lights, and the selection of background, that acceptable manual–visual video communication is possible even now with an affordable amount of channel capacity.

SUMMARY AND CONCLUSIONS

Three potential areas for development have been discussed: written language, sound transducers and translators, and video communications. The ratio of psychology to engineering is largest for the first and smallest for the last. The psychological and visual requirements of manual–visual video communication probably will not be difficult to specify; the problems are found in developing the technology to lower costs. The problem of building a sound transducer involves a more delicate balance between the limitations both of perception and of technology. But the problem of language transcription is strictly in the realm of psychology: All the tools we need are already at hand. And because a written language could fundamentally change the way its users think, I believe a solution to this problem would have the most profound effects on society in general, and on deaf people in particular.

REFERENCES

Bellugi, U. Studies in sign language. In T. O'Rourke (Ed.), *Psycholinguistics and total communication.* Silver Springs, Maryland: American Annals of the Deaf, 1972.

Bellugi, U., & Fischer, S. A comparison of sign language and spoken language. *Cognition: International Journal of Cognitive Psychology,* 1972, *1,* 173–200.

Brooks, L. Visual pattern in fluent word identification. In S. Reber & D. L. Scarborough (Eds.), *Toward a psychology of reading.* Hillsdale, New Jersey: Erlbaum, 1976.

Fujimura, O., & Kagaya, R. A pattern-structural code for Kanji. In *First USA Japan Computer Conference.* Montvale, New Jersey: American Federation of Information Processing Societies, Inc., 1972. Pp. 287–290.

Furth, H. G. *Thinking without language: Psychological implications of deafness.* New York: Free Press, 1966.

Lenneberg, E. *Biological foundations of language.* New York: Wiley, 1967.

Leong, C. K. Hong Kong. In J. Downing (Ed.), *Comparative reading.* New York: Macmillan, 1973.

Moores, D. Psycholingistics and deafness. *American Annals of the Deaf,* 1970, *115,* 37–48.

Nagao, M. Picture recognition and data structure. In F. Hake & A. Rosenfeld (Eds.), *Graphic languages.* Amsterdam: North Holland Publishing, 1972.

Nickerson, R. S. Speech training and reception aids for the deaf. Bolt Beranek and Newman, Inc. Report No. 2980, 1975.

Nickerson, R. S. & Stevens, K. N. Teaching speech to the deaf: Can a computer help? *IEEE Transactions on Audio and Electroacoustics,* 1973, AU-21, 445–455.

Sakamoto, T., & Makita, K. Japan. In J. Downing (Ed.), *Comparative reading.* New York: Macmillan, 1973.

Stokoe, W., Casterline, D., & Croneberg, C. *A dictionary of American Sign Language on linguistic principles.* Washington, D.C.: Gallaudet College Press, 1965.

Wang, W. S. Y. The Chinese language. *Scientific American,* 1973, *228,* 51.

7

On the Role of Vision in Language Acquisition by Deaf Children[1]

R. S. NICKERSON

That persons who have been profoundly deaf since birth or infancy tend to have severe communication problems is generally acknowledged. Such persons seldom acquire fluent speech (Calvert & Silverman, 1975; Nickerson, 1975) and only rarely read or write above a fourth-grade level (Furth, 1973; Brooks, Chapter 5, this volume). Furthermore, contrary to popular belief, only a small percentage of profoundly deaf persons become expert lipreaders (Furth, 1966, 1973).

It is also generally agreed that the communication problems of deaf people are symptomatic of a more basic difficulty, namely, poor language ability (Furth, 1966, 1973; Lenneberg, 1967; Moores, 1970). Facility with language clearly sets an upper bound on an individual's communication skills; the extent to which such facility also limits a person's cognitive abilities, more generally, is a matter of controversy. One position is exemplified by Bruner's (1966) argument that "language is a major instrument of thought [p. 104]," and that "in some unknown but considerable measure, the power of words is the power of thought [p.

[1] I am grateful to Marilyn Adams, David Green, A. W. F. Huggins, and Kenneth Stevens for helpful comments on a draft of this chapter.

105]." In contrast to this view is Furth's (1964) insistence on the separability of intellectual and verbal skills: "Various sources of empirical evidence confirm the theoretical position that just as language learning is not closely related to intellectual endowment so intellective performance is not directly dependent on language [p. 162]." But whatever position one takes, there can be no doubt that lack of language competence is a serious handicap. At best, it impedes an individual's ability to communicate with others; at worst, it precludes effective communication with oneself.

There are two striking facts about the way children usually acquire language. First, barring a sensory deficiency that prevents them from doing so, they rely primarily on information obtained by ear. It would be imprudent to argue that vision normally plays no role in language acquisition; however, the ease with which blind children become competent language users, compared with the difficulties experienced by deaf children, clearly demonstrates the sufficiency of the auditory channel and raises the question of whether hearing is not only a sufficient, but a necessary prerequisite to the development of normal language skills. Second, the language-acquisition process is normally quite spontaneous; although adults may provide some intentional instruction when a child begins to talk, for the most part adults simply provide samples for the child to mimic, volunteer names of objects and features of the child's world space, and perhaps correct persisting errors. Formal language instruction does not begin until the child has already become a functional language user. In other words, children normally are not *taught* language; instead; they *learn* it spontaneously as a consequence of exposure to language used more or less continuously.

The general question that motivates this chapter is how language acquisition by prelingually deaf persons—for whom the usual auditory route to language competence is precluded—might be facilitated by more effective use of vision. This general question prompts a number of more specific ones: Is vision an inherently poorer sensory channel for language acquisition than audition? How effective is manual signing as a medium for developing primary language skills and as a foundation for language-dependent aspects of thinking? To what extent can visual representations of speech, or of specific aspects of speech, facilitate speech perception by deaf people? How should reading be taught to deaf children? And, could reading serve as a vehicle for the acquisition of basic language skills, or does reading necessarily depend upon the prior acquisition of those skills?

Needless to say, this chapter does not answer these questions. Indeed, the answers to most of them will not be obtained without considerable research, inasmuch as they presuppose a much greater understanding of linguistic and cognitive development than we currently have. This chapter is meant to raise questions, to argue in some cases that what appear to have been accepted as working assumptions should be challenged, and to suggest some directions that research on these issues might take.

VISION AS A CHANNEL FOR LANGUAGE ACQUISITION

Although it does not answer the question of their relative merits as channels for language acquisition, a comparison of the visual and auditory systems as information-processing systems is at least suggestive. The human eye contains more than 130 million receptor cells, 125–130 million rods, and 6 or 7 million cones. These cells are mapped onto about 1 million fibers in the optic nerve, about 150 receptors per fiber. Compared to the eye, the human ear is poorly innervated; it contains less than 25,000 receptor cells—about 3500 inner and 20,000 outer hair cells—which map onto perhaps 25,000–30,000 ganglion cells in the auditory nerve. Thus the neuroanatomy of the eye permits it to deliver many times as much information to the brain per unit time as does that of the ear.

Both hearing and vision have great dynamic ranges. The ratio of the intensity of a stimulus that can just barely be detected to that of one that will cause pain is 12 or 13 orders of magnitude in hearing and 14 or 15 in vision. This comparison is somewhat misleading, however, inasmuch as vision is actually based on two sensory systems, mediated by two types of receptors: cones (photopic vision) and rods (scotopic vision). The dynamic range of the photopic system is 8 or 9 orders of magnitude, and that of the scotopic system about 7.

The dynamic range available for use at any given instant is much greater in hearing than in vision because the eye (especially the scotopic system) adapts to reductions in the level of stimulus intensity very slowly. Thus, the full range of sensitivity for very weak signals is not available until the eye has been dark-adapted for nearly 30 min. Even the photopic system requires about 5 min of dark-adaptation to reach maximum sensitivity. The threshold of hearing for weak stimuli, however, is affected for only a few milliseconds by the occurrence of a relatively loud sound. This lack of adaptation of the auditory system is one of the characteristics that makes it especially well-suited to processing signals, such as speech, whose intensity level may change abruptly by large amounts. An implication of this difference between hearing and vision for the visual encoding of speech is that intensity changes in the speech signal should not be represented directly by intensity changes in the visual code; instead, they should be mapped onto a visual dimension (e.g., gray scale, linear extent) that is not so subject to adaptation effects.

Another difference between the visual and auditory systems that may be particularly relevant to the processing of speech stimuli relates to their respective capacities to discriminate temporal relationships. Audition is usually thought of as being better than vision in this regard. Because speech is encoded in time, its decoding must depend, in part, on the perception of temporal patterns or on other patterns onto which temporal relationships have been mapped.

Consider what kind of temporal resolving power a system must have in order to decode speech. Speakers vary in the rate at which they talk, and a given speaker emits words at different rates under different conditions. Measured speech rates that have been reported in the literature all fall between 100 and 250 words a minute, with the majority between 125–175 words a minute. This corresponds to about three syllables, or 8–12 phonemes per second. Interpreting the order of occurrence of phonemes correctly would seem to be a requirement for understanding speech, and to satisfy this requirement it appears that the processing system must be able to recognize the order of two events whose onsets differ by about 80 msec. In fact, smaller temporal differences than this are important to speech understanding, because, although the durations of phonemes may average 100 msec or so, the variability around this average is considerable; moreover, some phonetic events that are important for distinguishing one phoneme from another may be as short as 10 or 20 msec.

Visual temporal acuity has usually been studied by measuring the critical fusion frequency (CFF), the frequency at which a series of equally spaced flashes is begun to be seen as fused rather than as flickering. The CFF depends upon such factors as intensity, size and spectral composition of the stimulus, state of adaptation of the eye; retinal locus of the stimulus image, and waveshape and duty cycle (relative durations of on and off phases) of the stimulus. A representative range for a foveal stimulus of intermediate intensity is 30–50 Hz. In other words, if successive visual stimuli are to be perceived as discrete events, their onsets must be separated by 20–30 msec.

Several attempts have been made to determine a critical flutter frequency, the auditory analog to the critical flicker frequency of vision. But this phenomenon has proved to be somewhat elusive, and not really analogous to its visual counterpart (see Geldard, 1972, for a discussion of the problem). More successful efforts to measure the temporal resolving

power of the ear have involved determining the shortest separation between two sounds that will permit an observer to distinguish the order of
their occurrence. Hirsh (1959) demonstrated that listeners could distinguish the order of events whose onsets differed by as little as 20 msec.
More recently, Patterson and Green (1970) have shown that under some
conditions they can distinguish onset time differences of only 2 msec.

In view of such evidence of the ability of both vision and hearing to
resolve small temporal differences, the difficulty that people have in
reporting the order of rapidly presented stimulus sequences in either
modality is somewhat surprising. When shown a sequence of letters at a
rapid rate (eight letters per second), for example, subjects are better at
reporting the letters that were presented than their order of occurrence
(Kolers, 1970). Particularly surprising is the finding of Warren, Obusek,
Farmer, and Warren (1969) and Warren and Warren (1970) indicating
that people have great difficulty reporting the order of a recurring series
of acoustic stimuli if the onsets between successive stimuli are less than
about .5 sec. This finding appears to be inconsistent with the fact that we
are able to decode the speech signal; a number of experimenters have
been sufficiently incredulous of it to go to the trouble of verifying it
themselves. Essentially, the same result has been obtained now several
times.

Warren's finding is not yet well understood, but there are several tentative accounts of it that make it consistent with our ability to perceive
speech. For the purposes of this chapter, the following observations will
suffice. First, a distinction should be made between perceiving the order
of stimuli and reporting it. Nickerson and Freeman (1974) have suggested that part of the difficulty subjects have with the Warren task may
stem from their inability to translate what they are hearing into an output code so that it can be remembered and reported. To the extent that
this conjecture is valid, it provides a basis for expecting very different
order–reporting performance for meaningless acoustic stimuli than for
speech; in the case of speech stimuli, remembering and reporting should
both be facilitated by the existence in memory of highly overlearned
linguistic units that preserve the order of the individual sounds. One
need not remember explicitly the order of the phonemes in "Saturday,"
for example; one simply remembers the word and in so doing assures
the correct reporting of the order of the individual sounds. Second,
because of the great redundancy of spoken language, it is not necessary
to perceive the order of individual phonemes precisely to understand, or
repeat, speech. Assuming approximately 40 phonemes in English, there
are more than 86 million ways to combine them into "words" of 5
phonemes each. Only a small fraction of these combinations (certainly

less than .1% of them) are, in fact, words in the language. Many of the possible combinations are unpronounceable, or otherwise violate the rules of word construction. The implication is that, given that people know they are listening to a word, they need not perceive every phoneme or the exact order of their occurrence to make a reasonable inference concerning what word they have heard. There are, of course, pairs of words that differ primarily with respect to phoneme order (e.g., *past–pats, split–spilt*), but they are exceptions, and, as a rule, any ambiguity that might exist regarding such words would be resolved by the semantic context in which the words occur. Third, the ability to perceive a stimulus that is decomposable into a set of ordered components is not the same as the ability to perceive the order of occurrence of a sequence of independent stimuli. The former may depend on pattern-recognition capabilities that are of no use with the latter.

There are two conclusions to be drawn from these considerations of the ability of the visual system to discriminate ordered stimuli such as those encountered in speech. First, it is not clear that the eye is very much worse than the ear in this regard. In particular, it is not clear that, given a proper visual coding scheme, the eye could not learn to distinguish among real-time visual analogs of the acoustic representations of words. Second, vision has an advantage over audition in that differences that are difficult to resolve temporally can be represented, and readily distinguished, spatially. The usual convention in representing time-varying variables visually is to represent time by one spatial dimension on a display. An advantage of such a representation is that it provides a memory, of sorts, of the time-varying event; consequently, features that could not be detected as they occurred may be perceived after the fact by examining the display. This point will be touched upon again in the section on visual representations of speech.

MANUAL SIGNING

Manual sign language is the most widely used nonoral means of communication among deaf adults. Until fairly recently, sign language had received relatively little attention from either linguists or psychologists. Consequently, little is yet known about how sign language compares with oral–aural language, either as a means of communication or as a foundation for language-dependent aspects of thinking. Moreover, nearly everything that has been written about sign language has been written by people who have learned sign as a second language, if at all. There is something mildly perverse about a hearing person passing judgment on the quality of a communication medium that can probably be fully appreciated only by an individual for whom it is the mother tongue. It should not be surprising that writers with normal hearing have often found it easy to make comparisons between speech and sign that show the latter to disadvantage. Speech might fare less well if the comparison were made by native users of sign; unfortunately, it might be difficult to convince the hearing world of the advantages of signs if they could be appreciated only by fluent signers, and even more so if the results of the comparison were communicated (as has been the custom) in the language of those making it.

Sign language has been considered by many to be inferior to oral–aural languages, in particular with respect to its ability to support abstract thinking; signing has been viewed as concrete, situation-specific, and conceptually impoverished as compared to oral–aural languages, such as English (Kohl, 1966). However, this opinion has been challenged as a result of the work of several investigators (Bellugi, 1972; Bellugi & Klima, 1972; Bellugi & Klima, Chapter 3, this volume; Lane, Boyes-Braem, & Bellugi, 1976; Stokoe, Croneberg, & Casterline, 1965). The position taken here is that it is not known whether manual sign language is inherently inferior to speech as a medium for representing and conveying ideas. It is conceivable to the writer that signing may prove to be superior in some respects.

Sign language does, however, have certain undeniable practical disadvantages: It occupies the hands and precludes them from performing other tasks while communicating, and, as it has no written form, it can be used only for face-to-face communication (Nowell & Liben, 1975). One can find arguments supporting the opposite case—sign language can sometimes be used to advantage in situations where speech is precluded by noise—but they seem weak by comparison.

Perhaps the most telling argument against sign language as an only means of communication is not an argument against the language per se, but a recognition of its limited uses in a hearing society. Because a very small percentage of the general population understands it, people who know *only* it are extremely limited with respect to the number of people with whom they can converse. And, although deaf children may acquire language through signing, at best their exposure to language usage will probably be much less than is that of hearing children, because relatively few of the people with whom they will come in contact are likely to be proficient signers.

Given that the vast majority of mankind depends on speech as its primary mode of communication and that there exist written representations of speech permitting the transmission of verbal information over indefinite distances and periods of time, speech must be the preferred means of communication for anyone for whom it is a possibility. What is not clear is that the hands and eyes are intrinsically less well-suited for real-time communication than are the mouth and ears. If all the world were deaf, manual–visual language might have evolved to the same level of sophistication and effectiveness as has speech, and orthographic systems could well have been developed to accommodate it (see Chapter 6 by Sperling, this volume). Such a possibility cannot be ruled out on the basis of what is known about human perceptual capabilities or about language.

THE VISUAL REPRESENTATION OF SPEECH

Tanner (1963) has suggested that the specificity of a sensory system may result solely from the characteristics of the transducer for that system and that the "processing mechanism" may be general. In this view, the function of any particular higher center, or processing mechanism, may be that of correlating the inputs from the nerves that feed into it with information obtained from other senses to establish the relationships between those inputs and relevant properties of the environment. The reason that the visual cortex gives rise to visual experience is that its transducer, the retina, transmits information regarding geometrical properties of the environment. Tanner speculates that *if* specificity is entirely a function of the sensory transducer, then it is conceivable that visual information might be processed effectively by the auditory center, or auditory information by the visual center, if the associated ascending nerves were able to accept signals from the transducers. "If it were possible to connect the auditory nerve to the retina and the optic nerve to the cochlea, the output of the auditory nerve would then contain information that would make possible discriminations specific to the 'visual' environment, and that of the optic nerve specific to audition [p. 215]."

If these speculations are correct, then the basic problem of sensory substitution is that of transducer design. More specifically, the problem in the case of substituting vision for hearing for the purpose of speech acquisition is that of designing a transducer than can deliver to the visual system those properties of the speech signal that are essential to the decoding of that signal as speech. Tanner cautions that if specificity is due to the transducer, and if a transducer that would permit the substitution of one sensory system for another were developed, the determination of whether or not it would work could be a very difficult task. This is, in part, because we do not know what to expect concerning how long it should take for the central processor to learn to interpret the substitutionary neural signals appropriately. Certainly, there is no reason to believe that signals from a substitute sensory system would be easier to interpret than those signals for which substitution is being made. Thus in the case of oral–aural language acquisition, we would expect that for any substitutionary encoding scheme to be effective, a child would need *at least* as much exposure to appropriate stimulation through it as the child without a hearing impairment must receive through the auditory channel to attain the same level of language proficiency.

There are at least three common ways to represent a speech signal visually. One way is to use a direct visual analog of the speech sound-pressure wave that simply shows how sound pressure at a given point varies over time. Such a representation contains precisely the same information that is contained in the sound-pressure wave itself. A second way is to show how the distribution of acoustic energy over the speech frequency range changes in time. In the conventional spectrogram, the vertical axis represents frequency, the horizontal axis represents time, and the relative darkness of the figure at any given point represents the relative amount of energy at the frequency indicated by the ordinate of the point at the time indicated by its abscissa. Information is lost by this representation in two ways: by the limited number of darkness levels that can be distinguished, and by the fact that a vertical cross-section of the figure at any given point represents an integration of frequency information over several milliseconds. The fact that a spectrographic display contains less information than a representation of the sound-pressure wave does not necessarily mean that it is a less useful representation. Some properties of the speech sounds are easily seen in the former that cannot be extracted visually from the latter. The basic goal of recoding is not to preserve all the information that is in the original signal, but to preserve the information that is critical for some purpose (in this case, for speech understanding) and to represent it in a form that can be interpreted.

A third way of representing a speech signal visually probably involves an even further reduction of information than does the spectrogram. In this case certain features of the signal—such as fundamental frequency, the amplitude envelope, the frequencies of several formants, and the presence of frication—are extracted and shown simultaneously but individually as functions of time.

The most widely used of these visual encodings of speech is the spectrographic display. Developed at the Bell Telephone Laboratories during the 1940s, the spectrograph is now one of the speech scientists's most useful tools (Koening, Dunn, & Lacey, 1946; Potter, Kopp, & Green, 1947). To the trained observer, a spectrogram can convey much information about the acoustic properties of speech. The fundamental frequency and formant frequencies of voiced sounds may be seen; unvoiced fricatives are relatively distinctive, as are the closures and releases of stop consonants. The extreme vowels, /i/, /a/, and /u/, are fairly easily discriminated, as are the durations of many phonetic elements and the spectral changes that take place at some phoneme boundaries.

Typically, spectrograms have been used to study speech after it has been produced, rather than during the production process. The speech is recorded, spectrograms are made from the recordings, and then the visual patterns on the spectrograms are scrutinized for the presence or absence of certain characteristics or features. One can imagine, however, a "real-time" display that would generate a spectrographic representation of speech as the speech is produced. Such a display might show, for example, the last N sec of speech, the rightmost edge of the display always representing the present. Viewing such a display would be analogous to looking through a window at an endless spectrogram that was moving below the window from right to left. At any given instant one would see a representation not only of the speech that was being generated at that instant but of that that had been produced during the last few seconds as well. No serious attempt has been made to use real-time spectrograms as speech-reception aids, although several researchers have investigated their usefulness in the context of remedial speech training (Kisner & Weed, 1972; Kopp & Green, 1948; Stark, Cullen, & Chase, 1968).

The development of a wearable real-time spectrographic display would require the solution of some difficult engineering problems. These problems are probably solvable, however, or will be as further advances are made in microprocessor technology. In any case, it is not the purpose of this chapter to focus on these types of problems. The question of interest here is: If a wearable real-time spectrographic display *could* be implemented, what is the likelihood that it could be an effective vehicle by which a deaf child could learn spoken language?

While direct evidence on the question is sparse, informed opinion is pessimistic. Speech spectrograms are very difficult to read, even by scientists who have worked with them over many years. Liberman, Cooper, Shankweiler, and Studdert-Kennedy (1968) have argued that this difficulty is not a matter of training or experience. They attribute it rather to the fact that speech is not a simple alphabet, which is to say that there is not a one-to-one correspondence between phonemes and acoustic patterns. Rather the acoustic representation of a given phoneme is likely to vary, depending on the context in which it occurs; moreover, the accoustic signal is not readily segmented into discrete phonemes, inasmuch as a single nonsegmentable feature in the signal often carries information about two adjacent phonemes. The ear, Liberman, Cooper, Shankweiler, and Studdert-Kennedy (1968) contend, is capable of recovering the individual phonemes from the speech signal in spite of these facts; however, the eye does not have a comparable decoding ability to apply to the spectrogram.

The fact is, however, that it is still not known how the ear, or rather the ear–brain system, accomplishes the decoding in the face of the difficulties that Liberman *et al.* note. The prima facie evidence of its decoding ability is that we do understand speech; if we did not, the problems that have been pointed out might be cited as reasons why the decoding by the auditory system of anything like a speech signal would be impossible!

It is worth noting that even the most experienced readers of spectrograms have spent relatively little time at this activity, compared with the amount of time a hearing child spends in acquiring speech. Further, spectrogram readers do not encounter their first spectrogram until they are well beyond the age at which language and speech competence is usually attained. And the motivation for learning is not that of acquiring a primary means of communication. It is not clear that a child could not learn to decode real-time spectrograms as speech if he or she had as much exposure to them, from birth, as the hearing child has to auditory speech signals.

Of course, as has already been noted, the spectrogram represents only one of many possible ways to encode speech visually. And, while it has proven to be a useful method for many purposes, there is no reason to assume that it is the best possible encoding for teaching speech to young children. One goal of research should be to explore alternative coding possibilities with a view to finding the visual representation that will maximize the chances that the eye–brain system can learn to interpret it.

READING

Reading ability is normally acquired in a very different way than is oral–aural language. Children do not, as a rule, spontaneously learn to read; they must be taught, and the teaching is not begun until the child has already become a relatively proficient language user. The methods that are used to teach reading presuppose competence in oral–aural language, and typically focus on orthographic–phonologic transformation rules. The assumption is that if children can transform spelling into speech, then they can understand what they say to themselves.

Unlike hearing children, deaf children cannot learn to read by learning to translate printed symbols into their phonological counterparts. Even if the children are among the small minority who are competent language users by virtue of knowing how to sign, they cannot learn to read in the same way as hearing children do, because printed words cannot be mapped onto signs in a one-to-one fashion as they can onto spoken words. As Furth (1973) notes, whereas hearing children learn to read by superimposing some new skills on their existing knowledge of language, for deaf children learning to read is tantamount to learning a language per se. And, unlike the case of language acquisition by the hearing child, the learning is not done as a result of being constantly exposed to people using this language as their primary means of communication. Moreover, the teaching of reading usually is not begun until well beyond the age at which the children would have acquired most of their basic language skills if they had normal hearing. It is not surprising, then, that deaf people are almost universally poor readers. Tests have shown that the average prelingually deaf individual reads at somewhere between a second- and fourth-grade level, and that one who can read at a fifth-grade level is a rare exception (Furth, 1973; Brooks, this volume).

There are two questions that should be raised regarding the teaching of reading to deaf persons:

1. How can teaching methods be improved to take better advantage of whatever language skills the deaf learner may have?
2. Could the teaching of reading to very young deaf children be an effective method of early language training?

It seems safe to say that neither of these questions has received the attention it deserves. Almost all the research on reading that has been motivated by an interest in the development of better teaching methods has concerned reading by hearing persons. And the methods that are used invariably assume a functional oral–aural language foundation on which to build. On the face of things, it seems absurd to assume that methods that are appropriate to use with hearing children who are competent oral–aural language users would also be appropriate for deaf children who not only lack this ability, but may not even have a clear notion of what a word is. Nevertheless, it appears that this is the assumption that has been made. At least, the lack of research aimed at finding more effective ways of teaching reading specifically to deaf persons suggests that there must be a consensus among researchers that the problem is not different in any significant respects from that of teaching reading to hearing persons.

There are at least three types of capabilities that underlie skilled reading: perceptual capabilities, short-term memory capabilities, and inferential capabilities. Children must be able to make the perceptual discriminations necessary to tell one letter from another. They must be able to hold part of a sentence in memory while decoding another part. And they must be able to apply their knowledge of the world, inferentially, to impose meaning on the sequences of words they read. The last-mentioned ability requires, of course, that the children *have* some knowledge of the world stored in long-term memory.

Unless a deaf child is known to be multiply handicapped, there is little reason to believe that that child's visual perceptual capabilities are inferior in any way to those of the child with normal hearing. Of course, the child's ability to identify letters of the alphabet by name or to recognize letter groups that define graphemes may be impaired by virtue of a general lack of oral–aural language. These impairments would severely limit one's ability to learn to read by means of the usual grapheme–phoneme translation process; however, it is not clear that they would impede learning by some means not dependent on a functioning phonological system.

The importance of the role that short-term memory plays in the reading process has been stressed by Conrad (1972), among others. He raises the question of why children who seem to have the perceptual prerequisites for reading by about age 4 seem unable to be taught to read much before age 6. His answer is that it is not until about 6 years of age that a child has a sufficiently well-developed auditory or articulatory short-term memory. Before this time the child would have to rely on visual short-term memory to support the comprehension process, and visual short-term memory is simply not adequate to the task. We should note that this hypothesis does not rule out the ability to learn to recognize individual words and to build a visual vocabulary before age 6. Moreover, its implications for the problem of teaching reading to the deaf are not clear. Assuming that a deaf child does not learn to read by recoding the visual symbology into a phonological representation, then the age at which a short-term memory that could be used to store the phonological representation normally becomes available is irrelevant. If it were possible to teach a child to read effectively without using the phonological system, then there seems no point in calibrating the training to the time at which phonological strings can be stored.

The assumption that a functional auditory–articulatory, or phonological, short-term memory is a necessary, or nearly necessary, precondition for learning to read is one that should be given very careful attention. If it is true, teaching deaf children to read will continue to be an exceptionally difficult task and efforts to this end will necessarily have limited success. If it is false, the challenge is to seek explicitly for teaching methods that do not presuppose such a memory and, rather, make effective use of the short-term memory capabilities that the child does have.

The evidence that hearing people often do recode visually presented linguistic stimuli into an auditory representation for storage in short-term memory is compelling. The first evidence of this came from the analysis of substitution errors made by people in verbal-recall tasks (Conrad, 1964; Wickelgren, 1966). The general finding was that the errors were more readily accounted for in terms of acoustic similarities between the erroneously reported items and the correct items that were missing, than in terms of visual similarities between these items.

It is not entirely clear why such a sight-to-sound recoding occurs, although there are some plausible conjectures. If the subject has to make a verbal response in a recall task, then a recoding is necessary at *some* point in order to articulate the visual stimulus with the verbal response. If this were the primary reason for the recoding, the recoding could take place just before the emission of the response, and the stimulus could be held in memory during the retention interval in the visual form. Alternatively, it could be recoded immediately after reception and the output code retained during the retention interval. The assumption that recoding is done simply because it is a necessary step before the response can be emitted does not favor either of these possibilities over the other.

Another plausible explanation of why the recoding is done is to facilitate rehearsing the material during the retention interval. This interpretation gains credence from the fact that, as Dainoff (1970) has pointed out, experiments that have provided evidence of auditory recoding typically have involved memory loads that approach the immediate memory span (say five to seven items). Evidence for such recoding has not been so readily obtained in studies in which the memory load has been small (e.g., a single item). But why should it be easier, or more effective, to rehearse material that is represented in an auditory form than to rehearse material that is represented visually? In particular, if rehearsal amounts to "listening" to memory images of the names of items, why should it be easier to listen to acoustic images than to "look" at visual ones? It seems to be generally assumed that rehearsal *is* easier with auditory stimuli, although several investigators have presented evidence that strongly suggests that people can generate visual as well as auditory images.

Since Conrad's and Wickelgren's initial studies that focused on recall errors as a source of cues concerning the coding process, several other research strategies have been applied to the investigation of visual and auditory encoding in short-term memory. The results of many of these studies seem to indicate that visual short-term memory is more robust than was once thought. Visual, as well as auditory, similarity has been shown to be a determinant of the time required to decide that the second of two sequentially presented letters is different from the first (Wood, 1974). Numerous experiments have shown that the time spent deciding that two sequentially presented letters have the same name is less if they have the same name and are in the same case (are physically the same) than if they only have the same name (Dainoff, 1970; Parks, Kroll, Salzberg, & Parkinson, 1972; Posner & Mitchell, 1967). Other experiments using "same"–"different" judgments have also shown that the physical correspondence between the stimuli affect performance even when it is incidental to the judgment that is required (Nickerson, 1976; Nickerson & Pew, 1973). Hintzman and Summers (1973) found that recognition memory for visually presented words was greater if the words were printed in the same case on both acquisition and test trials than if they were shown in one case on the acquisition trails and in another (at least 3 min later) on the test trials. Kolers (1974) had subjects attempt to distinguish among sentences that they had not read previously, sentences that reappeared in the same typography, and sentences that had been read in a different typography. The results indicated that subjects did retain information about the pictorial aspects of what they had read. Several studies have shown that the performance of a shadowing task (repeating what is heard over earphones) during the retention interval affects auditory memory detrimentally, while memory for visual or audio–visual stimuli may show little loss over 12 sec (Kroll, Parkinson, & Parks, 1972; Kroll, Parks, Parkinson, Bieber & Johnson, 1970; Parkinson, Parks, & Kroll, 1971). None of these results demonstrates that short-term visual memory could be as effective as auditory–articulatory memory in supporting the acquisition of reading skills. They do indicate, however, that the persistence of visual information is greater than has often been assumed, and they attest to the importance of attempting to find more effective ways using this fact in teaching reading to deaf children.

The third type of capability underlying skilled reading—the ability to apply general world knowledge inferentially to the interpretation of sequences of words—is only beginning to receive the attention it deserves. Consider the following simple story:

On Saturday the children took a bus to the zoo. They saw some animal shows. In one show a seal tossed a ball to its trainer. The trainer caught it and tossed it back. On the way home they had a flat tire, but they enjoyed the trip all the same.

In order to comprehend this simple story, children must have a fair amount of knowledge about the world. They must know, for example, that a bus is a vehicle that transports people. Otherwise, the first sentence could have been interpreted, 'the children carried a bus to the zoo', as one might take (carry) a watch to the jeweler's. They must know that a seal—at least the kind of seal that is found in a zoo and takes part in animal shows—and not a ball, is likely to have a trainer, or the referent for *its* in the third sentence would be ambiguous. Similarly, a ball—at least the kind of ball that is named in the third sentence—must be recognized as something that can be caught; otherwise each *it* in the fourth sentence could be interpreted as the seal, as it would be if the sentence read: *The trainer gave it a fish and shook its flipper.* Actually, the disambiguation of the first *it* in the fourth sentence is more subtle than this suggests, because a seal can be caught as well as a ball, albeit in a different sense. The sentence would in fact be ambiguous if it read: *The trainer caught it and threw it into the pool.* To make sense of the last sentence in the story, the reader must know that busses, and not children, as the sentence literally claims, have flat tires, and that such things tend to diminish the pleasantness of the occasions on which they occur.

Without this sort of general knowledge of the world, even such a simple story as this example would be incomprehensible. Normally, a child acquires this type of knowledge in part through direct experience in the world and in part through communication with other people. Reading itself can also be a means of acquiring more information about the world that will in turn provide a broader knowledge base to facilitate further the reading process, but this can probably happen only after the child's reading skill has been developed to a relatively high degree. Thus, deaf children are doubly handicapped regarding the use of world knowledge in reading: They have difficulty learning to read partly because of their limited knowledge of the world, and their knowledge of the world is limited partly because they cannot read. It seems especially important, therefore, that every possible avenue for increasing the deaf child's general knowledge base be pursued. Such knowledge certainly would be valuable to the child independently of its implications for reading; however, the important point for this chapter is the absolute necessity of this knowledge base for developing reading competence.

It is clear that relatively little is known about how best to go about teaching reading to children who lack oral–aural language. It is not clear that effective, or at least more effective, techniques could not be developed if the problem were given the attention it merits. There are many specific questions relating to the problem of teaching reading to deaf children that could be the foci of research. For example, are there inherent differences in the difficulty with which deaf children learn to read in different languages? In particular, are alphabetic languages more or less difficult than ideographic languages? What is the possibility of developing a pictorial or printed version of Ameslan, or other sign language, that might provide a bridge between the signer's native tongue and printed English? (See Chapter 6 by Sperling, this volume.) Would it be possible and desirable to develop a sign language that had a greater isomorphism with English orthography? Fingerspelling does not provide sufficient bandwidth to permit the transmission of information at an acceptable rate. Would it be possible to develop a system of signs onto which written material could be mapped more directly than it can onto Ameslan and which, at the same time, would be fast enough to serve as a practical communication medium? How can a deaf child best be given the basic concepts of grammar, the idea of a sentence, the distinction between different word types? To what extent is the sequential nature of language an accident of the necessarily sequential nature of speech? The importance of the temporal and rhythmic aspects of speech are well established; it is not known, however, to what extent such factors are important to language more generally. Nowell has commented on the rhythmic aspects of sign language in the discussions of this study group; and Brooks has suggested that rhythm and timing may play important roles in the acquisition of reading skills. The implications of these ideas for the teaching of reading to deaf children need to be investigated. What basic visual and cognitive skills must be developed before reading can be taught, and to what extent can the acquisition of these fundamental skills be facilitated by formal training techniques? What can be done to assure that the deaf child will gain the "common-knowledge" information base about his world that is necessary to make sense out of "meaningful" strings of words?

Because the vast majority of children are proficient users of oral–aural language before any attempt is made to teach them to read, it is natural to make use of this proficiency. It also seems natural to assume that this is the optimal approach. Moreover, there has been little motivation to challenge this assumption, inasmuch as the approach has worked (with hearing children) reasonably well. But is it not possible that there might be better ways to teach reading, or at least some aspects of reading, independently of oral–aural language skills? It would be ironic indeed if the attempt to find alternative ways to teach reading to deaf children resulted in the finding of better ways to teach reading generally.

REFERENCES

Bellugi, U. Studies in sign language. In T. O'Rourke (Ed.), *Psycholinguistics and total communication*. Silver Springs, Maryland: American Annals of the Deaf, 1972.

Bellugi, U., & Klima, E. The roots of language in the sign talk of the deaf. *Psychology Today*, 1972, *60*, 61–64; 75–76.

Bruner, J. S. *Toward a theory of instruction*. Cambridge, Massachusetts: Belknap Press, 1966.

Calvert, D. R. & Silverman, S. R. *Speech and deafness*. Washington, D.C.: A. G. Bell Association for the Deaf, 1975.

Conrad, R. Acoustic confusions in immediate memory. *British Journal of Psychology*, 1964, *55*, 75–84.

Conrad, R. Speech and reading. In J. F. Kavanagh & I. G. Mattingly (Eds.), *Language by ear and by eye: The relationships between speech and reading*. Cambridge, Massachusetts: M.I.T. Press, 1972.

Dainoff, M. J. Time course of visual and auditory encoding. *Journal of Experimental Psychology*, 1970, *86*, 214–224.

Furth, H. G. Research with the deaf: Implications for language and cognition. *Psychological Bulletin*, 1964, *62*, 145–164.

Furth, H. G. *Thinking without language: Psychological implications of deafness*. New York: Free Press, 1966.

Furth, H. G. *Deafness and learning: A psychological approach*. Belmont, California: Wadsworth, 1973.

Geldard, F. A. *The human senses*. New York: Wiley, 1972.

Hintzman, D. L., & Summers, J. J. Long-term visual trances of visually presented words. *Bulletin Psychonomic Society*, 1973, *1*, 325–327.

Hirsh, I. Auditory perception of temporal order. *Journal of the Acoustical Society of America*, 1959, *31*, 759–767.

Kisner, J. L., & Weed, H. R. The design of the Visual Vocoder. *Conference Record, 1972, Conference on Speech Communication and Processing, IEEE*, 1972, 259–262.

Koenig, W., Dunn, H. K., & Lacey, L. Y. The sound spectrograph. *Journal of the Acoustical Society of America*, 1946, *18*, 19–49.

Kohl, H. R. *Language and education of the deaf* (Policy Study 1). Center for Urban Education, 1966.

Kolers, P. A. Three stages of reading. In H. Levin & J. P. Williams (Eds.), *Basic studies on reading*. New York: Basic Books, 1970, 90–118.

Kolers, P. A. Two kinds of recognition. *Canadian Journal of Psychology,* 1974, *28,* 51–61.

Kopp, G. A., & Green, H. C. Visible speech. *Volta Review,* 1948, *50,* 61.

Kroll, N. E. A., Parkinson, S. R., & Parks, T. E. Sensory and active storage of compound visual and auditory stimuli. *Journal of Experimental Psychology,* 1972, *95,* 32–38.

Kroll, N. E. A., Parks, T. E., Parkinson, S. R., Bieber, S. L., & Johnson, A. L. Short-term memory while shadowing: Recall of visually and of aurally presented letters. *Journal of Experimental Psychology,* 1970, *85,* 220–224.

Lane, H., Boyes-Braem, P., & Bellugi, U. Preliminaries to a distinctive feature analysis of hand shapes in American sign language. *Cognitive Psychology,* 1976, *8,* 263–289.

Lenneberg, E. *Biological foundations of language.* New York: Wiley, 1967.

Liberman, A. M., Cooper, F. S., Shankweiler, D. P., & Studdert-Kennedy, M. Why are speech spectrograms hard to read? *American Annals of the Deaf,* 1968, *113,* 127–133.

Moores, D. Psycholinguistics and deafness. *American Annals of the Deaf,* 1970, *115,* 37–48.

Nickerson, R. S. Characteristics of the speech of deaf person. *Volta Review,* 1975, *77,* 342–362.

Nickerson, R. S. Short-term retention of visually presented stimuli: Some evidence of visual encoding. *Acta Psychologica,* 1976, *40,* 153–162.

Nickerson, R. S., & Freeman, B. Discrimination of the order of the components or repeating tone sequences: Effects of frequency separation and extensive practice. *Perception & Psychophysics,* 1974, *16,* 471–477.

Nickerson, R. S., & Pew, R. W. Visual pattern matching: An investigation of some effects of decision task, auditory codability, and spatial correspondence. *Journal of Experimental Psychology,* 1973, *98,* 36–43.

Nowell, R., & Liben, L. *Linguistic and communicative characteristics of American Sign Language.* Paper presented at the meeting of the New England Psychological Association, Worchester, Massachusetts, 1975.

Parkinson, S. B., Parks, T. E., & Kroll, N. E. A. Visual and auditory short-term memory: Effects of phonemically similar auditory shadow material during the retention interval. *Journal of Experimental Psychology,* 1971, *87,* 274–280.

Parks, T. E., Kroll, N. E. A., Salzberg, P. M., & Parkinson, S. R. Persistence of visual memory as indicated by decision time in a matching task. *Journal of Experimental Psychology,* 1972, *92,* 437–438.

Patterson, J. H., & Green, D. M. Discrimination of transient signals having identical energy specta. *Journal of the Acoustical Society of America,* 1970, *48,* 894–905.

Posner, M. I., & Mitchell, R. F. Chronometric analysis of classification. *Psychological Review,* 1967, *74,* 392–409.

Potter, R. K., Kopp, G. A., & Green, H. C. *Visible speech.* New York: Van Nostrand, 1947.

Stark, R. E., Cullen, J. K., & Chase, R. A. Preliminary work with the new Bell Telephone visible speech translator. *American Annals of the Deaf,* 1968, *113,* 205–214.

Stokoe, W., Croneberg, C., & Casterline, D. *A dictionary of American Sign Language.* Washington, D.C.: Gallaudet College, 1965.

Tanner, W. P., Jr. The simulation of living systems: On the question of substituting one sensory system for another. In L. L. Clark (Ed.), *Proceedings of the international Congress on Technology and Blindness* (Vol. 2). New York: American Federation for the Blind, 1963.

Warren, R. M., Obusek, C. J., Farmer, R. M., & Warren, R. P. Auditory sequence: Confusion of patterns other than speech or music. *Science,* 1969, *164,* 586–587.

Warren, R. M., & Warren, R. P. Auditory illusions and confusions. *Scientific American,* 1970, *222,* 30–36.

Wickelgren, W. A. Short-term recognition memory for single letters and phonemic similarity of retroactive interference. *Quarterly Journal of Experimental Psychology,* 1966, *18,* 55–62.

Wood, L. E. Visual and auditory coding in a memory matching task. *Journal of Experimental Psychology,* 1974, *102,* 106–113.

III

SOCIAL DEVELOPMENT

8

Impulse Control in Deaf Children: Research and Clinical Issues[1]

ROBERT I. HARRIS

In the past 10 years there has been a rapidly growing interest among developmental, clinical, and behavioral psychologists in identifying factors that contribute to the conceptual tempo of reflection impulsivity. This variable represents how long children consider alternative solutions in situations of high response uncertainty before committing themselves to one solution (Kagan, 1965c). *Impulsivity* refers to the tendency to make fast decisions and many errors, whereas *reflection* refers to the tendency to react slowly, with relatively few errors.

The primary instrument used to index the child's position on this bipolar dimension is the Matching Familiar Figures (MFF) test. The MFF test, de-

[1]A major portion of this chapter was written while R. Harris was affiliated with The University of Rochester Medical Center, Rochester, New York. The chapter was supported, in part, by a Rehabilitation Research Fellowship from Social and Rehabilitation Service, Department of Health, Education and Welfare; by the Graduate Fellowship Fund from Gallaudet College Alumni Association; by a Deaf–Blind Scholarship from Illinois Division of Vocational Rehabilitation; and by the Deaf Berger Scholar Program from Deafness Research and Training Center, New York University. I also wish to express my gratitude to Rue L. Cromwell, Louise Kaplan, and Lynn S. Liben for their constructively critical comments on earlier versions of this chapter.

DEAF CHILDREN: DEVELOPMENTAL PERSPECTIVES

veloped by Kagan (1965c), is a match-to-sample perceptual recognition task; the subject is shown a familiar object, such as a cowboy, tree, or house, and asked to choose which of six highly similar choices matches the standard. The 12-item MFF test assesses the degree to which a child reflects on solutions by measuring response latencies and rates. A child who scores above the median in response time and below the median in errors is classified as reflective, whereas a child who scores below the median in response time and above the median in errors is classified as impulsive.

Growing evidence from studies of reflection–impulsivity indicates that this bipolar dimension is directly related to several other aspects of a child's personality development. Greater reflectivity is associated with age (Kagan, 1965a), reading ability (Kagan, 1965b), adjustment (Weintraub, 1968), social class (Weintraub, 1968), and verbal control of motor behavior (Meichenbaum & Goodman, 1971). Highly reflective children are also typically (a) more highly motivated toward achievement (Kagan, Moss, & Sigel, 1963); (b) less likely to commit errors on serial learning tasks (Kagan, 1965b); (c) more persistent (Kagan, 1965a); (d) more confident in approaching intellectual tasks (Kagan, 1965a); and (e) capable of longer attention span and less likely to be easily distracted (Kagan et al., 1963; Kagan, Rosman, Day, Albert, & Phillips, 1964). An excellent review of MFF test studies can be found in Kagan and Kogan (1970).

Many studies have been conducted on reflection–impulsivity in children who have normal hearing, but there have been very few studies of reflection–impulsivity in children who are prelingually and profoundly deaf. This chapter focuses on reflection–impulsivity in the latter group, specifically those whose hearing loss (a) is congenital or occurred before normal speech and language were acquired; and (b) cannot be brought to functional level by auditory devices. There are approximately 56,000 such children in this country (Gentile & Rambin, 1973), a number which represents only 2.5% of children with hearing losses. The remaining 97.5% are able to use their residual hearing through the use of hearing aids, auditory training, and/or speech therapy (Mindel & Vernon, 1972). For readers unfamiliar with the impact profound deafness has upon a child's development, a brief summary of various readings on psychological and psychiatric aspects of deafness follows. More extensive reviews can be found in Mindel and Vernon (1971); Levine (1956); D. Wright (1969); Schlesinger and Meadow (1972); Altshuler (1971, 1974); and Rainer, Altshuler, Kallmann, and Deming (1963).

Although infants with a profound hearing loss may look normal in every respect, they often have other congenital handicaps, such as a neurological dysfunction. The profoundly deaf infant has no auditory equipment to transform sound impulses into meaningful experiences, thus there is a lag in his ability to transform a gross mass of undifferentiated perceptions and conceptions to a higher level of differentiation and integration. This means that there is also a lag in the growth of psychic structure in general, and impulse control in particular. The world of sound plays a powerful role in the infant's development in every respect—emotionally, socially, intellectually, linguistically, culturally, and physiologically. Because hearing loss is invisible and the child babbles and coos like a normal infant, hearing parents usually do not notice the infant's inability to process auditory information. Thus, the parent–infant interaction is typically normal for the first few months of the child's life (Altshuler, 1974; Lenneberg, 1967).

When the infant enters the second half of his or her first year, parental expectations, however, are not met. Because of deafness, the child is unable to channel auditory impulses into age-specific, socially appropriate behaviors. For example, the child does not turn toward the sound of the caretaker's voice. With age, the child's behavior begins to deviate increasingly from what is considered normal. When deaf infants reach their first birthday, parents expect them to say a few words, and when this fails to occur, parents become more anxious and puzzled. Often, without being aware of it, the parents feel rejected or deprived by their infant's failure to respond to their overtures. The infant's failure to respond to maternal stimulation often results in a decrease in that maternal stimulation. Hence, seeds of interruption in the parent–child interaction are sown.

The parents may think that the deaf infant is mentally retarded or autistic and consult a family doctor. More often than not, the doctor finds nothing wrong with the deaf infant and assures the parents that the infant will gradually outgrow developmental shortcomings. Relieved, the parents go home and expect that the deaf infant will eventually behave in a normal and age-appropriate fashion. However, more pronounced deviations in the child's behavior soon become manifest, and the parents become increasingly anxious, confused, and frustrated. Between the time the parents notice a deviation in the infant's behavior and the doctor's confirmation of deafness, many traumatic experiences have already occurred in the parent–child interaction.

Hearing loss is often discovered during the second year of a child's life, an age that is one of the most vulnerable periods of life. During this time the mother is expected to help the child relinquish infantile dependence on her and become more independent. Also, at this time, the mother's emotional availability for the facilitation of the child's separation from her is crucial. Unfortunately, a mother may be further emotionally traumatized when she learns of her child's deafness, and, as a result, she is often unable to help the deaf child internalize and modulate aggressive and libidinal impulses. Moreover, because the mother of a deaf child often suffers from a reactive depression, important processes of the child's development may be interrupted, resulting in emotional and cognitive problems that may not yield to later intervention.

At the same time, there is a marked lag in the child's development of structure formation that influences the acquisition of symbolic thought or verbal language (Altshuler, 1971, 1974; Levine, 1956; Mindel & Vernon, 1971; Schlesinger & Meadow, 1972). In addition to having limited vocal communication with their parents, the deaf child faces intense frustrations in communication in most educational situations. If the child has had no opportunity for formal preschool education, it is not until age 5 or 6 years that he or she even begins to learn verbal language. A hearing child of the same age would have already learned 25,000 words (Lenneberg, 1967).

In brief, deaf people typically have several emotional and linguistic disadvantages. First, they have not learned and used a language during their early years, and thus their language skills are inadequately developed. Second, they have missed the opportunity to communicate freely with their parents and peers, with detrimental consequences for emotional development generally (see Chapter 9 by Schlesinger, this volume). Correlatively, because of inadequate communication between parents and children, deaf children's outlets for venting frustrations, disappointments, and anger are narrowed, and their emotions are often expressed in an impulsive and immature manner. In turn, their impulsive disposition has an adverse effect upon later cognitive development and learning and, consequently, on social and vocational development.

Research on reflection–impulsivity or impulse control in this population is important for several reasons. First, in surveys of schools the percentage of deaf children classified as emotionally disturbed exceeds that of the general population. For example, Schlesinger and Meadow (1972) found that 12% of deaf children at a residential school for the deaf were classified by their teachers and counselors as having severe emotional disturbance, compared with 2.4% of hearing children so classified in general public schools in Los Angeles County. An additional 19.6% of the deaf children exhibited some degree of behavior problems that demanded a disproportionate share of teacher's time, compared with 7.5% of the hearing children. If the two types of behavior disturbance are combined, more than 30% of deaf students had various forms of emotional disturbance, compared with only 10% in the general student population. Poor impulse control may underlie these disturbances. In fact, poor impulse control and its correlates were the most frequently noted characteristics of these deaf children. Other investigators have reported similar findings (Goulder & Trybus, 1977; Meadow, 1975; Schein, 1975).

Second, deaf adults who apply for vocational rehabilitation services have been found to have a high incidence of impulse control deficits and related problems (Rodda, 1974). This implies that at least some deaf adults are characterized by occupational underachievement and that costly personal, social, and prevocational adjustment training programs are needed to help deaf clients become more employable.

Additional indication of the need for research on impulse control is provided in a study by Rainer *et al.* (1963). These investigators found that, although the incidence of schizophrenia was equivalent in deaf and hearing mental patients, more behavior problems were evident among deaf mental patients. These behavior disorders are characterized by impulsivity, poor insight, low frustration tolerance, poorly differentiated affective integrity, and limited empathy for others. Altshuler (1964) described a typical cluster of symptoms as

> lack of understanding of, and regard for the feelings of others (empathy) coupled with inadequate insight into the impact of their own behavior and its consequences in relation to others. With a generally egocentric view of the world and with demands unfettered by excessive control machinery (conscience), the adaptive approach is characterized by gross coercive dependence. The preferred defensive reactions to tension and anxiety are typified by a kind of primitive riddance through action. Behaviorally, this mode of handling tension is reflected in considerable impulsivity and the absence of much thoughtful introspection [pp. 63–64].

These reasons, then, support the need for research on impulse control in deaf children. One important aim of this research is to identify factors that account for some deaf children's success in impulse control and others' failures. This chapter will review previous literature on impulse control in deaf people, will offer suggestions regarding the areas in which future research is needed, and will suggest ways in which findings may aid in the diagnosis and training of deaf children.

RESEARCH ON IMPULSE CONTROL IN DEAF CHILDREN: A REVIEW

Several studies have systematically examined the variations of impulse control in deaf children (Altshuler, Deming, Vollenweider, Rainer, & Tendler, 1976; Binder, 1970; R. I. Harris, 1976; Moores, Weiss, & Goodwin, 1973). Most reports of such characteristics as emotional immaturity, short attention span, poor impulse control, and hyperactivity across all ages of deaf samples were based upon nonstandardized observations (Altable, 1947; Altshuler, 1971; Baroff, 1963; Gordon, cited in Binder, 1970; Hefferman, 1955; Hess, 1960; Klaber & Falek, 1963; Levine, 1956; McAndrew, 1948; Myklebust, 1960; Neyhus, 1962; Zivkovic, 1971). Three recent investigations have, however, included standardized assessment of impulse control.

In one of these studies, Binder (1970) examined the relationship between verbal ability and impulse control in 10–15-year-old deaf children using the verbal portion of the Wechsler Intelligence Scale for Children to assess language ability, and the Porteus Maze·test and tambour movement to measure impulse control. She hypothesized that high-verbal deaf children would have higher impulse control scores than low-verbal peers. However, she found no significant differences between the two groups and concluded that verbal language is not related to impulse control.

In another study, Altshuler et al. (1976) assessed impulse control in 15–17-year-old deaf and hearing adolescents in the United States and Yugoslavia to see if auditory loss was related to short-sighted actions, with little planning and a relative lack of internal controls. The tests used were (a) Porteus Maze test; (b) Szondi test; (c) Id–Ego–Superego (IES) test; (d) Rorschach test, (e) Draw-A-Person test; and (f) Draw-A-Line test.

Both the deaf American and Yugoslavian adolescents were less able to draw a line slowly, made more errors in the Porteus Maze test, and showed lowered ego responses on all subtests of the IES than their hearing peers. The differences between the deaf and hearing adolescents were of nearly the same magnitude and proportion in each country, with the Yugoslavs starting at a higher baseline level of impulsivity than the Americans on each test. In addition, despite the fact that each of these tests differentiated deaf and hearing adolescents as a group, there were no systematic correlations between individuals' scores on the various tests of impulsivity. The findings led Altshuler et al. (1976) to conclude that impulsivity was probably multifactorial and that the tests differentiated a number of aspects of personality, any one of which could be evidenced clinically as impulsive behavior. In addition, the Rorschach findings for the deaf adolescents were (a) a higher $F\%$ (form responses); (b) a lower $F + \%$ (good form response); (c) overproduction of A (animal responses); and (d) lower Total R (general productivity). These findings, as well as separately calculated comparisons of developmental, hostility, and anxiety levels (DL, HL, AL: Friedman's system and Elizur's Rorschach Contest test) fit the hypothesized greater impulsivity in the deaf adolescents. On the basis of the overall findings, Altshuler et al. concluded that loss of auditory input has a retarding effect on the development of impulse control in a deaf child.

A third study of impulse control and deafness was conducted by Moores *et al.* (1973), who used the MFF test to assess impulse control in a deaf population. Using Kagan's (1965c) criteria for categorizing deaf children as impulsive and reflective, 22 reflectives and 22 impulsives were identified from a group of 70 deaf children between the ages of 5 and 7. The two groups did not differ significantly on the basis of sex, IQ, age, etiology, or program. Since the MFF test has been used previously in reading research (Kagan, 1965b), Moores *et al.* (1973) hypothesized that the prereading skills of the reflective deaf children would be superior to those of the impulsive deaf children. To test this hypothesis, the deaf subjects were given the Copying, Matching, and Alphabet portions of the Metropolitan Readiness test and the Printed Word subtest of the Receptive Communication Scale.

The reflective deaf children had significantly higher scores on the Matching and Copying tests. However, there were no significant differences in the scores on the Alphabet or Printed Word tests. Similarities between the MFF test and some Illinois Test of Psycholinguistic Abilities (ITPA) subtests led the investigators to compare the performance of reflective and impulsive deaf children on the five ITPA subtests. Reflective deaf children were found to be significantly superior on only one subtest—Visual Closure. One interesting part of the results on the MFF test was that the three tests on which the reflective and impulsive deaf children differed significantly (Copying, Matching, and Visual Closure), are all timed measures. These findings prompted Moores *et al.* (1976) to conclude that it is the ability to function well on a timed test, rather than superiority of prereading or reading skills, that differentiates reflective and impulsive deaf children.

In summary, these three studies indicate that (*a*) loss of auditory input appears to have a retarding effect on the development of impulse control in deaf adolescents (Altshuler *et al.*, 1976); and (*b*) verbal language is not associated with impulse control in deaf children (Binder, 1970; Moores *et al.*, 1973). These statements, taken together, suggest the following question: Is it auditory input itself, auditory input combined with verbal language, or verbal language itself that contributes significantly to the development of impulse control? An examination of clinical studies of mental illness in deaf patients helps to answer this question.

ETIOLOGY OF POOR IMPULSE CONTROL IN DEAF PEOPLE: THEORETICAL ALTERNATIVES

Altshuler's hypothesis on the role of auditory input in a child's psychic structure in general, and impulse control in particular, fits well with theories on the causes of obsessionalism, depression, and impulsivity. In a review of more than 400 deaf patients at New York State Psychiatric Institute, Altshuler (1971) found a disproportionately low incidence of obsessional traits and various forms of depression. He noted, however, that impulsivity was a frequent symptom among deaf patients. From these findings, Altshuler concluded that "audition is somehow necessary for internalized control of rage [p. 1521]." He also explained that language development is important for the development of obsessionalism and depression. The following summarizes his views on the role of auditory feedback and language in the development of impulse control:

> It is likely that it is no accident for language development to concur in time with the evolution of impulse control and internalization of rage and self-constraint. Words or signs bring with them the first substitution of smaller for larger units of action, as the pointing finger or the word for milk replaces gross undifferentiated motor signals of frustration. . . . So it would seem that language, in conjuction with audition per se, serves as both model and a means of embedding the internalized constraints necessary for both obsessionalism and depression [pp. 1524–1525].

These findings and Altshuler's interpretation raise the following question: Is audition itself or verbal language necessary for impulse control? Verbal language may be an important tool in containing and refining impulses, in transforming primitive responses into higher-level coping styles. Thus, the audition hypothesis may not account for the impulse control deficits often found in deaf people. The following observations suggest that auditory input per se may not be necessary for developing impulse control.

First, an alternative sensory modality—for example, vision as utilized in early manual communication—may have the necessary ingredients for acquisition of impulse control. Work by Freedman and his colleagues (Freedman, 1971, 1972; Freedman, Canady, & Robinson, 1971) indicates that this is possible. On the basis of longitudinal observations of six congenitally deaf girls between the ages of 2 and 5, Freedman (1971) concluded:

> That spoken language is not a prerequisite or even a significant factor in this early phase of personality development. My subjects are friendly, outgoing youngsters who show age-appropriate relations with other children as well as adults. They have developed internalized regulators of behavior and have made identifications and shown interests typical of their age and sex [p. 1544].

These findings also led Freedman (1972) to state that "lack of speech and hearing is by no means incompatible with the process of differentiation of psychic structure [p. 66]." Freedman explained that other sensory modalities were utilized to offset the retarding influence of auditory loss on differentiation of psychic structure in general, and impulse control in particular.

Second, some deaf children have sufficient self-control, whereas others do not. This fact has been largely ignored. Only two studies have attempted to analyze systematically the intragroup variability (Binder, 1970; Moores *et al.*, 1973), but no significant differences were found in either study. These studies, then, are unable to suggest what types of intervention might help deaf children in achieving self-imposed control.

Third, side effects of hearing loss, rather than the hearing loss itself, may account for poor self-control of rage in deaf people. These side effects may include (*a*) rearing practices not tailored to the needs of the deaf child; (*b*) negative attitude of parents toward disability in general, and deafness in particular; (*c*) poor parent personality pattern in coping with unexpected crises and stresses; and (*d*) inability of hearing parents to communicate manually to meet the needs of a deaf child. Klein (1962) suggested a clear distinction between two varieties of deprivation: (*a*) a specific sensory restriction or deficit; and (*b*) an isolation from the environment. Klein pointed out that it is the interpersonal isolation, not the sensory deficit alone, that disrupts the synthetic function of a child's ego or personality development. One approach to studying these two effects is discussed in the next section.

PARENTAL HEARING STATUS: IMPLICATIONS FOR IMPULSE CONTROL

One of the best ways to untangle the effects of hearing loss per se from the usual side effects of hearing loss is to compare the development of deaf children who have deaf parents with the development of deaf children who have hearing parents. Although both groups of children suffer auditory loss, those with deaf parents typically avoid most of the usual negative side effects of deafness, as deaf parents are rarely traumatized by their child's deafness, are able to communicate manually with their children, and so on.

There has been a long tradition of comparing deaf children of deaf and hearing parents on a variety of linguistic and cognitive measures. Several studies have indicated that deaf children of deaf parents have better language skills than deaf children of hearing parents. Quigley and

Frisina (1961) studied 16 nonresidential deaf children of deaf parents (manual group) and 16 nonresidential deaf children of hearing parents (oral group) and found that the manual group performed significantly higher on vocabulary and fingerspelling tests than the oral group. Although the differences were not significant, the manual group showed higher educational achievement than the oral group. The oral group performed significantly better on speech tests. No significant differences were found on lipreading tests.

Stevenson (1964) collected data from school files for the years 1914 and 1961 to compare educational achievement of deaf children of deaf versus hearing parents. He found that 90% of the deaf-parent group attained a higher educational level than the hearing-parent group, with 30% of the former group attending college compared with only 9% of the latter groups.

Using a matched-pair design to compare deaf children of deaf versus hearing parents on various school achievement tests, Stuckless and Birch (1966) found no significant differences on speech intelligibility tests or psychosocial adjustment rating scales. However, deaf children of deaf parents performed significantly better on speechreading, reading, and writing tests. In a similar study, Meadow (1968) compared 56 deaf children of deaf parents (manual group) with 56 matched children of hearing parents (oral group). The manual group was significantly better than the oral group on reading, math, overall educational achievement, social adjustment, and written language tests. No significant differences were found in speech and speechreading tests.

These researchers attributed better performance in deaf children of deaf parents to the parents' early use of manual communication at home. Vernon and Koh (1970) questioned this conclusion, however, since other differences between the two groups may also exist. Specifically, they suggested that deaf children of hearing parents might more commonly have undetected neurologic dysfunctions than deaf children of deaf parents, whose deafness was more likely to be hereditary and hence unassociated with other damage. In an investigation that controlled for such effects, Vernon and Koh again found that those exposed to manual communication performed significantly better in reading, paragraph meaning, vocabulary, and written language tests. No significant differences were found on speech intelligibility, speechreading, or psychosocial adjustment tests.

It should be noted, however, that early manual communication may not be the sole factor leading to better language competence in deaf children of deaf parents. To separate the effects of parents' use of manual communication from parents' hearing status per se (related to acceptance of deafness, role models, etc.), Corson (1973) included deaf children of *oral* deaf parents in his work. Corson matched four groups of deaf children by such factors as age, sex, IQ, amount and type of hearing loss, and etiology. One group of children had deaf parents and the second had hearing parents, but both these first two groups of parents reported using only oral communication with their children. The third group consisted of deaf children of deaf parents who used manual communication at home. The fourth group included deaf children of hearing parents who used only oral communication at home.

The results indicated that both groups of deaf parents exhibited significantly more positive acceptance of deafness than did the hearing parent. Regardless of school placement, deaf children of deaf parents received significantly higher scores on reading, arithmetic, and speech-reading tests than deaf children of hearing parents. No significant differences were found among the four groups on speech intelligibility and self-image tests.

On the basis of these findings, Corson (1973) concluded that the use of manual communication alone cannot fully account for the superior performance of deaf children of deaf parents on various tests, but that, in addition, deaf parents' better acceptance of their deaf children contributes significantly to their children's higher school performance.

In a later study, Brasel and Quigley (1975) hypothesized that the *amount* of language stimulation given to a deaf child plays a more important role in his later learning of the English language than the particular method of communication used. Thus, parental language competence and parental hearing status were the two main variables in this study. Various school achievement tests were administered to compare four groups of deaf children. The first two groups had deaf parents who used manual communication at home. One of these groups, the "manual English" group, had deaf parents who had a good command of English (as indicated by their written responses to an open-ended questionnaire), whereas the second, "average manuals," had deaf parents who did not have a good command of English. The third and fourth groups had hearing parents; the third, "intensive oral," were children who had received oral preschool education, the fourth, "average oral," were children who had not had oral preschool education.

Using analyses of covariance to partial out the effects of socioeconomic status, nonverbal intelligence, and age, Brasel and Quigley found that in every test, the two deaf-parent groups scored significantly higher than the two hearing-parent groups. In addition, the manual English group scored significantly better on many tests than the two oral groups, while the manual English group scored significantly better than the average manual group on several measures. No significant differences were found between the average manual group and the intensive oral group, nor between the intensive oral and average oral groups.

These findings led Brasel and Quigley to conclude that parental language competence influences the child's developing ability through the early use of manual communication. They also concluded that having deaf parents does not mean that deaf children will necessarily have a large academic or syntactic advantage over those who have hearing parents; the greatest advantage emerges when parents are competent in standard English and use manual English communication with and around the deaf child. Finally, they concluded that there is some advantage in the early use of manual communication regardless of its degree of deviation from standard English syntax.

In summary, the studies reviewed here show that deaf children of deaf parents perform better than deaf children of hearing parents on a wide variety of linguistic and cognitive tasks. This conclusion suggests several parallel questions about impulse control: First, do deaf children of deaf parents have better impulse control than deaf children of hearing parents? Second, does the early use of manual communication by deaf parents contribute significantly to the child's impulse control? Third, is a deaf child's facility in language significantly associated with his facility in monitoring his impulses?

In one study designed to answer these questions, R. I. Harris (1976) investigated the relationship of impulse control to parent hearing status, manual communication, and academic achievement in deaf children. The MFF test was administered to 324 6–10-year old deaf children to assess two aspects of impulse control: (a) response time; and (b) error score. The Draw-A-Man-Time test was also given to analyze two variables analogous to those in the MFF test to determine the generality of the Kagan MFF test as a measure of impulse control. Time to draw a whole man and the quality score based on Goodenough–Harris Point Scale (D. B. Harris, 1963) were recorded. In addition, questionnaires were mailed to the parents regarding social class, parental hearing status, methods of communication practiced at home before and after learning that their child was deaf, and the age at which the subject was first exposed to manual communication.

The results uniformly confirmed that deaf children of deaf parents ($N·= 50$) obtained greater impulse control scores in all four measures than deaf children of hearing parents ($N = 274$). Specifically, children who had deaf parents had significantly longer response times and made significantly fewer errors on the MFF test than children who had hearing parents. Moreover, children of deaf parents took more time, although not significantly, in drawing a whole man and obtained significantly higher quality scores for their drawing than did those of hearing parents.

The results also indicate that the younger the age at which the deaf children were exposed to manual communication, the longer their response times, the fewer their errors, and the longer the time taken to draw a whole man. No significant correlation was found between the age of exposure to manual communication and quality score for drawing a whole man. Regardless of parent hearing status, the MFF response time was positively correlated (.23 to .76) with many subtests of the Stanford Achievement test, Metropolitan Achievement test, and Gates Primary Reading test. Also, the MFF error was found to be negatively correlated (−.21 to −.70) with many achievement subtests. Thus, the reflective deaf children tended to obtain higher achievement scores. The result also indicated that older and brighter deaf children tended to take longer and made fewer errors on the MFF test. They spent more time in drawing a whole man and received higher quality scores for their drawings. Social class was not significantly correlated with the measures of impulse control.

In summary, deaf children of deaf parents were found to have better impulse control than those of hearing parents, paralleling the results reviewed earlier on language development and academic achievement. These results suggest that auditory feedback is not the only sensory modality that contributes to the development of adequate impulse control, contrary to the suggestion made by Altshuler (1971). Perhaps alternative sensory modalities (e.g., visual or visual–proprioceptive) help deaf children acquire better impulse control.

Some researchers (Altshuler, 1974; R. I. Harris, 1976; Meadow, 1968) have concluded that the better impulse control and their correlates (e.g., maturity, responsibility, independence, fewer toilet training problems), are primarily the result of the deaf parents' use of manual communication. Exposure to manual communication during infancy may help deaf children to develop cognitive and linguistic skills that are useful in modulating impulses more constructively. The significant relationship between early manual communication and impulse control found by R. I. Harris (1976) does suggest that early manual communication is a significant contributor to adequate impulse control.

It is probable, however, that the use of manual communication is not the only factor leading to more adequate impulse control in deaf children of deaf parents. The frequency of the use of manual communication and the use of English in manual communication may play a crucial role in the development of impulse control. For example, as a hearing child who is bombarded with auditory input, the deaf child of deaf parents is "bombarded" with visually-oriented linguistic stimulation in his home environment.

Furthermore, the emotional satisfaction received both by deaf parents and their deaf child through the early use of manual communication may lay the groundwork for a rewarding and meaningful relationship between the parent and the child and therefore create a healthy atmosphere for the deaf child to develop adequate impulse control (see Chapter 9 by Schlesinger, this volume). In the book, *A Deaf Adult Speaks Out*, Leo M. Jacobs (1974) describes growing up as a deaf child of deaf parents:

> I was born deaf of deaf parents who had an older deaf son. Therefore, my family was entirely deaf, and we lived in a world of our own, where manual communication was the order of the day. I grew up in a loving atmosphere and never knew any deprivation of communication; my parents knew my wants, and I knew just how far I could go without bringing their wrath down on my head. The conversation was full and interesting at the dinner table. I attended a residential school as a day pupil. I did not have any communication difficulties because they followed the "combined method" of instruction. My only communication difficulties arose when I began doing business with the outside world, but I thought nothing about them because I had observed my parents' methods of overcoming those barriers. I merely followed the same road—that of employing a pad and pencil to convey my wishes, and attempting to read lips at first, then offering the pad and pencil to the other party if I failed to understand him [p. 11].[2]

In contrast, as discussed earlier, hearing parents are often at a loss as to how to communicate with their deaf child. Often, without being aware of it, the parents may feel rejected or deprived by their infant's failure to respond to their overtures and they may stop trying to elicit responses from the child. As a result, the deaf child is doubly deprived, the first deprivation arising from this deafness and the second from the effect of his handicap upon the environment (Chess, 1975). Moreover, hearing parents frequently resort to physical punishment and restraint, rather than verbal discipline and explanation (Chess, 1975; Mindel & Vernon, 1971; Schlesinger & Meadow, 1972). Consequently, the deaf child sees few options for channeling aggressive impulses or frustrations, and has a poor foundation for transforming impulses into socially acceptable outlets.

Another condition that may contribute to more adequate impulse control in deaf children of deaf parents is that these parents more readily accept their child's disability. R. I. Harris (1976) found that deaf parents

[2] Reprinted by permission from L. M. Jacobs, *A deaf adult speaks out*. Washington, D.C.: Gallaudet College Press, 1974.

tended to suspect their child's hearing difficulties about 5 months sooner than did hearing parents, receiving confirmation of their child's deafness about 9 months sooner. Meadow (1967) also found that deaf parents suspect and accept the child's hearing problems quickly, whereas hearing parents tend to prolong and intensify their denial of the child's deafness.

In conclusion, the results of the relationship of parental hearing status to impulse control in deaf children, as well as the findings on the use of early manual communication, suggest that the audition hypothesis proposed by Altshuler (1971) is inadequate. More specifically, the results reviewed here suggest that the retarding effects of auditory loss on deaf children's acquisition of impulse control are less apparent when the child's parents are deaf. This may result from the early use of manual communication, which provides the child with a tool for monitoring impulses (for example, instead of throwing a temper tantrum, the child may use a hand gesture to indicate a desire for milk).

It should be understood that the findings on the relationship between parent hearing status and impulse control do not imply that parents must be "physically" deaf for their deaf child to acquire self-control. Rather, what is needed is two-way communication between child and parents and a loving and caring relationship. Absence of either impedes the development of impulse control and results in a personality in which impulsive satisfaction is the guiding rule.

IMPLICATIONS FOR INTERVENTION

As reviewed earlier, studies on reflection–impulsivity in hearing children have found that reflective children have advantages in emotional, academic, and attentional areas. It would be useful in planning educational programs to know whether these relationships hold for deaf children as well. Educators and mental health specialists might routinely incorporate the MFF test and related measures in the psychoeducational and psychosocial evaluation of deaf children (e.g., using tests developed by Harrison & Nadelman, 1972; Lewis, Rausch, Goldberg, & Dodd, 1968; Ward, 1968; J. C. Wright, 1974). Impulse control scores may help predict reading and academic potential and could also help specialists to develop programs for improving deaf children's control of motor behavior. Several studies with hearing children have demonstrated that impulsive tempo may be modified (Briggs, 1966; Debus, 1970; Kagan, Pearson, & Welch, 1966; Meichenbaum & Goodman, 1971; Nelson, 1968;

Ridberg, Parke, & Hetherington, 1971; Sklerov, 1974; Yando & Kagan, 1968). Meichenbaum and Goodman (1971), for example, found that an impulsive child exercises less verbal control over his motor behavior and uses private speech in a less instrumental fashion than does a reflective child. They found two conditions necessary for engendering self-control in impulsive children: (a) a self-instruction agent that the child can model, and (b) rehearsal in self-instruction. Additional research is needed to determine if sign language and/or fingerspelling can be similarly used for self-instruction in controlling one's motor behavior. (See also Chapter 12 by A. Harris, this volume.)

A third area of interest concerns the relationship between syntax and impulse control. It would be interesting to know whether different forms of manual communication such as Ameslan, The Rochester Method, and Signing Exact English (SEE) (see Chapter 11) have differential impact upon development of impulse control in deaf children.

In conclusion, many specialists in the field of aural rehabilitation, speech pathology, special education, and deafness, recognize that hearing loss has a profoundly retarding effect upon the child's language and personality development. Intensive preschool programs on auditory training and speech therapy have often been regarded as the single most important area of instruction for deaf children. Few specialists, however, recognize that training impulse control is also an important part of deaf children's education. The research reviewed in this chapter and the questions posed indicate that more research and intervention on impulse control are needed.

The research reviewed in this chapter suggests that the use of early manual communication by deaf parents partly minimizes the retarding effects of hearing loss upon the child's impulse control. The positive relationship between verbal language and impulse control in hearing children is encouraging and suggests that attention and effort should be directed toward developing parent-education programs and preschool curricula that help deaf children to monitor their impulses constructively. The incidence of deaf children now having deficits in impulse control is alarmingly high and should no longer be ignored.

REFERENCES

Altable, J. P. The Rorschach psychodiagnostic as applied to deaf mutes. *Rorschach Research Exchange,* 1947, *11,* 74–79.
Altshuler, K. Z. Personality traits and depressive symptoms in the deaf. In J. Wortis (Ed.), *Recent advances in biological psychiatry* (Vol. 6). New York: Plenum Press, 1964.

Altshuler, K. Z. Studies of the deaf: Relevance to psychiatric theory. *American Journal of Psychiatry*, 1971, *127*, 1521–1526.

Altshuler, K. Z. The social and psychological development of the deaf child: Problems and treatment. In P. J. Fine (Ed.), *Deafness in infancy and early childhood*. New York: Medcom Press, 1974.

Altshuler, K. Z., Deming, W. E., Vollenweider, J., Rainer, J. D., & Tendler, R. Impulsivity and profound early deafness: A crosscultural inquiry. *American Annals of the Deaf*, 1976, *121*, 331–345.

Baroff, G. S. Rorschach data and clinical observations. In J. D. Rainer, K. Z. Altshuler, F. J. Kallman, & W. E. Deming (Eds.), *Family and mental health problems in a deaf population*. New York: Columbia University Press, 1963.

Binder, P. J. The relationship between verbal language and impulsivity in the deaf (Doctoral dissertation, Wayne State University, 1970). *Dissertation Abstracts International*, 1971, *32*, 5614B–5615B. (University Microfilms No. 71–384)

Brasel, K. E., & Quigley, S. P. *The influence of early language and communication environments on the development of language in deaf children*. Urbana–Champaign: University of Illinois, Institute for Research on Exceptional Children, 1975.

Briggs, C. H. An experimental study of reflection-impulsivity in children (Doctoral dissertation, University of Minnesota, 1966). *Dissertation Abstracts*, 1968, *28*, 3891B–3892B. (University Microfilms No. 68-1610)

Chess, S. Behavior problems of children with congenital rubella. In D. Naiman (Ed.), *Needs of emotionally disturbed hearing impaired children*. New York: New York University School of Education, Health, Nursing, and Art Professions, 1975.

Corson, H. J. Comparing deaf children of oral deaf parents and deaf parents using manual communication with deaf children of hearing parents on academic, social, and communication functioning (Doctoral dissertation, University of Cincinnati, 1973). *Dissertation Abstracts International*, 1974, *34*, 6480A. (University Microfilms No. 78-8454)

Debus, R. L. Effects of brief observation of model behavior on conceptual tempo in impulsive children. *Developmental Psychology*, 1970, *2*, 22–32.

Freedman, D. A. Congenital and perinatal sensory deprivation: Some studies in early development. *American Journal of Psychiatry*, 1971, *127*, 1539–1545.

Freedman, D. A. On hearing, oral language and psychic structure. In R. R. Holt & E. Peterfreund (Eds.), *Psychoanalysis and contemporary science*, (Vol. 1). New York: Macmillan, 1972.

Freedman, D. A., Canady, C., & Robinson, J. R. Speech and psychic structure: A reconstruction of their relation. *Journal of American Psychoanalytic Association*, 1971, *19*, 765–779.

Gentile, A., & Rambin, J. B. *Reported causes of hearing loss for hearing impaired students, United States: 1970–1971* (Series D, No. 12). Washington, D.C.: Office of Demographic Studies, Gallaudet College, 1973.

Gordon, J. E. Ego deficit in deaf children (Research relating to children, 15-T-23) Washington, D.C.: U. S. Government Printing Office, 10/61-7/62. Unpublished data. In P. J. Binder, The relationship between verbal language and impulsivity in the deaf. (Doctoral dissertation, Wayne University, 1970). *Dissertation Abstracts International,* 1971, *32,* 5614-5615B. (University Microfilms No. 68-1610)

Goulder, T. J., & Trybus, R. J. *The classroom behavior of emotionally disturbed hearing impaired children* (Series R., No. 3). Washington, D.C.: Office of Demographic Studies, Gallaudet College, 1977.

Harris, D. B. *Children's drawings as measures of intellectual maturity.* New York: Harcourt, Brace and World, 1963.

Harris, R. I. The relationship of impulse control to parent hearing status, manual communication, and academic achievement, (Doctoral dissertation, New York University, 1976). *Dissertation Abstracts International,* 1977, *37,* 4682B. (University Microfilms No. 77-5410)

Harrison, A., & Nadelman, L. Conceptual tempo and inhibition of movement in black preschool children. *Child Development,* 1972, *43,* 657–668.

Hefferman, A. A psychiatric study of fifty children referred to hospital for suspected deafness. In G. Caplan (Ed.), *Emotional problems of children.* New York: Basic Books, 1955.

Hess, D. W. *The evaluation of personality and adjustment in deaf and hearing children using a non-verbal modification of the Make-A-Picture Story (MAPS) Test.* Unpublished doctoral dissertation, University of Rochester, 1960.

Jacobs, Leo M. *A deaf adult speaks out.* Washington, D.C.: Gallaudet College Press, 1974.

Kagan, J. Individual differences in the resolution of response uncertainty. *Journal of Personality and Social Psychology,* 1965, *2,* 154–160. (a)

Kagan, J. Reflection-impulsivity and reading ability in primary grade children. *Child Development,* 1965, *36,* 609–628. (b)

Kagan, J. Impulsive and reflective children: Significance of conceptual tempo. In J. D. Krumboltz (Ed.), *Learning and the educational process.* Chicago: Rand McNally, 1965. (c)

Kagan, J., & Kogan, N. Individual variation in cognitive processes. In P. H. Mussen (Ed.), *Carmichael's Manual of child psychology* (3rd ed., Vol. 1). New York: Wiley, 1970.

Kagan, J., Moss, H. A., & Sigel, I. E. Psychological significance of styles of conceptualization. *Monographs of the Society for Research in Child Development,* 1963, *28* (2, Serial No. 86).

Kagan, J., Pearson, L., & Welch, L. The modifiability of an impulsive tempo. *Journal of Educational Psychology,* 1966, *57,* 359–365.

Kagan, J., Rosman, B., Day, D., Albert, J., & Phillips, W. Information-processing in the child: Significance of analytic and reflective attitudes. *Psychological Monographs,* 1964, *78* (1, Whole No. 578).

Klaber, M., & Falek, A. Delinquency and crime. In J. D. Rainer, K. Z. Altshuler, F. J. Kallmann, & W. E. Deming (Eds.), *Family and mental health problems in a deaf population.* New York: New York State Psychiatric Institute, Columbia University Press, 1963.

Klein, G. S. Blindness and isolation. *Psychoanalytic Study of the Child,* 1962, *17,* 82–93.

Lenneberg, E. H. *The biological foundations of language.* New York: Wiley, 1967.

Levine, E. S. *Youth in a soundless world.* New York: New York University Press, 1956.

Lewis, M., Rausch, M., Goldberg, S., & Dodd, C. Error, response time, and I.Q.: Sex difference in cognitive style of preschool children. *Perceptual and Motor Skills,* 1968, *26,* 563–568.

McAndrew, H. Rigidity and isolation. A study of the deaf and the blind. *Journal of Abnormal and Social Psychology,* 1948, *43,* 476–494.

Meadow, K. P. The effects of early manual communication and family climate on the deaf child's development (Doctoral dissertation, University of California, Berkeley, 1967). *Dissertation Abstracts,* 1968, *28,* 4205A. (University Microfilms No. 68-05785)

Meadow, K. P. Early manual communication in relation to the deaf child's intellectual, social, and communicative functioning. *American Annals of the Deaf,* 1968, *113,* 29–41.

Meadow, K. P. *Studies of the behavioral problems of deaf children.* Paper presented at the First National Symposium on the Mental Health Needs of Deaf Adults and Children, Chicago, June 1975.

Meichenbaum, D., & Goodman, J. Training impulsive children to talk to themselves: A means of developing self-control. *Journal of Abnormal Psychology,* 1971, *77,* 115–126.

Mindel, E. D., & Vernon, M. *They grow in silence: The deaf child and his family.* Silver Springs, Maryland: National Association of the Deaf, 1971.

Mindel, E. D., & Vernon, M. Out of the shadows and the silence. *Journal of the American Medical Association,* 1972, *220,* 1127.

Moores, D. F., Weiss, K. L., & Goodwin, M. W. *Evaluation of programs for hearing impaired children: Report of 1972–1973* (Research Project No. 57, Project No. 332189, Grant No., OE-332189-4533). Minneapolis: University of Minnesota Research, Development and Demonstration Center in Education of Handicapped Children, 1973.

Myklebust, H. R. *The psychology of deafness: Sensory deprivation, learning, and adjustment.* New York: Grune & Stratton, 1960.

Nelson, T. F. The effects of training in attention development on observing behavior in reflective and impulsive children (Doctoral dissertation, University of Minnesota, 1968). *Dissertation Abstracts,* 1969, *29,* 2659B. (University Microfilms No. 68–17, 703)

Neyhus, A. The personality of socially well adjusted adult deaf as revealed by projective tests (Doctoral dissertation, Northwestern University, 1962). *Dissertation Abstracts,* 1963, *23,* 2589. (University Microfilms No. 63–1326)

Quigley, S. P., & Frisina, R. Institutionalization and psychoeducational development of deaf children. *Council for Exceptional Children Research Monograph,* 1961, Series A., No. 3.

Rainer, J. D., Altshuler, K. Z., Kallmann, F. J., & Deming, W. E. (Eds.). *Family and mental health problems in a deaf population.* New York: Columbia University Press, 1973.

Ridberg, E. H., Parke, R. D., & Hetherington, E. M. Modification of impulsive and reflective cognitive styles through observation film-mediated models. *Developmental Psychology,* 1971, *5,* 360–377.

Rodda, M. Behavioral disorders in deaf clients. *Journal of Rehabilitation of the Deaf,* 1974, *7,* 1–13.

Schein, J. D. Deaf students with other disabilities. *American Annals of the Deaf,* 1975, *120,* 92–99.

Schlesinger, H. S., & Meadow, K. P. *Sound and sign: Childhood deafness and mental health.* Berkeley: University of California Press, 1972.

Sklerov, A. The effect of preschool experiences on the cognitive style of reflection-impulsivity of disadvantaged children. *Graduate Research in Education and Related Disciplines,* 1974, *7,* 77–91.

Stevenson, E. A study of the educational achievement of deaf children of deaf parents. *California News,* 1964, *80,* 143.

Stuckless, E. R., & Birch, J. W. The influence of early manual communication on the linguistic development of deaf children. *American Annals of the Deaf,* 1966, *111,* 452–460, 499–504.

Vernon, M., & Koh, S. D. Early manual communication and deaf children's achievement. *American Annals of the Deaf,* 1970, *115,* 527–536.

Ward, W. Reflection-impulsivity in kindergarten children. *Child Development,* 1968, *39,* 867–874.

Weintraub, S. A. Cognitive and behavioral impulsivity in internalizing, externalizing, and normal children (Doctoral dissertation, University of Minnesota, 1968). *Dissertation Abstracts International,* 1969, *30,* 395B. (University Microfilms No. 69-11, 47)

Wright, D. *Deafness.* New York: Stein and Day, 1969.

Wright, J. C. *Reflection-impulsivity and information processing: From three to nine years of age.* Paper presented at the meeting of the American Psychological Association, New Orleans, 1974.

Yando, R., & Kagan, J. The effect of teacher tempo on the child. *Child Development,* 1968, *39,* 27–34.

Zivkovic, M. Influence of deafness on the structure of personality. *Perceptual and Motor Skills,* 1971, *33,* 863–866.

9

The Effects of Deafness on Childhood Development: An Eriksonian Perspective

HILDE S. SCHLESINGER

Profound childhood deafness is more than a medical diagnosis; it is a cultural phenomenon in which social, emotional, linguistic, and intellectual patterns and problems are inextricably bound. Despite the normal potential of the deaf child and advances in medicine, audiology, and education, it is still the case that scholastic retardation and psychological "uniqueness" are frequent among deaf children and adults.

Psychologically, the most frequently stated generalization about deaf individuals is that they seem to reflect a high degree of "emotional immaturity." Levine (1956) describes this complex in terms of pronounced underdevelopment in conceptual forms of activity, emotional underdevelopment, substantial lag in understanding the dynamics of interpersonal relationships and of the world, a highly egocentric life perspective, a markedly constricted life area, and a rigid adherence to book-of-etiquette code rather than an inner sensibility as a standard for behaving and even for feeling. Myklebust (1960) finds that the deaf are immature in "caring for others." Altshuler (1964) characterizes the deaf as showing egocentricity, lacking empathy, displaying gross coercive dependency, being impulsive, and not practicing thoughtful introspection. The consistency of these observations by independent investigators working with

157

populations of varying ages and backgrounds, both normal and malad-
justed, adds credence to their existence.

Our clinical work corroborates these findings. Given this consensus,
understanding the source of these characteristics becomes crucial for
intervention. Does the absence of early auditory stimulation, feedback,
and communication in itself create a propensity toward these behavioral
and achievement patterns, or does early profound deafness elicit particular responses from parents, teachers, siblings, and friends that contribute to a particular set of cognitive and behavioral deficiencies?

In our book, *Sound and Sign* (Schlesinger & Meadow, 1972), we traced
the impact of the auditory deficit through the developmental steps: the
"critical moments" that Erikson has so eloquently defined. Erikson maintains that the whole life cycle, the eight stages of man, can be seen as an
integrated psychosocial development in a sequence of critical phases. A
critical phase can be described as a biologically motivated process of
maturation that requires psychological adaptation to achieve a new level
of development. Each phase is characterized by phase-specific development that must be solved; the foundation for the solution is prepared in
the previous stages and is worked out further in the subsequent ones.
Each critical phase can be described in terms of extremes of successful
and unsuccessful solutions, although the usual outcome is a balance between these two extremes: basic trust versus mistrust; autonomy versus
shame and doubt; initiative versus guilt; industry versus inferiority;
identity versus identity diffusion; intimacy versus isolation; generativity
versus stagnation; integrity versus despair.

Throughout our work we have indicated that the resolution of each
critical phase by the deaf child depends on the difficulty of the crisis as
influenced by the degree, onset, and shape of his hearing loss, and the
individual, parental, and societal resources that are immediately available to him. This chapter discusses the first three critical stages of
development in relation to prelingual deafness. We suggest that the child
must have meaningful, reciprocal, and largely positive interactions with
his environment in order to resolve the first three critical stages successfully.

INFANCY: THE DEVELOPMENT OF TRUST

The basic task of infancy, the period from birth to 18 months, is to
establish a trust in the world that later will become a feeling of hope
about oneself and the world. To *survive,* all infants (animal and human)

need to have their most urgent physiological needs met. Infants are known to survive even when these needs are met haphazardly, passively, negatively, unpredictably, or primarily through mechanical contact (Bettelheim, 1967; Harlow & Harlow, 1965). But it would appear that in order to thrive, to *live* rather than to survive, infants must have their physiological, cognitive, and affectional needs met meaningfully, reciprocally, and joyfully.

Optimally, early physiological needs must be met in largely consistent, positive, and predictable ways through mutual regulation with a living being. Apparently only an adult of the species (rather than a sibling or a machine) can optimally engage in mutually regulatory behavior with the infant that will culminate in his active participation in the satisfaction of his needs. The infant needs to learn that he is not a passive recipient of the riches of the environment and the people that inhabit it, but that *his* actions on his own behalf contribute to optimal need satisfaction. Reciprocally, his cries of pain will contribute to obtaining relief, his cries of hunger and his active sucking to food intake, his clinging to cuddling, his smiles to evoking satisfying excitement on the part of others.

More and more evidence is accumulating that the infant has cognitive needs that are almost as urgent as the physiological ones. These have been variously termed "intrinsic motivation," "a need for the senses to take in what feels good," or a drive for competency (Erikson, 1968; Hunt, 1961; White, 1959). Again, the environment must satisfy these needs by providing varied sensory and cognitive input. The food for the body has to be rich enough but digestible enough for ongoing growth, varied enough to contain all the necessary ingredients at age-appropriate levels, and obtainable by the infant through his own actions with the help of others. The food for thought similarly must be appropriately rich but not overpowering (White & Held, 1966); familiar enough to become emotionally important; varied enough to satisfy the need for novelty. Again, it appears crucial that the infant produce the changes in sensory stimulation by his own actions. Visual depth-perception in human infants (Bower, 1966) and normal visual–motor development in kittens (Held & Hein, 1963) was found to be linked to self-induced movements rather than to externally produced motion of the visual stimuli.

This discussion of the infant's urgent needs and their satisfaction through the environment has only tangentially referred to the need for an affectional system represented by a specific, usually maternal, object in the environment. Bowlby (1969) gathers a wealth of material and sensitively weaves it into a theoretical tapestry that illuminates the most modern concept of mothering. An infant does not long remain indiscriminately interested in all objects or humans who satisfy his needs.

Very early the infant prefers cuddly to cold contact, live to inanimate contact. The infant's cries of distress can be calmed by rocking and sucking almost from birth but also by the human voice (Hetherington & Parke, 1975). It appears that even young infants can discriminate among faces and voices and that they have demonstrable preferences based upon these discriminations.

The infant thus develops early attachment behavior toward the mother demonstrated by his early preference for her face, voice, and touch and the discriminating appearance of "social" behaviors such as crying, smiling, babbling, and reaching. Later, preferential attachment is evident in the increased protest at her departure, as well as the increased delight at her arrival. Among many others, the maternal figure will typically provide greater comfort, and the infant in turn will preferentially seek her out with both eyes and movements; the infant will flee to her for safety and cling to her even upon punishment. Most importantly, the infant will vocalize more and explore the environment more freely in her presence.

So far we have described an intact infant living in an environment that enables him actively to obtain food for body, thought, and affect in the presence of the mother. We are primarily interested, however, in infants with inadequate auditory contact with the environment. Without active intervention their food for thought will be impoverished and may be insufficient. Active intervention can help the deaf child to approximate Piaget's aphorism (Hunt, 1964) "the more a child has seen and heard, the more he wants to see and hear." With modern advances in audiology and hearing aids, auditory contact with the environment can be increased for most, if not all, deaf children.

Depending on the pattern and severity of the hearing loss, some youngsters will learn to appreciate environmental sounds; to discriminate between speech and environmental sounds, between male and female voices, and between cheerful and angry voices, and some will actually be able to eventually repeat words—even unfamiliar ones—with good approximation. Even if the auditory route remains blocked, the deaf child may benefit from compensatory visual and tactile input very much as blind infants benefit from compensatory auditory contact (Burlingham, 1964, 1967).

During the attachment phase of infancy, communication between parent and child occurs primarily through such nonverbal means as voice quality, touch, and smile. In moving to the next stage of development, however, symbolic, linguistic communication assumes a more important role.

EARLY CHILDHOOD: AUTONOMY VERSUS SHAME AND DOUBT

The basic task of early childhood, the period from 18 months to 3 years, is to develop a sense of autonomy, the sense of being a separate human being who has control over his body and who can influence the environment increasingly more maturely. This autonomy is accompanied by a feeling of good will toward self and environment. The successful resolution of this critical phase depends on mutual regulation between parent and child so that the child may develop a feeling of "I am what I will freely." During this period the child has strong and conflicting impulses to hold on or to let go in a variety of situations. His abilities to withhold and expel are increased through the "rapid gains in motor and sphincter controls."

Behaviorally, the child at this stage is frequently described as stubborn, alternately clinging to mother and violently pushing her away, alternatively accepting and refusing the "power struggle" of toilet training. It appears as if the child were saying "I want to do with my muscles, my words, and my sphincters (which all have recently and laboriously come to be under my control) what feels good to me." Therein lies the conflict, for the mother frequently holds different views about if, when, and how the child should indulge in or refrain from acting on these urges. Ideally the mother will gradually help the child to place adequate restraints on these strong urges. For "man must learn to will what can be, to renounce as not worth willing what cannot be and to believe he willed what is inevitable [Erikson, 1964, p. 118]." The child is helped in this achievement by outer controls that are firmly reassuring, gradually applied, and flexible. Outer controls applied too severely, too rigidly, or too early will rob the child of his own gradual learning control and may result in a double rebellion and double defeat (Erikson, 1968).

The outer controls designed to help the child delay, substitute, or prohibit satisfaction of his urges, become more often accompanied by linguistic symbols and communication. Similarly, the child's impulsive acts begin to be replaced by his own verbal prohibitions.

The important role of language has been recognized by people in a wide variety of disciplines. Psychiatrists have focused on substituting or supplementing deeds with words (Fraiberg, 1959; Greenacre, 1971) and on transmitting, clearly or ambiguously, the communicative techniques of the culture to the child (Lidz, Fleck, & Cornelison, 1965). Some cognitive theorists have suggested that language shapes thought (Vygotsky, 1962); others have suggested that although thought precedes language, language does provide freedom from immediacy (Furth, 1969). Other researchers have presented evidence that maternal linguistic styles affect both the cognitive and affective realm of the child. For example, Bernstein (1970) and Hess and Shipman (1965) have postulated that the restricted and positional maternal linguistic codes most prevalent among "lower class" mothers tend to transmit the culture of poverty to their children, who in turn develop cognitive and behavioral stances at odds with the middle-class educational system. Others have noted that cognitive structuring—clear statements of parental rules, reasons for these rules, and consequences of breaking them—is crucially important in teaching the child to forego, postpone, or modify strongly motivated activity. Effective discipline in nursery schools has been related to the use of reasoning in a generally nurturant and nonpunitive atmosphere, with rewards for self-control and firmly enforced rules (Baumrind & Black, 1967). Parke (1969) has found that cognitive structuring dilutes and overrides other parameters of punishment such as timing, intensity, and nurturance levels.

The developing deaf child, however, faces many difficulties associated with language. Most deaf children are born to hearing parents who expect to socialize their child through the modality of spoken English. This process is enormously difficult, especially for youngsters whose auditory contact with the environment is inadequate for speech discrimination. Despite recent advances in audiology, linguistic input for many deaf children is limited to what can be lipread. Lipreading is difficult, even for persons with well-developed English skills, because only about 40% of spoken English is visible on the lips. For the young deaf child, this difficulty is compounded further by difficulties in attending to the relevant stimuli. Bruner, Olver, and Greenfield (1966) have suggested that young children's visual perception is characterized by unsteady attention and is organized around a minimal number of cues—usually the concrete ones to which the child can most readily point. Children are ill-equipped to reconstruct a whole from partial cues, such as those available in lipreading. Furthermore, perception in young children is said to be "stuck" (Bruner et al., 1966) or "centered" (Piaget & Inhelder, 1969), so that the child finds it difficult to shift his set. Thus, young deaf children have difficulty in learning English and in communicating with others.

Consequently, there are delays in language acquisition and deficits in age-appropriate linguistic competence and performance, with these problems often leading to cumulative deficits as the child matures. How do these linguistic deficiencies relate to, or cause, other intellectual or psychological maladaptations? What happens to the meaningful, reciprocal, and joyful communication that we have postulated is of crucial importance in this stage of development?

The hearing parents of a deaf child, frustrated by limitations in communication, frequently resort to restrictive, imperative, positional linguistic codes. It is easier to say "no" to a deaf child than to patiently help the child understand by qualifying the "no" with "not this time, not in this place, not in this way." These maternal linguistic codes do not provide freedom from immediacy and may contribute to the deaf child's resemblances to the "child of poverty" or the "experientially deprived [Furth, 1966]." Words are slow to substitute for acts and do not as easily distinguish between fantasy and reality. Discipline has inadequate cognitive structuring and must rely on timing and intensity.

Hearing parents of deaf children do, however, put a premium on their deaf child's verbalization, a premium that must appear one-sided to the child. Power struggles usually seen in the battle of toilet-training occur in the battle of words. There is clinical and research evidence that noncognitive psychological forces also play their role in the mutism of many deaf individuals. The literature on hearing, but mute, children indicates that mutism can have an interpersonal origin associated with delayed autonomy (Filippi & Rousey, 1968; Levy, 1955). Interestingly enough, these hearing, mute youngsters demonstrate signs of negativism, impulsive aggressiveness, fearfulness of adult disapproval, and provocation of adult nurturance and overprotection, all of which can be seen as sequelae of an unresolved crisis of autonomy. The deaf child frequently shows such negative mutism when words are anxiously and insistently forced by the parent. Joy and reciprocity both suffer.

In comparing the interactions between deaf and hearing children and their mothers, we noted that as a group the mothers of the hearing children were more flexible, permissive, encouraging, and creative; they were less frequently didactic and intrusive. As a group, the hearing children were more buoyant, more compliant, more creative, and showed more enjoyment in the interaction with their mothers and more pride in their achievements. However, within the group of deaf children, some revealed evidence of more successful and gratifying communication with their mothers.[1] These understanding–understood chil-

---

[1] The reasons for the more successful communication are under investigation. Although the degree of hearing loss was comparable among the deaf children, the shape of the audiograms differed widely (and may, in fact, indicate a more important variable), and the history of audiological help varied. Furthermore, some youngsters had had early access to a combination of sign language and speech.

dren more closely resembled hearing children and their mothers (Schlesinger & Meadow, 1972).

Teachers, parents, and mental health professionals who have frequent contact with deaf children have commented that those children often fall into one of two bipolar behavior patterns, one categorized as "goody two-shoes," excessively obedient or compliant, and the other as "Attila the Hun," active and excessively defiant. Our own psychiatric experience with parents and children tends to corroborate these generalizations. Patterns of mother–child communication may well be related to the development of these behavior patterns. In examining the relation between communication and behavioral patterns, it is useful to consider Bernstein's (1972) division of communicative modes into four contexts:

1. The regulative context, in which the child is made aware of rules and of authority relationships
2. The instructional context, in which the child learns about the objective nature of objects and persons, and acquires skills of various kinds
3. The imaginative or innovating context, in which the child is encouraged to experiment and recreate the world on his own terms and in his own way
4. The interpersonal context, in which the child is made aware of affective states, both his own and others'

The regulative, imaginative, and interpersonal context appear most vulnerable to linguistic deficiencies. As cognitive structuring is more difficult for the mother of a deaf child, the rules of the moral order are more difficult to clarify. Cheyne (1971) found that cognitive structuring enables one to link punishment to a specific response, thereby reducing the risk of generalized inhibition. This finding suggests an interesting question: Does a reduction of cognitive structuring in the deaf child produce the two extremes of behavior, obedience and rebellion?

In response to confusion, the growing child must find ways to establish some meaning and order. This can be accomplished by emphatic obedience to parental dicta so that meaning resides in the authority. It can also be accomplished by defying all that the "superior" person says and does, so that meaning resides in the very act of opposition.

Meaning can be less ambiguous in the world of objects. For the young deaf child, meaning may reside in an obsessional manipulation of the physical environment in which the interplay of thought and action can progress more satisfactorily than it can in the world of persons.

Behaviorally, this more lucid understanding of the physical world than the social world may have some noxious consequences with overinsistence on orderliness in terms of space, sequence, and tempo. Sandler (1960) notes that obsessional manifestations may constitute an attempt to achieve by magical means a degree of security and safety (by excessive controlling and ritualistic behavior).

It is interesting to note that there are some theoretically important parallels between the dysfunctional thought processes of the obsessional (Barnett, 1972) and some of the psychological characteristics of the deaf that were mentioned earlier. Ambiguity in early family situations, constricted thinking, a tendency to label rather than to think, a bipolarity of passivity and occasional compulsive acting out, confusion between blame and responsibility are common in both. Indeed, the word "deaf" could be substituted for "obsessional" in the following:

> With such ambiguous premises, the interpersonal world becomes a morass of poorly grasped and inadequately understood occurrences. The obsessional, despite his frequently high intelligence, often finds it difficult to understand even relatively simple interpersonal events and is surprisingly inept in performing simple functions in his personal relationships [Barnett, 1972, p. 345].

Cognitively, there are more felicitous outcomes. It may be argued that those areas of cognition that are least subject to ambiguous input are most likely to function at age level. Thus, Brown (1965) notes that for universal concepts, social mediation is not likely to be important since they are learned from direct manipulation of the physical world. This greater ability to establish logical connections in the physical world (in contrast to the interpersonal world) may also explain Furth's (1970) data indicating that the deaf are not retarded on certain cognitive tasks which may require symbolic thought, but are not bound to language per se. It may also account for some of the parallels of "disadvantaged" children and deaf children: many of these children are better at doing and seeing than at talking and hearing; they often appear to achieve better on performance tests than on verbal ones; they appear to think in spatial terms, rather than temporal ones, and they often have poor time perspective (Riessman, 1962).

But the reality for the child resides not only in the world of objects and their static and dynamic *relations*, but also in the world of people, with their enormously more complex dynamics. The next stage illuminates additional difficulties.

LATER CHILDHOOD: INITIATIVE VERSUS GUILT

The task of childhood from 3 to 6 years is to develop a sense of initiative with a feeling of the purposefulness of life and of one's own self. With optimal resolution of the previous stages, the child has reached a more advanced kind of identification; he is by now convinced that he is a person on his own and must now find out the kind of person he may become (Erikson, 1968). The chant of this age could be, "I am what I can imagine I will be." Does the deaf child at this age encounter, produce, or enhance meaningful reciprocal and joyful communication?

This stage is characterized in the normal youngster by marked verbal and motor exuberance. In the deaf child, this exuberance is doubly inhibited—the verbal exuberance is almost invariably diminished by a paucity of symbols, but the feelings remain exuberant, and it is not surprising that youngsters "deprived of the ability or opportunity to express powerful feeling in words . . . usually erupt in actions [Katan, 1961]." The motor exuberance is thus potentially increased for the deaf youngster, but in practice is further inhibited.

A child incessantly in action cannot or will not focus attention on adults who need or wish to communicate with him. Parents who urgently need to communicate about potential dangers and about prospective plans will tend to force the child into a motionless attentiveness. Teachers who feel the need to "pour" language into the deaf child will also place a premium on immobility, discouraging self-initiated, exploratory maneuvers so valuable for development.

Furthermore, "poured in" language decreases self-initiated and reciprocal communication. Teaching based on rote drill and unceasing imitation interfere both with the joyfulness and the meaning of communication. No teacher, no child, can remain vitally interested when the same worn label is invariably attached to a well worn object.

One further factor looms important in the inhibition of joyful communication. Each human being is unique and is consequently different from any other in a multitude of ways. Many clinicians (Fromm, 1939; Horney, 1937; Rogers, 1951; Sullivan, 1953) have emphasized the intimate connection between acceptance of self and acceptance by others. The growth of self-acceptance is accompanied by early awareness of human differences, which ideally can be accepted either joyfully or neutrally. We have noted that many parents attempt to force their youngsters into a normalcy not available to them. Some parents abhor any vestige of difference and forego the hearing aid, inhibit gestures and voice. Their children learn early that their deficiencies—hearing aids, vocal quality, use of gestures—are devalued by the overall society.

SUMMARY

The patterns of development described in this chapter suggest that the typical deaf child of hearing parents suffers in the resolution of each of the three early phases identified by Erikson. Other developmental patterns are, however, evident in some groups of deaf children. For some years we have studied the development of deaf children of deaf parents, whose mother tongue is American Sign Language. These children have demonstrated better overall functioning and we have become convinced that this advantage is related to an earlier onset of successful communication (Meadow, 1967; Schlesinger, 1972; Schlesinger & Meadow, 1972). More recently we have studied deaf youngsters of hearing parents who have communicated with each other through a combination of speech and signs during the crucial stages described above. The findings thus far indicate that their communication is more meaningful, joyful, and reciprocal, and that these youngsters have traversed the first three Eriksonian stages more successfully and with more hope, more will, and more purpose.

REFERENCES

Altshuler, K. Z. Personality traits and depressive symptoms in the deaf. In J. Wortis (Ed.), *Recent advances in biological psychiatry* (Vol. VI). New York: Plenum Press, 1964.

Barnett, J. Therapeutic intervention in the dysfunctional thought processes of the obsessional. *American Journal of Psychotherapy*, 1972, *26*, 338–351.

Baumrind, D., & Black, A. Socialization practices associated with dimensions of competency in preschool boys and girls. *Child Development*, 1967, *38*, 291–327.

Bernstein, B. B. A sociolinguistic approach to socialization with some references to educability. In Williams, F. (Ed.), *Language and poverty*. Chicago: Markham, 1970. Pp. 25–61.

Bernstein, B. B. Social class, language, and socialization. In S. Moscovici (Ed.), *The psychosociology of language*. Chicago: Markham, 1972.

Bettelheim, B. *The empty fortress*. New York. New York: Free Press, 1967.

Bower, T. G. R. The visual world of infants. *Scientific American*, 1966, *215*, 80–92.

Bowlby, J. *Attachment and loss* (Vol. 1). New York: Basic Books, 1969.

Brown, R. W. *Social psychology*. New York: Free Press, 1965.

Bruner, J. S., Olver, R., & Greenfield, P. M. *Studies in cognitive growth*. New York: Wiley, 1966.

Burlingham, D. Hearing and its role in the development of the blind. *Psychoanalytic Study of the Child*, 1964, *19*, 95–112.

Burlingham, D. Developmental considerations in the occupations of the blind. *Psychoanalytic Study of the Child*, 1967, *22*, 147–162.

Cheyne, J. A. Some parameters of punishment affecting resistance to deviation and generalization of a prohibition. *Child Development,* 1971, *42,* 1249–1261.

Erikson, E. H. *Insight and responsibility.* New York: Norton, 1964.

Erikson, E. H. *Identity, youth and crisis.* New York: Norton, 1968.

Filippi, R., & Rousey, C. L. Delay in onset of talking—a symptom of interpersonal disturbance. *Journal of the American Academy of Child Psychiatry,* 1968, *7,* 316–328.

Fraiberg, S. H. *The magic years.* New York: Scribners, 1959.

Fromm, E. Selfishness and self-love. *Psychiatry,* 1939, *2,* 507–523.

Furth, H. G. *Thinking without language: Psychological implications of deafness.* New York: Free Press, 1966.

Furth, H. G. *Piaget and knowledge.* Englewood Cliffs, New Jersey: Prentice-Hall, 1969.

Furth, H. G. A review and perspective on the thinking of deaf people. In J. Hellmuth (Ed.), *Cognitive studies.* New York: Brunner/Mazel, 1970.

Greenacre, P. *Emotional growth: Psychoanalytic studies of the gifted and a great variety of other individuals.* International Universities Press: New York, 1971.

Harlow, H. F., & Harlow, M. K. The affectional systems. In A. Schrier, H. Harlow, & F. Stolhitz (Eds.), *Behavior of nonhuman primates* (Vol. 2). New York: Academic Press, 1965.

Held, R., & Hein, A. Movement-produced stimulation in the development of visually guided behavior. *Journal of Comparative and Physiological Psychology,* 1963, *56,* 872–876.

Hess, R. D., & Shipman, V. C. Early experience and the socialization of cognitive modes in children. *Child Development,* 1965, *36,* 869–886.

Hetherington, E. M. & Parke, R. D. *Child Psychology.* New York: McGraw-Hill, 1975.

Horney, K. *The neurotic personality of our time.* New York: Norton, 1937.

Hunt, J. M. *Intelligence and experience.* New York: Ronald Press, 1961.

Hunt, J. M. How children develop intellectually. *Children* (Vol. 2). Washington, D. C.: Department of Health, Education and Welfare, 1964.

Katan, A. Some thoughts about the role of verbalization in early childhood. *Psychoanalytic Study of the Child,* 1961, *16,* 184–188.

Levine, E. S. *Youth in a soundless world.* New York: New York University Press, 1956.

Levy, D. M. Oppositional syndrome and oppositional behavior. In P. Hock (Ed.), *Psychopathology of childhood.* New York: Grune & Stratton, 1955.

Lidz, T., Fleck, S., & Cornelison, A. R. *Schizophrenia and the family.* New York: International Universities Press, 1965.

Meadow, K. P. *The effect of early manual communication and family climate on the deaf child's development.* Unpublished doctoral dissertation, University of California, Berkeley, 1967.

Myklebust, H. *The psychology of deafness.* New York: Grune & Stratton, 1960.

Parke, R. D. Effectiveness of punishment as an interaction of intensity, timing, agent nurturance and cognitive structuring. *Child Development,* 1969, *40,* 211–235.

Piaget, J., & Inhelder, B. *The psychology of the child.* New York: Basic Books, 1969.

Riessman, F. *The culturally deprived child.* New York: Harper & Row, 1962.

Rogers, C. R. *Client-centered therapy.* Boston: Houghton Mifflin, 1951.

Sandler, J. The background of safety. *International Journal of Psychology,* 1960, *41,* 352–356.

Schlesinger, H. S. Meaning and enjoyment: Language acquisition of deaf children. In T. J. O'Rourke (Ed.), *Psycholinguistics and total communication: The state of the art.* Washington, D. C.: American Annals of the Deaf, 1972.

Schlesinger, H. S., & Meadow, K. P. *Sound and sign: Childhood deafness and mental health.* Berkeley: University of California Press, 1972.

Sullivan, H. S. *Conceptions of modern psychiatry.* New York: Norton, 1953.

Vygotsky, L. S. *Thought and language.* Cambridge: M.I.T. Press, 1962.

White, B. L., & Held, R. Plasticity of sensorimotor development in the human infant. In J. Rosenblith & W. Allinsmith (Eds.), *The causes of behavior* (2nd edition). Boston: Allyn and Bacon, 1966.

White, R. W. Motivation reconsidered: The concept of competence. *Psychological Review,* 1959, *66,* 297–333.

IV

EDUCATIONAL AND
CULTURAL CONTEXTS

10

Current Research and Theory
with the Deaf:
Educational Implications[1]

DONALD F. MOORES

In discussing the application of research findings to educational practice it is always prudent to begin by noting the lack of contact between those individuals conducting research and those educating children. Research and education are frequently perceived as independent activities with no need for cross-fertilization. It is obvious that any paradigm concerning the application of research represents an ideal to be pursued rather than the reality of the present.

The gap between research and application is wider in the field of special education than in general education. And within special education, this gap is broadest in the area of deafness. In a review of research trends in special education in the United States, Hurder (1973) reported that among all categories of handicaps funded by the Bureau of Education for the Handicapped over a 5-year period, hearing impairment was the only handicap in which more grants were made for demonstration projects than for research projects, suggesting that service concerns ex-

[1] The preparation of this paper was supported, in part, by a grant from the Bureau of Education for the Handicapped, U. S. Office of Education, Department of Health, Education and Welfare to the Research, Development and Demonstration Center in Education of Handicapped Children, University of Minnesota.

173

ceed research concerns in this area. Hurder states:

> If this is true, it presents an unusual paradox when examined in the perspective of the potential contribution of our understanding of human behavior inherent in the resolution of such issues as the relationship of oral/aural language to cognitive development. Were a culture discovered in which all human communication took place in the complete absence of oral/aural inputs and outputs, it would surely arouse great interest within the scientific community. . . . Such individuals are interspersed throughout all oral/aural cultures; yet they seemingly provoke relatively little interest among those who seek knowledge of human cognitive development and function [p. 194].

This chapter is designed to explore educational implications of the effects of deafness on the individual and to suggest the areas of investigation the author believes are most in need of study. An attempt has been made to deal with new issues or to treat existing issues in different ways. The author has not attempted to duplicate recent reviews or summaries treating in detail various facets of educating the deaf. For extensive background information the reader should refer directly to earlier reviews concerned with educational implications of deafness (Bonvillian, Charrow, & Nelson, 1973; Moores, 1972a, 1975), educational research on manual communication (Moores, 1971, 1974, 1975; Rodda, 1972), psycholinguistics and deafness (O'Rourke, 1973), and early childhood education for the deaf (Moores, 1974; Moores, Weiss, & Goodwin, 1978).

The material presented here is related to topics covered in several other chapters—particularly those concerned with American Sign Language, relationships between language and thought, and the impact of deafness on the child and his or her family—although an effort has been made to minimize redundancy. Furthermore, this chapter is specifically oriented toward implications for educational practice. That is, the same content may be considered from several perspectives. The most obvious example relates to investigations of American Sign Language (ASL). Analyses of ASL within linguistic and developmental psycholinguistic frameworks overlap, but do not coincide completely with the goals and procedures involved in deciding what place ASL or one of its variants should have in an educational system.

THE RESEARCH TO APPLICATION PROCESS

The conceptual framework that follows for the development of strategies for applying research to education is an expansion of Gallagher's (1968) 5-step sequence beginning with "basic" research and ending in educational adoption, as presented by Moores (1973a).

The process by which the discovery of new knowledge is accomplished and eventually translated into educational innovation is a complex one, extending over a series of identifiable stages. Gallagher identifies five phases: research, development, demonstration, dissemination, and adoption into an ongoing educational operation. Each phase requires a different emphasis, concentration of professional skills, and organizational support.

The ultimate criteria of successful educational research must be changes in the educational system that are of demonstrable benefit to children. A major component of any educational research must be careful consideration of how results can be used to ameliorate existing problems.

The current time lag in American education between the initiation of research activities and the adoption of changes can be attributed to a number of factors. One basic obstacle is that the research and the adoption ends of the continuum have been perceived as separate domains by both universities and public schools, organizations that differ in their priorities. At the university level, priorities and reinforcements have been arranged to encourage concentration on research to the exclusion of other stages. High-status university educational researchers generally do "basic" research, resulting in a closed system in which research is usually conducted for the benefit of other researchers. Thus, an individual might conceive of a problem, develop a design, run an experiment, and report the results in esoteric jargon, which is incomprehensible to the educational practitioner. Two outcomes of this process have been:

1. Much educational research has been done that is irrelevant to education.
2. Much of the relevant research has not been educationally beneficial because there are no mechanisms for translating this basic knowledge into behavior.

Figure 10.1 illustrates the situation that exists when the interaction between universities and schools is nonexistent and when the translation of knowledge to action is blocked by the lack of cooperation between the two systems and by the absence of activity in the demonstration phase.

The breakdown occurs at that point where university–public school cooperation should be at the maximum level, namely the demonstration stage which, in Gallagher's terms, involves an effective conjunction of organized knowledge and child. To be believable, any such conjunction must be accomplished in a school or home setting. Without an effective bridge, there is little confluence of knowledge and practice.

Progress by schools requires them to be open to input from several sources, with universities providing a significant impetus for innovation.

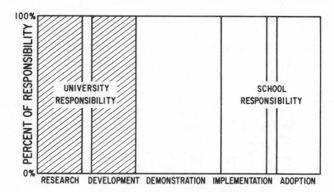

Figure 10.1 Perceived disjunction of the missions of universities and public school.

If the universities are to exert a major influence they must adopt a learner's role and be more sensitive to the needs of children and to the realities of the home and classroom. Acceptance of an idea comes only after it stands the test of empirical verification in the field.

Ideally, schools and universities should function as partners in all phases of the research-to-adoption continuum. Although the universities should assume the major responsibility for the first stages, the schools must be able to influence the type of research undertaken. At the other end, the universities should contribute their unique skills to the evaluation and modification of programs that have been adopted into the ongoing educational operation. Figure 10.2 presents an ideal university–school relationship.

Within this context, the following sections of this chapter delineate issues for future study and consider implications of current knowledge for educational practice. The first section concerns the potential contributions of ethological approaches to understanding the successful adaptation of a deaf child.

CONTRIBUTIONS OF ETHOLOGY[2]

During the past 10 years, educational programs for deaf children have been serving increasingly younger children. Today, most large met-

[2] I would like to acknowledge the contribution of William Charlesworth, colleague at the Research, Development and Demonstration Center in Education of Handicapped Children, Professor at the University of Minnesota Institute of Child Development, and member of the *Humanethologie Arbeitsgruppe, Max Planck Institute für Verhalten Physiologie,*

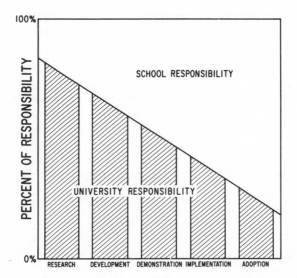

Figure 10.2 Ideal sharing of responsibility between universities and public schools.

ropolitan areas provide some type of educational service to the child and family as soon as the hearing loss has been identified. It must be recognized, then, that educational intervention extends into the home and involves not only the deaf individual, but also the complete family unit. Except for the work of Meadow and Schlesinger (Meadow, 1968a,b, 1969; Schlesinger & Meadow, 1971) there have been few efforts to observe systematically the impact of deafness on a child and his family.

An example of the importance of examining the interaction between deaf children and their environments is found in trying to interpret the consistent research finding that deaf children of deaf parents are superior in academic achievement and English language abilities to deaf children of hearing parents (Meadow, 1968; Stevenson, 1964; Stuckless & Birch, 1966; Vernon & Koh, 1970). These differences generally have been attributed to the use of manual communication with deaf children. Although the role of manual communication is probably important, the environment of a deaf child of deaf parents probably differs from that of a deaf child of hearing parents in many other ways. Moores (1973b) has

---

West Germany. His work at the University of Minnesota's RD&D Center on applications of ethological principles to observations of retarded children and their families has led me to become acquainted with ethology and to consider the use of ethological methods to study deaf children and their families.

postulated that part of the superiority also may be explained by the easier acceptance of deafness by deaf parents and the resulting reduction of strain during transitional stages of the life cycle. (Additional discussions of these issues is found in Chapter 8 by R. Harris, this volume.)

There is an obvious need for careful, detailed observation of the behavior of deaf children in natural settings to determine whether the enviornmental challenges for deaf children are different from those for hearing children and to determine to what extent such differences require different modes of adaptation. In applying an ethological approach to the study of human beings, we need to describe the individual's intelligent behavior as well as the cognitive demand characteristics of the environment (Charlesworth, 1974). The cognitive demand characteristics not only daily challenge the individual to act intelligently, but also influence the development of his intelligence. Therefore we must study both the deaf individual and the demands made on that individual by the environment.

Intelligent behavior, then, may be seen as a mode of adaptation to everyday environmental demands. Within this context, Hinde (1966) has argued that if a species appears to be deficient in some faculty, as defined by a particular test, one must refer back to the natural situation to assess the extent to which this is compensated for by the development of other faculties. Applying similar reasoning to the study of human beings, Charlesworth (1974) argues that if a psychologist or anthropologist goes into a lower socioeconomic section of town—into a ghetto, into the jungles of the Amazon, even into the back wards of a mental institution—he should assume that the individuals in these places have already adapted.

By extending such reasoning to deafness, it should be possible to (a) identify environments that encourage optimal development of deaf children; and (b) identify those areas in which deafness per se has implications for the development of the individual. The most important theoretical and practical issues to which this approach may be applied concerns the nature of human communication and language. The basic issue is whether the auditory–vocal channel lies at the heart of human language, or if instead, the auditory–vocal channel has merely been the most convenient and most common mode of communication. Phylogenetically, Homo sapiens have acquired elaborate acoustic–articulatory mechanisms that enable the development of spoken language. It is uncertain to what extent a nonfunctioning or partially functioning acoustic mechanism prevents a child from realizing linguistic competence. The use of observational techniques in naturalistic settings could contribute to the resolution of this issue.

Ethological methodology might help us to identify what and how often environmental demands require adaptation of the deaf child's cognitive skills. Such an approach would involve the use of minute categorical and episodic observations and would lead to the construction of ecologically valid test items or situations capable of tapping basic skills. Although such research would be tedious and time consuming, it is imperative to move beyond the laboratory if we wish to identify natural basic cognitive skills and fundamental problem-solving processes that are significantly related to successful adaptation. The politial benefits justify a major commitment in this direction.

RELATIONSHIP OF THOUGHT, LANGUAGE, AND DEAFNESS

Language and Thought: The Work of Furth

The publications of Furth (1964, 1966, 1969, 1971, 1973, 1974) have made educators of the deaf aware of Piaget's work and have been influential in modifying many educators' concepts of language, thought, and deafness. Of greatest impact, perhaps, has been Furth's assertion that despite the fact that deaf children receive inadequate instruction in English, speech, and school subjects; that their parents are miscounseled and misled; that they face prejudice, distrust, and discrimination— despite all of this—the majority of deaf individuals adequately adjust to the world. They marry, raise children, pay taxes, contribute to the good of the community, fight, watch television, and entertain themselves in much the way as everyone. The survival and endurance of deaf people in the face of a generally indifferent or hostile world that must be dealt with daily is a tribute to the human spirit.

Furth, among others, has contributed to a decreasing tendency to view deafness and deaf individuals with models of deviancy, deficiency, or pathology, substituting, instead, a healthier and more positive approach of identifying strengths and fostering optimal development with those strengths. (See also Chapter 12 by A. Harris, this volume.) Furth has affirmed the idenpendence of thinking from language, at least through concrete operational thinking, and has advocated a reordering of priorities in the education of the deaf (as well as in general education) in which education for thinking would take priority over instruction in language. Without denying the importance of language, Furth (1971) argues that the appropriate medium for helping the developing mind is not verbal language, but is rather experience in concrete situations. Projects such as a thinking laboratory for deaf children (Furth, 1969) and a book on games without words (Wolff & Wolff, 1974) have been based on this position.

If one were to play devil's advocate, however, it should be noted that many of Furth's statements tend to be cateogorical assertions of fact. These assertions are sometimes left unqualified or are qualified only in other writings, thus causing confusion in the unwary reader. Some examples are provided in the direct quotes below:

> Piaget is the one great psychologist who holds a theory of thinking that makes sense of the fact that deaf children can grow up into thinking human beings even though they do not know much language [Furth, 1971, p. 9].

> The inferior performance of the deaf on some tasks is parsimoniously attributed to either lack of general experience which is no longer manifest by adulthood or to specific task conditions which favor linguistic habits [Furth, 1964, p. 145].

> Language refers to the living languages as heard and spoken in our society [Furth, 1964, p. 147].

> We use the term experiential deficiency to describe the intellectual poverty in which deaf children grow up [Furth, 1973, p. 259].

> Sign language is the natural language of the deaf [Furth, 1974, p. 267].

> Language is a principal and preferred medium of thinking for a developed mind, for a mind that has reached, as Piaget calls it, the formal operating stage [Furth, 1971, p. 11].

> Where deaf persons in general fall short is at the formal operative level. More precisely what happens is that they barely reach formal operating thinking, and then they cannot develop their minds much further because they do not have the tool of language [Furth, 1971, p. 12].

These quotations contain several inconsistencies and unquestioned assumptions which should be challenged. Of primary importance is the belief, implicit and explicit, that deaf individuals typically do not know much language. Furth has referred to the extensive literature regarding low levels of reading achievement to justify his position that deaf individuals tend to be linguistically deficient. However, reading achievement scores do not necessarily reflect linguistic functioning. Considering his reliance on reading achievement scores and his reference to living language as heard and spoken in our society, it appears that Furth means that deaf people tend to be deficient in standard middle-class American English. Given his statement that sign language is the natural language of the deaf, it would seem that his statements on the lack of language in the deaf must be qualified pending intensive investigations of the nature and functions of sign language. For example, when the author was a classroom teacher beginning to learn sign and to teach through the use of simultaneous signs and speech, I found that in the case of difficult concepts, or concepts difficult for me to communicate, if one student could get the concept, the student could convey the ideas, no matter how difficult, easily and efficiently through sign language. In my own readings of studies of intellectual functioning of the deaf, I have come to the conclusion that in those cases where the deaf have shown inferior performance, the most parsimonious explanation may be neither lack of language nor experiential deficiency, but rather the very real possibility that *the experimenters were unable to communicate effectively with the deaf subjects*. Therefore, I believe serious reservations must be entertained concerning Furth's position because:

1.   He has not demonstrated that deaf persons lack language.
2.   He has not demonstrated that deaf persons "fall short" at the formal operational level.

Given this position, I also must question the claim that only Piaget's theory of thinking can explain the existence of thought without language in the deaf, not because of any basic disagreement with Piaget, but because the deaf, as a group, cannot be considered to be without language.

It should be pointed out also that Piaget is not the only theorist who does not consider intelligence to be language based. As Furth (1964, p. 145) himself acknowledges, William James in 1890, and Binet and Simon in 1905 suggested that thought processes in a deaf person were developed prior to language. A review of articles in the *American Annals of the Deaf* suggests a consistent interest in the relationships between thought and language beginning with an article in the first volume by Ray (1848) titled "Thoughts of the deaf and dumb before instruction." As may be expected, opinions were diverse, and there were frequent exchanges of what one editor (Peet, 1855, p. 27) felt constrained to describe as a "friendly discussion." The most ambitious undertaking was a translation from the German of Schneider's "The thought and language of the deaf-mute," which was published in nine installments of the *Annals* from 1908 to 1911.

Even outside the field of education of the deaf, it is inaccurate to state that Piaget's is the only theory that does not consider intelligence to be language based. Osgood (1963, 1966, 1968), for example, has consistently argued for the primacy of meaning. Furth's statement also ignores the extensive recent work on semantic bases of language, and attention to the primacy of cognitive development over language (e.g., Antinucci & Parisi, 1973; Bloom, 1970; Bowerman, 1970; Brown, 1973; Clark, 1973; McNamara, 1972; Schlesinger, 1971; Slobin, 1973).

In his survey of cognition in handicapped children, Suppes (1974) commented that Furth does not really make a strong theoretical point because his analysis is concerned entirely with command of a standard natural language. Noting Furth's acknowledgment that the processes deaf children use are not clear, Suppes reasoned that process-oriented approaches to cognitive skills seem to argue strongly that some sort of language is being used internally, even if the language is not that of the society in which the children live.

Suppes goes on to state that the experiments on logical reasoning on which Furth bases his conclusions are all extremely elementary. Suppes summarized his position as follows:

> The real test will be not successful efforts to transform more sophisticated forms of inference into nonverbal contexts, because this seems *prima facie* impossible, but rather to test the ability to communicate and to handle such inferences in sign language. These more developed forms of inference are not primarily auditory in nature but visual; for example, there is very little development of mathematical proofs in purely auditory fashion [pp. 162–163].

An alternate approach: The Soviet view. Since this chapter is oriented to educational implications for the deaf, it is appropriate to consider the position of Lev Vygotsky, a theorist whose work has already influenced educational procedures with deaf children. In *Thought and Language* (which first appeared in 1934 and was translated into English in 1962), Vygotsky (1962) concluded:

1. In their ontogenetic development, thought and speech have different roots.
2. In the speech development of the child, we can with certainty establish a preintellectual stage, and, in his thought development, a prelinguistic stage.
3. Up to a certain point in time, the two follow different lines, independently of each other.
4. At a certain point, these lines meet, whereupon thought becomes verbal and speech rational [p. 44].

Because Vygotsky's work has been so influential with Soviet educators of the deaf, who have, in turn, been critical of Furth's position (Shif,

1969), I will outline some areas in which Soviet techniques differ from Furth's. It might be fruitful if the effects of these different procedures on the general development of deaf children examined.

It should first be noted that in the Soviet Union it is customary not to treat language and thought separately, but rather to address the complex dialectical interdependence of thought and language. Shif (1969), for example, has criticized Furth for studying the interaction between language and thinking outside the context of developmental changes in their relationship. He argues that behind grammatical activities, which occur so quickly in hearing children, are complex mental processes. Another characteristic of the Soviet position is the belief that complex mental processes, or complex functional systems, are formed during the child's associations with adults (Luria, 1969). Third, it is believed that the child is a social being from the beginning who must develop a means of communication as quickly as possible.

To a large extent, the type of activities used in the Soviet Union are similar to those advocated by Furth. Instruction concentrates on practical activities to encourage independence (Moores, 1972b). There is extensive use of manipulative toys and materials such as paper, plastic, textiles, papíer-mâché and Plexiglas. Arts and crafts are emphasized to develop concepts of position and color as well as to develop creativity. Activities with practical application include work with illustrations and figures. There are numerous measuring and counting experiences. Much of the child's early education is devoted to organized observation of the environment.

Despite these similarities, the goals of Soviet educators of the deaf represent a different set of priorities (Moores, 1972b). They are:

1. To give the child tools of communication, especially expressive communication, at an early age.
2. To change a passive youngster to an active one with initiative in learning.
3. To free the child and his language from the immediate situation.

In illustrating the principle of communication, Zukov, during a discussion with me (Moores, 1972b), represented the interdependence of language and subject matter by showing language as the hub of a wheel with spokes radiating out to the circumference (Figure 10.3). Language is considered the most important dimension of the first stage of education and is included in all subjects. Without language, Zukov (1962) argued, other subjects cannot be taught effectively. Language is a means of communication in itself and must be taught as such. Just as language can be used to teach all subjects, all knowledge can also be used to enrich

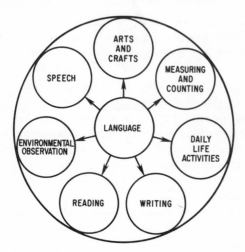

Figure 10.3 The principle of communication (Zukov).

language development. Because early education is centered around everyday needs, the first words taught to the child are those that can be used to influence the environment. Typically, the first word taught is "give" (note the similarity to Premack) and is introduced in the context of toys. Initial emphasis is on such action words as *come, go, eat, drink, sleep, sit,* and *walk*.

Summary

The material reviewed is a response to the assumption implicit in the approach of Furth and others that deaf individuals can either develop their language or their thought, but not both. As a psychologist, Furth is interested in studying the nature of thought without language. In my opinion, deaf individuals are not appropriate candidates for such investigations because they *do have* language. The review of an approach based on Vygotsky's work is an attempt to illustrate that there are alternatives to the current systems of education of the deaf child.

The available evidence suggests that the condition of deafness imposes no limitations on the intellectual capabilities of individuals. In addition, there is no evidence to suggest that deaf persons think in more "concrete" ways than the hearing or that their intellectual functioning is in any way less sophisticated. As a group, deaf people function within the normal range of intelligence and they exhibit the same wide variability as the hearing population.

In conclusion, it appears that efforts to use deaf subjects to study interaction between language and thought are misdirected. Deaf people do not lack language abilities—regardless what scores are obtained on standardized tests of reading achievement—and in no way can they be considered alinguistic.

MANUAL COMMUNICATION, SIGN LANGUAGE, AND TOTAL COMMUNICATION

Any chapter on research needs and applications in educating the deaf must consider the role of manual communication. Manual communication encompasses gestural systems from primitive idiosyncratic gestures to highly complex forms that in every way may be considered legitimate language systems. American Sign Language (ASL) is defined here as including those systems used throughout the United States and Canada that have a high degree of mutual intelligibility. Standard ASL may be thought of as a linguistic system possessing its own rules that do not necessarily follow the same constraints as the formal English system. (Some of the linguistic characteristics of ASL are described by Bellugi & Klima, Chapter 3, this volume.) Other manual systems, with varying approximations to English, also exist.

Using manual communication, it is possible to present a word in two different ways. One is with fingerspelling, that is, using the manual alphabet to spell each word letter by letter. The rate is equivalent to a comfortable rate of speech.

A second means of manual communication is with signs, each of which represents a complete idea. Following a classification system developed by Stokoe (1958), each sign consists of three elements: (a) the position(s) of the hands; (b) the configuration(s) of the hands; and (c) the movement(s) of the hands to different positions.

Proficient users of manual communication have a variety of options at their disposal. They can communicate completely through signs using no fingerspelling or they can communicate completely through fingerspelling. Most individuals tend to use a combination. Generally, the more informal the situation, the greater is the tendency for signs to dominate. As a situation becomes more formal there is an increasing tendency to use spelling.

Table 10.1 presents a classification of manual communication systems currently used in the United States. Native Sign Language or Ameslan (Fant, 1972) represents systems in which a minimum of spelling is employed, the copula is omitted, and word order does not necessarily follow English. Much information is presented through context, facial expression and body posture. These are the systems that have been studied by

TABLE 10.1

Major Systems of Manual Communication Currently Used in the United States

Standard	Formal	Pedagogical (prescriptive)
Native Sign Language	Signed English	Seeing Exact English
Ameslan	Manual English	Signing Essential English

such linguists as Stokoe (1958, 1972a,b) and Bellugi (Bellugi, 1972; Bellugi & Klima, 1972, Chapter 3, this volume). Signed English, a formal variant, expresses all aspects of English, including the copula, bound morphemes and English word-order. Independent of signed English, which uses a mixture of signs and fingerspelling, would be manual English, which is pure spelled English.

Although Native Sign Language and signed English are presented here as representing two ends of a continuum, elsewhere it has been argued that ASL is distinct from English and constitutes a separate language (Bellugi & Klima, 1972, Chapter 3, this volume; Stokoe, 1972a). One could regard ASL and English as two languages and argue that a deaf child should first learn ASL and later, in school, learn English as a second language. This is a position advanced by Cicourel and Boese (1972). Regarding the uniqueness of ASL, Bellugi and Klima (1972) state, "In its deepest and most interesting respects, sign seems to be a language in its own right, with properties that are different from spoken language in general and English in particular [p. 61]."

Two systems recently developed for pedagogical purposes should also be mentioned. They are Signing Exact English (Anthony, 1971) and Seeing Essential English (Gustafson, Pfetzing, & Azwolkow, 1972). Their primary deviations from other systems are new signs developed for bound morphemes such as *ing, ment,* and *ness,* and for such function words as *of* and *by,* which traditionally have been spelled.

Probably no researcher is more misunderstood than one studying some aspect of sign language. The work of linguists is often misinterpreted, because educators fail to realize that, to a great extent, the question of whether ASL is or is not a language independent from English is a separate issue from whether manual communication should be used in the classroom. Unfortunately, the work of such linguists as Bellugi and Stokoe showing that ASL is not isomorphic with English has been cited (Alexander, 1974) as justification for prohibiting signs with young children. Within this context, Kates (1972) argues that since ASL constitutes a different language from English, its use detracts from learning and using English. Similar arguments have been made in other countries and for other languages. For example, in the Soviet Union, early instruction is entirely through fingerspelling (Moores, 1972b). Shif (1969) states that in Russian sign language there are no word changes nor helping words and that signs cannot be connected with definite parts of speech. Depending on the context, the same gesture can mean 'knife' or 'to cut', 'glass' or 'to drink', 'teeth' or 'white'. Also, the structure of what is considered the minic-gesticulatory system differs from spoken sentence structure. Therefore, Shif argues, sign language does not prepare deaf children for learning the grammatical structure of the spoken language. (Speculation on the opposite effect, that is, that learning sign language may have a positive effect on learning English, is discussed by Sperling, Chapter 6, this volume.)

In view of the negative evaluation of sign language by most hearing educators, it is somewhat disconcerting to note that

1.   The majority of deaf adults in all countries apparently use sign language.
2.   Deaf children in the United States who use signs from birth are superior in *English* usage to deaf children who do not (see reviews by R. Harris, Chapter 8, this volume; Moores, 1971; Rodda, 1972).

The situation just described is a classic example of the separation of research and application and illustrates how educators minunderstand the goals and implications of "basic" research.

In defense of educators, it should be noted that almost no research had been conducted on the educational use of signs with young children. This can be explained by the fact that signs have not been permitted within the classroom with young deaf children until very recently.

Moores and his associates (Moores, 1970; Moores & McIntyre, 1971; Moores, McIntyre, & Weiss, 1972, 1973; Moores, Weiss, & Goodwin, 1973a,b, in press) have conducted a longitudinal study of seven preschool programs for the deaf that use the following methods of instruction:

1.   Oral-Aural Method. In this method, the child receives input through speechreading (lipreading) and amplification of sound, and he expresses himself through speech. The use of signs and fingerspelling are not part of the educational process.
2.   Rochester Method. This is a combination of the Oral-Aural Method and fingerspelling. The child receives information through speechreading, amplification and fingerspelling, and expresses himself through speech and fingerspelling. When prac-

ticed correctly, the teacher spells every letter of every word in coordination with speech.

3. Total Communication. This approach (also known in this context as the Simultaneous Method) is a combination of the Oral–Aural Method plus fingerspelling and signs. The child receives input through speechreading, amplification, signs, and fingerspelling. He expresses himself through speech, signs, and fingerspelling. A proficient teacher will sign in coordination with the spoken word, using spelling to represent elements of language for which no signs exist.

One aspect of the study has been the relative efficiency of receiving information through different modes. For the 1972 test period, a receptive communication test was developed to assess five different, but not mutually exclusive, modes of communication: (a) sound alone; (b) sound plus speechreading; (c) sound and speechreading plus fingerspelling; (d) sound and speechreading plus signs; and (e) the printed word.

The results of testing in the Receptive Communication scale showed:

1. The least efficient mode was speech alone (34% understood). Performance increased with the addition of each component, jumping to 56% with the addition of speechreading, 61% with fingerspelling, and 71% with signs. The mean score on reception of the printed word was 38%.
2. Children with the highest scores in reception of speech plus speechreading were from programs using manual and oral communication from the time the children started their education, suggesting that instead of inhibiting the reception of spoken language, early manual communication probably facilitates it.
3. Scores on the Receptive Communication Scale were significantly correlated to hearing loss for children in oral-only programs ($r = .58$, $p < .01$) but not for children in combined programs ($r = .24$, n.s.).
4. Significant differences were found between children in the lower quartile in hearing from oral programs and children in the upper quartile in hearing from combined programs on receptive communication. No other significant differences were found. These data suggest that early manual communication does not hinder children with substantial residual hearing and that the lack of manual communication retards receptive ability of children with minimal amounts of residual hearing.

5. On tests of articulation, no differences were found between programs. Whether the children had oral–manual or oral-only instruction at the beginning does not appear to be a factor. Success in this area seems to be more a function of program priorities. Children from combined programs represent two of the top three programs in this category.

6. Pearson product–moment correlation coefficients were computed between all modes. Sound and speech plus fingerspelling correlated with the printed word ($p < .01$), speech plus speechreading ($p < .05$), and speech plus speechreading plus signs ($p < .05$). There were no negative correlations. The fact that the test with sound alone produced no significant correlations with any other test suggests that the use of residual hearing by deaf children is relatively unaffected by manual communication and depends on other factors operating in an educational program.

Before definite answers can be given to the role of signs in the education of deaf children, intensive investigations need to be conducted along a number of dimensions including study of rates of presentation of signs and speech; effects of the addition of "new" elements such as signs for bound morphemes; effects of signs on the development of speech and utilization of residual hearing; processing of messages presented simultaneously by vocal and gestural means, and relative benefits of signing in English compared with signing in other sign systems (e.g., ASL).

SUMMARY

A research–to–application paradigm was suggested as an ideal in developing interdependent relations between researchers and educators. Three broad areas were identified as fruitful avenues of inquiry related to the education of the deaf and suggestions were made concerning educationally beneficial types of activities. The areas of inquiry are:

1. Applications of ethological principles to the study of the development of deaf individuals

2. Investigations of the implications of different theories on language–thought interactions relating to education of the deaf

3. Examination of the roles of manual communication and sign language in educating the deaf

REFERENCES

Alexander, A. Effectiveness of visible English and the combined system in language acquisition. In *Proceedings of the 1973 Convention of American Instructors of the Deaf.* Washington, D. C.: U. S. Government Printing Office, 1974. pp. 53–74.

Antinucci, F., & Parisi, D. Early language acquisition: A model and some data. In C. Ferguson & D. Slobin (Eds.), *Studies of child language development.* New York: Holt, Rinehart and Winston, 1973.

Anthony, D. *Seeing Essential English.* Anaheim, California: Anaheim School District, 1971.

Bellugi, U. Studies in sign language. In T. O'Rourke (Eds), *Psycholinguistics and total communication.* Silver Springs, Maryland: American Annals of the Deaf, 1972.

Bellugi, U., & Klima, E. The roots of language in the sign talk of the deaf. *Psychology Today,* 1972, *6,* 60–64.

Bloom, L. *Language development: Form and function in emerging grammars.* Cambridge: M.I.T. Press, 1970.

Bonvillian, J., Charrow, V., & Nelson, K. Psycholinguistic and educational implications of deafness. *Human Development,* 1973, *16,* 321–345.

Bowerman, M. *Learning to talk: A cross-linguistic study of early syntactic development, with special reference to Finnish.* Unpublished Doctoral Dissertation, Harvard University, 1970.

Brown, R. *A first language: The early stages.* Cambridge, Massachusetts: Harvard University Press, 1973.

Charlesworth, W. *Human intelligence as adaptation: An ethological approach.* Paper presented at the University of Pittsburgh Conference on the Nature of Intelligence, March 1974.

Cicourel, A., & Boese, R. Sign language and the teaching of deaf children. In D. Hymes, D. Cazden, & V. John (Eds.), *Functions of language in the classroom.* New York: Teachers College Press, 1972.

Clark, E. How children describe time and order. In C. Ferguson & D. Slobin (Eds.), *Studies in Child Language Development.* New York: Holt, 1973.

Fant, L. *Ameslan.* Silver Springs, Maryland: National Association of the Deaf, 1972.

Furth, H. Research with the deaf: Implications for language and cognition. *Psychological Bulletin,* 1964, *62,* 145–164.

Furth, H. *Thinking without language.* New York: Free Press, 1966.

Furth, H. *A thinking laboratory for deaf children.* Washington, D.C.: Catholic University, 1969.

Furth H. Education for thinking. *Journal of Rehabilitation of the Deaf,* 1971, *5,* 7–71.

Furth, H. *Deafness and learning: A psychological approach.* Belmont, California: Wadsworth, 1973.

Furth, H. The role of language in the child's development. In *Proceedings of the*

1973 Convention of American Instructors of the Deaf. Washington, D.C.. U. S. Government Printing Office, 1974. pp. 258–261.

Gallagher, J. Organization and special education. *Exceptional Children,* 1968, *34,* 435–441.

Gustafson, G., Pfetzing, D., & Azwolkow, E. *Signing exact english.* Rossmoor, California: Modern Signs Press, 1972.

Hinde, R. *Animal behavior.* New York: McGraw-Hill, 1966.

Hurder, W. United States of America. In J. McKenna (Ed.), *The present situation and trends of research in the field of special education.* Paris: UNESCO, 1973. pp. 147–270.

Kates, S. *Language development in deaf and hearing adolescents.* Northampton, Massachusetts: Clarke Institute for the Deaf, 1922.

Luria, A. Speech development and the formation of mental processes. In M. Cole & I. Maltzman (Eds.), *A handbook of contemporary Soviet psychology.* New York: Basic Books, 1969.

McNamara, J. Cognitive basis of language learning in infants. *Psychological Review,* 1972, *79,* 1–13.

Meadow, K. Early manual communication in relation to the deaf child's intellectual, social and communicative functioning. *American Annals of the Deaf,* 1968, *113,* 29–41. (a)

Meadow, K. Parental responses to the medical ambiguities of deafness. *Journal of Health and Social Behavior,* 1968, *9,* 299–309. (b)

Meadow, K. Self image, family climate and deafness. *Social Forces,* 1969, *47,* 428–438.

Moores, D. Evaluation of preschool programs: An interaction analysis model. *Proceedings of the International Congress in Education of the Deaf* (Stockholm), 1970, *1,* 164–168.

Moores, D. *Recent research on manual communication.* Occasional paper No. 7. Minneapolis: University of Minnesota Research, Development and Demonstration Center in Education of Handicapped Children, 1971.

Moores, D. Neo-oralism and education of the deaf in the Soviet Union. *Exceptional Children.* 1972, *38,* 377–384. (b)

Moores, D. Communication—some unanswered questions and some unquestioned answers. In T. O'Rourke (Ed.), *Psycholinguistics and total communication.* Silver Springs, Maryland: American Annals of the Deaf, 1972. pp. 1–11. (c)

Moores, D. *Moving research to relevancy.* APA Symposium Paper on Research and Relevancy. University of Minnesota Research, Development and Demonstration Center in Education of Handicapped Children, Occasional Paper No. 24, December, 1973. (a)

Moores, D. Families and deafness. In A. Norris (Ed.), *Deafness annual* (Vol. III). Washington, D.C.: Social and Rehabilitation Service, 1973. (b)

Moores, D. Non-vocal systems of verbal behavior. In R. Schiefelbusch (Ed.), *Language acquisition: Retardation and intervention.* Baltimore: University Park Press, 1974. pp. 277–418.

Moores, D. Review of research in education of the hearing impaired. In L. Mann & D. Sabatino (Eds.), *Reviews of special education.* Boston: Houghton Mifflin, 1976. pp. 19–52.

Moores, D. *Educating the deaf: Phychology, principles, and practices.* Boston: Houghton Mifflin, 1978.

Moores, D., & McIntyre, C. *Evaluation of programs for hearing impaired children: Report of 1970–1971.* University of Minnesota Research, Development and Demonstration Center in Education of Handicapped Children, Research Report No. 27, December, 1971.

Moores, D., McIntyre, C., & Weiss, K. *Evaluation of programs for hearing impaired children: Report of 1971–1972.* University of Minnesota Research, Development and Demonstration Center in Education of Handicapped Children, Research Report No. 39, September, 1972.

Moores, D., Weiss, K., & Goodwin, M. *Evaluation of programs for hearing impaired children: Report of 1972–1973.* University of Minnesota Research, Development and Demonstration Center in Education of Handicapped Children, Research Report No. 57, December, 1973. (a)

Moores, D., Weiss, K., & Goodwin, M. Receptive abilities of deaf children across five modes of communication. *Exceptional Children,* 1973, *39,* 22–28. (b)

Moores, D., Weiss, K., & Goodwin, M. Early intervention programs for hearing impaired children. *ASHA Monographs,* 1978.

O'Rourke, T. (Ed.) *Psycholinguistics and total communication.* Silver Springs, Maryland: American Annals of the Deaf, 1973.

Osgood, C. On understanding and creating sentences. *American Psychologist,* 1963, *18,* 735–751.

Osgood, C. Meaning cannot be an r_m. *Journal of Verbal Learning and Verbal Behavior,* 1966, *5,* 402–407.

Osgood, C. Toward a wedding of Insufficiencies. In F. Dixon & D. Horton (Eds.), *Verbal behavior and general behavior theory.* Englewood Cliffs, New Jersey: Prentice-Hall, 1968. Pp. 495–519.

Peet, H. Notions of the deaf and dumb before instructions, *American Annals of the Deaf,* 1855, *8,* 1–44.

Ray, L. Thoughts of the deaf and dumb before instruction. *American Annals of the Deaf,* 1848, *1,* 149–157.

Rodda, M. *Research on total communication.* Paper presented at Alexander Graham Bell Annual Convention, Chicago 1972.

Schesinger, I. The grammar of sign language and the problem of language universals. In J. Morton (Ed.), *Biological and social factors in psycholinguistics.* Cambridge, Massachusetts: Logos Press, 1971, Pp. 217–241.

Schlesinger, H., & Monson, K. *Deafness and mental health.* San Francisco: Langley Porter Neuropsychiatric Institute, 1971.

Shif, Zh. *Language learning and deaf children's thought development.* Moscow: Institute of Defectology, 1969.

Slobin, D. Cognitive prerequisites for the development of grammar. In C. Pearson & D. Slobin (Eds.), *Studies in child language development.* New York: Holt, 1973. Pp. 175–208.

Stevenson, E. A study of the educational achievement of deaf children of deaf parents. *California News,* 1964, *80,* 143.

Stokoe, W. Sign language structure. *Studies in linguistics.* Occasional Paper No. 8. University of Buffalo, 1958.

Stokoe, W. *Semiotics and human sign languages.* The Hague: Mouton, 1972. (a)

Stokoe, W. *The study of sign language.* Silver Springs, Maryland: National Association of the Deaf, 1972. (b)

Stuckless, E., & Birch, J. The influence of early manual communication on the linguistic development of deaf children. *American Annals of the Deaf,* 1966, *111,* 452–460.

Suppes, P. A survey of cognition in handicapped children. *Review of Educational Research,* 1974, *44,* 145–176.

Vernon, M., & Koh, S. Effects of manual communication on deaf children's educational achievement, linguistic competence, oral skills, and psychological development. *American Annals of the Deaf,* 1970, *115,* 527–536.

Vygotsky, L. *Thought and language* (E. Hanfmann & G. Vakar, Eds. and trans.). Cambridge: M.I.T. Press, 1962.

Wolff, S. Piaget workshop. In *Proceedings of the 1973 Convention of American Instructors of the Deaf.* Washington, D.C.: U.S. Government Printing Office, 1974. Pp. 628–630.

Wolff, S., & Wolff, C. *Games without words.* Springfield, Illinois: Charles C Thomas, 1974.

Zukov, S. *Textbook for deaf children.* Moscow: Institute of Defectology, 1962.

11

Developmental Perspectives on the Experiential Deficiencies of Deaf Children

LYNN S. LIBEN

Investigators have compared performance by deaf and hearing children on a wide range of cognitive and social tasks. Although some studies have found that deaf children perform as well or better than their hearing peers, most have found that deaf children show performance deficits. Deficits have been reported on tests of classification, concept formation, and problem solving (e.g., Furth & Milgram, 1965; Michael & Kates, 1965; Oléron, 1953; Templin, 1950; Van der Woude, 1970); sequential memory (e.g., Blair, 1957; Olsson & Furth, 1966; Pitner & Paterson, 1917); Piagetian concepts (e.g., Furth, 1964; Oléron & Herren, 1961; Robertson & Youniss, 1969); and reading (Chapter 5 by Brooks, this volume; Furth, 1966; Wrightston, Aronow, & Moskowitz, 1963). Deficits have also been observed in the emotional realm, with deaf subjects being described as more egocentric, having poorer impulse control, and being generally less mature (see Chapter 12 by A. Harris, Chapter 8 by R. Harris, and Chapter 9 by Schlesinger, this volume).

The inferiority of deaf subjects has traditionally been explained as the result of language deficiencies. This explanation is consistent with classical psychological theories that have argued that thought is directly dependent on language. Watson (1913), for example, suggested that

DEAF CHILDREN: DEVELOPMENTAL PERSPECTIVES

"thought processes are really motor habits in the larynx." Russian psychologists and educators have also argued that language—particularly spoken language—is necessary for abstract thought:

> The deaf-mute who has not been taught to speak indicates objects or actions with a gesture; he is unable to abstract the quality or action from the actual object, to form abstract concepts, to systematize the phenomena of the external world with the aid of the abstracted signals furnished by language but which are not natural to visual, practically acquired experience. . . . The educational observations of teachers of deaf-mutes show . . . how much effort must be spent to restore these serious defects in complex psychological processes by continuous teaching of verbal speech [Luria & Yudovich, 1959, p. 32].

Recently, many people have begun to reconsider the language-impoverishment hypothesis as an explanation of the deaf child's cognitive deficits. One impetus for this reexamination is the growing popularity of Piagetian theory in which sensorimotor actions—not language—are assumed to lay the foundation for logical thought. Thus, even without language, the child's interactions with the physical world should permit the development of fundamentally normal cognitive skills, at least through the concrete operational period.

Another impetus for the reexamination of the language-deprivation hypothesis is a growing dissatisfaction with the position that deaf people are a group "without language," as had been asserted in earlier work (e.g., Furth, 1966). There are two bases for questioning this assertion. First, although deaf people rarely become fully competent in English, they often possess the English skills applicable to particular experimental tasks. Second, many deaf children and most deaf adolescents and adults have at least some competence in American Sign Language (ASL or Ameslan). Although it had earlier been assumed that Ameslan is only a loose, ungrammatical collection of iconic gestures, recent work (see Bellugi & Klima, Chapter 3 of this volume; Frishberg, 1975; Hoffmeister, Moores, & Best, 1974; Stokoe, Casterline, & Croneberg, 1965) has led linguists to reject this earlier assumption. Ameslan has been found to have a considerable degree of systematicity and hierarchical organization comparable to that found in spoken languages. Once it is recognized that it is incorrect to equate language with speech (e.g., see Slobin, 1971) and that Ameslan is a full-fledged, grammatical language, it becomes apparent that it is illegitimate to indiscriminately categorize deaf people as language-deficient.

If thought is not necessarily dependent on language and/or if deaf people are not necessarily deficient in language, a new explanation is needed for why deaf people with normal intelligence typically perform relatively poorly on cognitive and social tasks. One such explanation, suggested by Hans Furth (1966), is that deaf children face "a blending of social, emotional, and intellective neglect [p. 120]," or "experiential deficiencies."

The concept of experiential deficiency, however, has tended to be too general and post hoc to be theoretically or pragmatically useful. When deaf and hearing subjects perform equivalently, the data have been cited as evidence that oral language is not required for thought. In contrast, when deaf subjects perform worse than hearing subjects, the data have been explained as a consequence of deaf people's experiential deficiencies. It is the goal of this chapter to enumerate more specifically what kinds of experiential deficiencies actually occur in the deaf child's environment, particularly when viewed in the context of theories, methods, and empirical data of developmental psychology.

A PIAGETIAN PERSPECTIVE ON EXPERIENTIAL DEFICIENCIES

The discussions of experiential deficiencies that follow have been organized from the perspective of Piagetian theory. This perspective has been chosen for several reasons. First, since the experiential-deficiency hypothesis is meant as an alternative to the language-deficiency hypothesis, it is most useful to approach it with a theory such as Piaget's in which language is *not* hypothesized to be an important cause of development. Because such theories must propose other mechanisms that foster development, they necessarily suggest nonlinguistic aspects of the deaf child's environment that should be examined for possible deficiencies. Second, research and theory from the Piagetian tradition may be directly applicable to the problems of deafness, just as it has been useful in conceptualizing and treating the problems of blindness (Fraiberg, Siegal, & Gibson, 1966), emotional disturbance (e.g., Pimm, 1975), learning disabilities (e.g., Ariel, 1975), and education generally (e.g., Furth, 1970; Weikart, Rogers, Adcock, & McClelland, 1971). Third, Piagetian theory provides a useful structure for organizing relevant theory and research from other traditions of developmental psychology.

Piaget (1964, 1970; Piaget & Inhelder, 1969) has identified four factors as causal agents of development: maturation, experience with objects, social experience, and equilibration. With respect to maturation, Piaget notes the importance of organic growth, particularly of the nervous and endocrine systems. Certain behavioral patterns (for example, the coordination of vision and prehension) are dependent on the development of organic structures (Piaget & Inhelder, 1969). Although Piaget recognizes some direct influences of maturation, the most important influence of maturation on cognitive development is indirect, since it serves to increase the range of behaviors available to the child for interacting with the environment. Piaget's position is thus different from that of traditional maturationists such as Gesell (see Gesell & Ilg, 1949), in which organic maturation per se is taken to be a direct cause of cognitive growth.

The second factor identified by Piaget—experience with objects—is divided into two components. The first of these, physical experience, concerns knowledge about *objects* themselves. For example, the child learns that cotton is light and that metal is heavy through experience in manipulating these materials. The second, logicomathematical experience, concerns knowledge derived from and about the *actions* on objects. For example, by counting a heap of marbles in several different sequences, the child learns that the outcome of counting is unaffected by the order in which items are iterated.

The third factor—social experience—may also be divided into two components. First, social interaction provides the opportunity for transmission of the society's knowledge, traditions, mores, values, etc., through both formal and informal means, for example, schools and family. Second, social interaction provides the opportunity for the child to develop social–cognitive skills. Interactions with adults and peers force the child to recognize that others' viewpoints may differ from his or her own, thus helping the child to decenter from the egocentric perspective of preoperational thinking (Chandler, 1977; Flavell, 1974; Shantz, 1975).

The fourth factor—equilibration—is the self-regulating process that serves to coordinate the activities and outcomes of the other three factors, allowing the child to compensate for external disturbances to his or her current cognitive structure.

In the discussion that follows, the deaf child's environment is examined in the context of each of the change agents identified by Piaget.

THE DEAF CHILD'S ENVIRONMENT

Maturation

Maturation has received relatively little attention with respect to the development of deaf children. In the most direct application of maturational concepts to deafness, Griffiths (1957) suggested that maturational lags in some children prevent myelinization of the neural pathways. To remediate this problem, Griffiths recommends extremely early amplification. In one application of this procedure, Griffiths placed hearing aids on 42 infants (ranging in age from 1 to 8 months) who had been diagnosed as having a hearing loss. By the end of 1 year, 31 of these infants had normal hearing, while only 11 still required aids. This research has been criticized because the "cures" may simply reflect the unreliability of the early diagnosis of hearing loss and because others have not been able to replicate these findings (Wiley, 1971). Nevertheless, Griffiths' work suggests the need for further exploration of early physiological development in deaf children.

In addition to considering the role of maturational lags as a cause of hearing loss, it is also important to consider maturational deficits as an outcome of loss. In research on early experience there have been many animal studies concerned with the effects of early visual experience on later physiological and behavioral development. This work has been reviewed by Hunt (1961), and more recently, by Thompson and Grusec (1970). Although controversies regarding the scope and permanence of effects persist, an acceptable generalization is that enriched early experience (e.g., visual stimulation in cages) leads to better performance on a variety of tasks, apparently effecting both anatomical and biochemical changes. In contrast, early deprivations (e.g., rearing animals in darkness) lead to physiological deterioration and to retardation in performance.

In contrast to the vast literature on the effects of early visual experience, there has been relatively little work on the effects of early auditory deprivation and enrichment. This area has, however, now begun to attract attention (e.g., Clopton & Winfield, 1976; Killackey & Ryugo, 1977; Moore & Aitkin, 1975; Webster & Webster, 1976). This research suggests that an acoustically deprived or biased environment (e.g., one in which a loud tone of a constant frequency is always present) has neurophysiological and neuroanatomical effects that parallel those of the visual system.

Experience with Objects

Audition and Exploration

It is interesting that, whereas vision is readily recognized as an important channel for the reception of information and as an impetus for exploration, audition has not been comparably evaluated. Nevertheless, it is clear that sound also has important implications for the quantity, quality, and effectiveness of the child's experience with objects. With the absence or severe attenuation of sound, the deaf child is deprived of knowledge about the sound-making qualities of objects and actions. Furthermore, insofar as noises made by objects and by actions upon objects excite the child toward exploration, the absence of an auditory channel might be expected to limit the motivation for exploration and, hence, retard cognitive growth. Many of the observations made by Piaget suggest that sounds are important for the child's sensorimotor exploration. The following examples from *Origins of Intelligence* (Piaget, 1952) illustrate how audition may play an important role in encouraging exploration and in the generalization of schemes:

> *Observation 102.*—At 0;4 (15) Lucienne grasps the handle of a rattle in the shape of a celluloid ball. The movements of the hand in grasping the rattle result in shaking it and producing a sudden and violent noise. Lucienne at once moves her whole body, and especially her feet, to make the noise last. She has a demented expression of mingled fear and pleasure, but she continues. . . . This reaction lasts a few days but then Lucienne, when she is in possession of the rattle, limits herself to shaking it with the hand that holds it. But—a curious thing—at 0;5 (10) and again at 0;5 (12) she accompanies this movement of the hands with shakes of the feet analogous to those she makes to shake a hanging object.

> *Observation 104.*—At 0;3 (29) Laurent graps a paper knife which he sees for the first time; he looks at it a moment and then swings it while holding it in his right hand. During these movements the object happens to rub against the wicker of the bassinet: Laurent then waves his arm vigorously and obviously tries to reproduce the sound he has heard, but without understanding the necessity of contact between the paper knife and the wicker and, consequently, without achieving this contact otherwise than by chance [pp. 168–169].

These and other observations made by Piaget (1952) suggest that auditory feedback provides important information about objects, and acts as an important impetus for actions upon objects.

Little experimental work has been addressed to the role of early audition on exploration and on cognitive development in children. This research vacuum is not surprising as deafness, unlike blindness, is only rarely diagnosed during the early stages of the sensorimotor period (see Chapter 2 by Meadow, this volume). Some animal research, however, has been directed toward examining the effects of early auditory experiences on later performance on various tasks. Wolf (1943) deprived one group of albino rats of hearing and another group of vision for 10–15 days during infancy. Later tasks using either auditory or visual signals showed differential performance from the two groups in the expected direction: Auditory-deprived animals succeeded better when the signal was visual, and vice versa.

The effects of early auditory experiences on exploratory behavior have also been studied in animal research. MacDougall and Rabinovitch (1972) compared genetically deaf and hearing mice from the same litters on several measures of exploration. While there were no differences between the two groups on any measures at 2 months, there were significant differences at the 5–6 month period, with hearing mice walking more than deaf mice, and deaf mice grooming more than hearing mice. The fact that differences were not observed until the later test period indicates the importance of examining long-term as well as short-term effects of sensory deprivation.

MacDougall and Rabinovitch (1972) note that their findings contrast with earlier work by Zucker and Bindra (1961) that had shown no differences in exploratory behavior between sensory-deprived (blind) and sensory-normal mice. MacDougall and Rabinovitch suggest that the failure to find a difference in the Zucker and Bindra study occurred because the environment of the sensory-deprived group had been enriched. While early enrichment may, indeed, have compensated for sensory deprivation, other differences between the two studies (e.g., blindness versus deafness, different times of testing, different age of onset of deprivation, etc.) render the contrasts inconclusive. Additional research with both animal and human populations is needed to study the effects of early auditory experience.

It should be noted that if exploration patterns are affected by early auditory deprivation, the "prelingual" versus "postlingual" distinction normally used in deafness (see Chapter 1, this volume) may be too gross. Research is needed to examine whether exploration patterns differ in early or late infancy as a function of the age of hearing loss, even within the sensorimotor period. In compensating for auditory deficiencies, the deaf infant's environment could be enriched with objects that are visually interesting. It would be particularly useful to employ objects that change visually as a function of the child's own activities, for example, light displays that vary in color, intensity, and duration as a function of the pitch, volume, and length of sounds produced by the child. A visual stimulus controlled by speech sounds might also be useful for providing rhythmic information about language, which Brooks (Chapter 5, this volume) suggests may be an important component in the development of language skills. If interventions like those described here are to be developed exclusively for deaf infants, it will be necessary to improve techniques for earlier diagnosis of deafness. However, the effectiveness of supplementing the range of coordinated visual and auditory stimuli for all infants—both hearing and deaf—might also be explored.

Exposure to Stimuli

As already discussed, the early sensory deprivation of deafness may lead to indirect restrictions in the child's environment because of reduced organismic exploration. In addition, restrictions in the environment occur as a direct consequence of deafness. Specifically, since the visual system is bound to the immediate environment, the absence of audition prevents the individual from receiving information from removed sources such as the next room. Similarly, there are reductions in information because the deaf person cannot receive information from two channels simultaneously, whereas the hearing person can process auditory information while attending to a visual stimulus (Nowell & Liben, 1975).

In addition to organismic and physical restrictions, the environment may be reduced for the deaf child as a consequence of caretaking practices. Within the family setting, parents are likely to overprotect their deaf children, thus reducing the range of experiences and objects available for manipulation. Schlesinger and Meadow (1972b), for example, have noted that parents of deaf children tend to restrict their child's intrusions into the outside world by innumerable safety limits. In questionnaires concerning socialization for safety, Schlesinger and Meadow (1972a) found that in an effort to avoid street accidents, parents with deaf children were more likely to control the environment (by setting physical restrictions on movement) than were parents with hearing children. As Schlesinger and Meadow note, greater restrictions are often justified (here, for example, deaf children are indeed more vulnerable to street accidents since they cannot hear traffic noises), but restrictions are often unnecessarily excessive. Furthermore, in the context of the present discussion, it matters little whether such restrictions are justified: The range of experience is nevertheless reduced.

The overprotectiveness and restrictiveness of the home environment is usually continued and exacerbated by the school residential environment. Research on institutional care of infants has shown the devastating outcomes of severe perceptual and social deprivations (e.g., Bowlby, 1965; Dennis, 1960; Spitz, 1945). More subtle effects of institutionalization have also been reported in mentally retarded children. Zigler (1966), for example, suggested that institutionalization may increase dependency and decrease motivation, with negative consequences for cognitive growth. Although deaf children's residential environments are never as severely restricted as the stimulus-deprived infant care facilities of earlier decades, they may have more subtle restrictions.

Deaf students living in residential settings have relatively limited exposure to diverse settings outside their school. Evans (1975), for example, reports that in the residential school he studied, "older girls are bused to a local shopping center every other Saturday for "exposure" to the outside and for shopping needs. Neither sex is permitted to walk unchaperoned to a downtown movie, restaurant or drugstore and since chaperones are few (or busy), such contacts are infrequent [p. 549]."

That residential schools for the deaf provide restricted environments has also been noted by deaf adults themselves (Reich & Reich, 1973) and has been suggested as a contributing factor to cognitive deficits of the deaf (e.g., Templin, 1950). Research comparing academic performance of day versus residential students is consistent with this view, with the former group usually performing significantly better than the latter (Pitner & Reamer, 1920; Quigley & Frisina, 1961; Upshall, 1929). It is, however, difficult to determine whether such differences are the outcome of residential living, the reflection of prior differences between day and residential populations (see Chapter 2 by Meadow, this volume), or some interaction of these variables. Again, research from mentally retarded populations suggests that the effects of residential settings interact with the child's preinstitutional history (Balla, Butterfield, & Zigler, 1974). Specific research is needed to determine to what extent and in what ways residential schools for the deaf are restrictive and how these restrictions can be eliminated. The approaches of the early intervention programs in this country (e.g., see review by Horowitz & Paden, 1973), as well as those of communal facilities in other cultures (e.g., the kibbutzim of Israel) may provide good models for improving the experiences and outcomes of residential living.

Social Experience

Social experience is important for transmitting knowledge (through formal and informal instruction), for teaching role-appropriate behaviors and values, and for encouraging the transition from egocentric to decentered perspectives. For the deaf child, these processes may be seriously impeded by the scarcity of appropriate role models and by inadequacies in the quantity and quality of communication. Deficiencies in these realms, their outcomes, and their susceptibility to intervention are discussed in the following pages.

Role Models

Major developmental theories recognize the importance of models in the child's acquisition of knowledge, behaviors, goals, and values. In psychoanalytic theory, the process of identification is essential for the child's acquisition of societal values and behaviors such as those related to sex and morality (see Hall, 1954). As identification is enhanced by similarity between the model and child (narcissistic identification), the entire process is presumably strengthened if the deaf child is in contact with deaf adults. Similarly, empirical work within the tradition of social learning theory (see Mischel & Mischel, 1971) has demonstrated that imitation is enhanced by similarity between model and observer. Similarity between child and model is also important from the perspective of cognitive-developmental theory as illustrated by the process of sex-role development. Kohlberg (1966) suggests that children begin by labeling themselves as "boys" or "girls." Cognitive consistency then requires that the child value "male" or "female" things, respectively, in turn leading the child to assume appropriate behaviors and values. This paradigm is readily extended to deafness. Here, the child labels him or herself as "deaf," and then seeks to incorporate behaviors and values of significant other deaf people.

Traditionally, however, there have been few deaf adults available as models for the developing deaf child. Only about 10% of deaf children have deaf parents. Deaf teachers are also rare, particularly in the elementary grades. Administrators have tended to avoid hiring deaf teachers (in fact, until recently, deaf teachers were prohibited in California elementary schools) on the assumption that deaf teachers would be less able to provide satisfactory instruction in speech. Furthermore, few deaf adults are in professions likely to provide services to deaf children (e.g., medicine), and deaf adults rarely received attention in the national media. (However, this trend is now changing with the increasing popularity of the National Theatre of the Deaf, deaf people on "Sesame Street" and "Mr. Rodgers," and similar events.) Probably the most consistent opportunity for interaction between deaf children and adults is in the residence halls of the schools for the deaf, where deaf adults often serve as counselors. (Additional discussion of issues related to the availability of deaf adults as role models is included in Chapter 8 by R. Harris, this volume.) Thus, although older deaf children are available as models for their younger schoolmates, deaf adults often are not.

Communication: Quantitative Deficiencies

Many of the social deprivations of the deaf child may be traced to difficulties in communication between adults and children, and among peers. Most simply, there are delays and quantitative reductions in communication. For the 90% of deaf children who have hearing parents, there is typically no system for communication in early childhood other than primitive, iconic, home-made gestures and nonverbal communication. Even after the child enters school, oral skills are slow to develop and only rarely develop adequately enough to support meaningful communication with those who have not learned some form of manual communication. Schlesinger and Meadow (1972a) found that when mothers with deaf children were asked about problems of child-rearing, over half mentioned difficulties in communication. Data collected by Evans (1975) indicate that communication barriers continue at least through adolescence. Of deaf adolescents questioned, 49% reported poor communication with their parents. For example, 37% said that their parents had difficulty explaining their recent experiences to them, while 41% reported difficulty telling their parents of their own recent experiences. Deficits in the onset, depth, and quantity of adult–child communication can be reduced noticeably if parents and significant others learn and use some form of sign language.

One of the most predictable outcomes of the delay and reduction in communication is a reduction in the transmission of information. The general knowledge level of deaf people appears to be reduced, as indicated by poor performance on various achievement measures (see Chapter 1 by Liben). The results of research by Nass (1964) may also be interpreted as evidence of a reduction in the information available to deaf children. Nass studied the ability of deaf and hearing children to deduce agents of causality when the agents either were, or were not, accessible to direct experience (Levels 1 and 2, respectively). Nass found that 8–10-year-old deaf and hearing children gave comparable explanations of Level 1 phenomena (e.g., How come leaves fall off the trees? "How do we get shadows?"), but that deaf children gave more primitive explanations than their hearing peers for Level 2 phenomena (e.g., "How does the snow come?" "How is it that the stars shine?"). By age 12, differences between the two groups were no longer evident. Although Nass suggested that the early differences indicate that young deaf children have less adequate reasoning abilities than hearing children, it seems equally plausible that the findings simply result from inadequate information. Many of the questions about Level 2 phenomena are precisely the sorts of questions normally asked during the incessant "whys" of early childhood. The deaf child often does not have the communication skills needed to ask these questions, nor to understand the explanations when they are given.

Informational deficiencies may also occur in the classroom as a simple function of the curriculum planned for the students. Deaf adults often complain that too little was expected of them in school. Reich and Reich (1973) reported that about one-fifth of the adults they surveyed made comments about low expectations such as; "'English in school for deaf should be equal to hearing (schools)' . . . . 'In deaf school, when finished reading, teacher asked 'What did the boy do?'—in hearing school asked 'What was the climax?'. . . . 'History was the same every year, boring' [p. 74]." Furthermore, so much of the formal curriculum in schools for the deaf is devoted to teaching speech and language skills per se that there is necessarily a reduction in the amount of instruction devoted to other disciplines.

Communication among peers may also be reduced in deaf children. Stokoe (1960) noted that deaf children typically have fewer playmates than their hearing peers and engage more in solitary play. Even deaf children in residential settings apparently experience a delay in formal linguistic communication with their peers. Of deaf adults surveyed by Reich and Reich (1973), the mean age reported for having learned sign language was 13.7 years for day students and 7.11 years for residential students. By adulthood, 99% of the residential students could communicate with sign (which continued to be the most common method for communicating with other deaf people in adulthood), although only 69% of the day students could do so. Thus, formal linguistic communication is apparently delayed between deaf peers as it is between deaf children and hearing adults.

The opportunity for communication among peers—particularly between peers of the opposite sex—may also be reduced in the residential setting. Approximately one-third of the adults surveyed by Reich and Reich (1973) objected to the lack of social freedom they had experienced in their schools. In a residential school studied by Evans (1975), for example, social interactions between boys and girls were permitted only in recreation rooms (in groups) at limited and specified times, and on weekend "date nights" under supervision. Evans (1975) suggests that social restrictions such as these are the primary factors contributing to deaf adolescents' relative ignorance of norms related to dating behavior, family relationships, and customer roles.

Communication: Qualitative Deficiencies

In addition to deficiencies in the quantity of communication between the deaf child and significant others, there are also deficiencies in the quality of communication. Three areas of qualitative deficiencies may be identified. First, adult–child communication tends to be more didactic and less mutual. Second, the deep, semantic aspects of communication tend to be distorted or lost by excessive attention to the surface features of the communicative exchange. Finally, the expectation and goals communicated may be dysfunctional for optimal development. A discussion of each of these areas follows.

The tendency toward insufficient mutuality of communication is evident in a variety of settings. In a study of communicative patterns in classes for deaf children, Craig and Collins (1970) found that communication was overwhelmingly dominated by teachers. For language-dependent instruction (e.g., literature, social studies) at the primary grades, almost 80% of classroom communication was teacher-generated, while only 3% of the communication was student-initiated. Even when students did initiate communication, teacher-responsiveness was low: Teachers' responses accounted for less than .4% of communication. Results from other instructional areas and from intermediate and high school levels were comparable. It seems clear that a teacher-dominated setting such as this could not be sufficiently responsive to the individual child's needs, questions, and interests. Furthermore, such an environment would seem expecially unsuited for the development of communication skills, presumably a "hidden" curriculum of any content lesson.

The form of parent–child communication also has a significant impact on cognitive development. In examining social class differences, Hess and Shipman (1968) identified two major types of maternal control strategies: the "cognitive–rational" control strategy in which reasons are provided for rules or demands, future payoffs are emphasized, etc., and the "imperative–normative" strategy in which rules are given without justification. Hess and Shipman's findings suggest that controls that include rationales are more conducive to cognitive development than controls that are based simply on authority. The difficulties faced by parents in communicating with their deaf children might well be expected to lead to the use of imperative–normative control strategies. Data collected by Schlesinger and Meadow (1972a) support this interpretation in that mothers with deaf children reported using a narrower range of discipline techniques than did mothers with hearing children. Of those with deaf children, 71% reported feeling comfortable with using spanking, sometimes adding that spanking is "the only thing the deaf child understands [p. 104]." In contrast, only 25% of mothers with hearing children reported feeling comfortable with spanking. Similarly, Barsch (1968) found that of the hearing parents with deaf children interviewed, only 5% reported that they felt spanking was ineffective, whereas 20% considered that "explaining what was wrong to the child" was ineffective. More generally, Schlesinger and Meadow (1972a) found that mothers with deaf children were more controlling, didactic, and intrusive than mothers with hearing children.

In addition to avoiding the need for extended, logical communicative exchange by using imperative–normative strategies, parents of deaf children may also circumvent complex communication by avoiding situations of conflict. Informal comments by teachers, parents, and residential counselors suggest that there is a tendency for parents to avoid frustrating the child by acceding to the child's demands. Since conflict situations are valuable for teaching children that others' viewpoints may differ from their own, avoidance of conflict may encourage the maintenance of the socially and cognitively immature egocentric perspective. Indeed, as noted earlier, clinicians have observed that deaf children are emotionally more egocentric than their hearing peers (see Chapter 12 by A. Harris, Chapter 8 by R. Harris, and Chapter 9 by Schlesinger). In an experimental setting, young deaf children have been found to perform worse than their hearing peers on a communication task in which it was necessary for the subjects to recognize that other children's perspective differed from their own (Hoemann, 1972).

A second major difficulty in the quality of communication in the deaf child's environment concerns excessive attention to the surface form of the communicative exchange. First, parents are often encouraged by speech therapists and educators to continue speech and language lessons at home. Although it is important for the home environment to reinforce what the child learns in the school setting, too much emphasis on providing formal instruction can interfere with normal parenting functions. Schlesinger and Meadow (1972a) report that many of the mothers of deaf children they studied used potentially playful situations as opportunities for language instruction. For example, mothers were observed to refrain from giving their children snacks until appropriate language had been elicited. Negative outcomes of such interactions are also discussed by Schlesinger, Chapter 9 in this volume.

The emphasis on linguistic structure is even more noticeable in the classroom. First, as noted earlier, a large portion of the formal curriculum is devoted to teaching language skills directly, and thus the time for instruction in other content areas is reduced. More important, perhaps, teachers often correct the form of children's language during interactions and instruction in other areas.

Constant correction for language errors may cause children to lose interest in the subject matter, lose their train of thought, and associate communication with unpleasant affect. Furthermore, attempts to teach language through constant correction are unlikely to be successful. The famous annecdote reported by McNeill (1966) illustrates the futility of forced imitation.

> Child: *Nobody don't like me.*
> Mother: *No, say "nobody likes me."*

> Child: *Nobody don't like me.*
> (eight repetitions of this dialogue)
> Mother: *No, now listen carefully;* ***"nobody likes me."***
> Child: *Oh! Nobody don't likes me.*

Also relevant is research by Cazden (1965) in which language development was examined as a function of whether childrens' utterances were expanded or modeled by adults. In the expansion group, children's utterances were expanded into grammatical sentences, whereas in modeling, the children's utterance were reacted to conversationally. For example, if the child said "Doggie bite," an expansion might be "The doggie is biting," whereas a model might be "Yes, he's very mad." Although a small gain in linguistic performance was shown by the expansion group relative to a control group, a much greater gain was evident in the modeling group. One possible interpretation of these findings (for other interpretations see Dale, 1976; McNeill, 1970) is that children may simply filter out what are essentially boring repetitions of their own statements. Constant corrections of the deaf child's language might be similarly ignored and, thus, ineffective.

It is more consistent with current theories of language acquisition to emphasize, instead, exposure to a wide range of language experiences. There seems to be a tendency among educators of the deaf to limit the range of linguistic constructions used in spoken or written materials, as they know that the deaf child does not understand them. This tendency, however, creates a vicious cycle: Without exposure to the appropriate linguistic data, the child cannot possibly extract the relevant linguistic rules, but without the linguistic rules, the child cannot understand the content. Nickerson (Chapter 7, this volume) discusses related problems with respect to reading. If a full range of language experience could be provided for deaf children from a young age, it would not be necessary to censor later educational materials in order to eliminate advanced linguistic constructions.

Finally, it is important to consider what expectations are communicated to the child by the kinds of communication patterns used. Highly directive, intrusive communication of the kind described as common in classroom and family settings is likely to convey an evaluation of helplessness to the deaf child and to inhibit independent thinking. This is consistent with a tendency to infantalize handicapped children and to set lower goals for them (Hobbs, 1975). For example, Chess, Korn, and Fernandez (1971) found that rubella children (not all of whom were deaf) were far more capable of self-help tasks than they typically performed, suggesting a lack of encouragement from parents and other caretakers. Personal observation also indicates that teachers often significantly underestimate the abilities of the deaf children to perform new tasks. Research on the expectations conveyed by adults to deaf children is needed, perhaps using the paradigms and methodologies of the literature of the development of sex differences. For example, Hoffman (1972) has suggested that when faced with difficult problems, girls are rewarded for inducing someone to help them, whereas boys are rewarded for mastering the problems themselves. Parallel differences may occur between deaf and hearing children with comparably negative outcomes.

Equilibration

To compensate for situations or outcomes that do not fit current oper-ational structure, existing schemes are expanded and integrated through the equilibration process. While equilibration, itself, may be presumed to function normally in deaf children, the impetus for cogni-tive restructuring is probably attenuated because of a diminished oppor-tunity for external disturbances. It is also possible that the motivational aspect of equilibration—the drive toward cognitive balance—is reduced in deaf children as a consequence of the lack of encouragement for cognitive independence. Thus, deficiencies in equilibration are probably best conceptualized as by-products of the physical and social deficiencies described earlier.

SUMMARY AND CONCLUSIONS

A developmental approach to the experiential deficiencies of deaf children suggests several areas for further research and intervention. First, continued medical and physiological work is needed to provide maximum sensory input as early as possible. Second, it is important to develop ways to compensate for missing auditory information and incen-tives for exploration by providing visually interesting stimuli, particu-larly stimuli that change in response to the child's own actions. Third, it is necessary to consider ways in which the child's environment—both at home and school—is unnecessarily restrictive and insufficiently challeng-ing, and to modify these environments appropriately.

Finally, many of the deficits identified in this chapter may be under-stood as direct or indirect consequences of inadequate communication between deaf children and those around them (parents, teachers, peers). One potential solution to this problem is to use some form of manual communication. The early use of manual communication has often been discouraged for fear that it would interfere with the development of oral–aural skills. Empirical evidence, however, has not documented deficits in the linguistic, social, or cognitive realms as a consequence of early manual communication (see Chapter 1 by Liben, Chapter 8 by R. Harris, and Chapter 10 by Moores). In addition, recent work by linguists (e.g., see Chapter 3 by Bellugi & Klima) has exploded the myth that sign language restricts its users to the expression of concrete ideas. Additional evidence that early acquisition of sign language need not prove detrimental is provided by examining the development of hearing children of deaf parents. These children acquire sign language as a native language with no apparent interference with the development of English or cognitive skills. (It should be noted, however, that this generalization needs empirical validation, since to date there has been a dearth of research on this population.) Related evidence is provided by experimental programs in which hearing and deaf children are integrated within the same classroom. Both groups of children acquire and use sign language without apparent linguistic or cognitive decrements. In light of these observations, the fear of using manual communication with young children—even if a diagnosis of severe loss has not yet been confirmed—seems largely indefensible.

In emphasizing the potential contribution of manual language, it may appear that we have completed a circle and returned to the language-deficiency hypothesis ostensibly dismissed at the beginning of this chapter. In one sense this is true, in that language skills have been shown to be of crucial importance in the child's acquisition of knowledge, in socialization, and in the establishment of affective relationships. In another crucial sense it is not true. Rather than proposing that language affects thought directly, as stated in the original formulation, language here is hypothesized to have its effect on cognition indirectly, being mediated through interactions with family, peers, teachers, and society in general. Perhaps it is time to relinquish our belief that only oral languages can fulfill communicative and cognitive needs, and to encourage the use of combined manual and spoken language systems. By doing so, it should be possible to reduce a large component of the experiential deficiencies now encountered by deaf children.

REFERENCES

Ariel, A. Piaget, behavior modification, and the adolescent with learning disabilities. In G. Lubin, J. Magary, & M. Poulsen (Eds.), *Piagetian theory and the helping professions*. Los Angeles: University of Southern California, 1975.

Balla, D., Butterfield, E., & Zigler, E. Effects of institutionalization on retarded
    children: A longitudinal cross-institutional investigation. *American Journal of
    Mental Deficiency*, 1974, *78*, 530–549.
Barsch, R. *The parent of the handicapped child.* Springfield, Illinois: Charles C
    Thomas, 1968.
Blair, F. A study of the visual memory of deaf and hearing children. *American
    Annals of the Deaf*, 1957, *102*, 254–263.
Bowlby, J. *Child care and the growth of love* (2nd ed.). Baltimore: Penguin, 1965.
Cazden, C. *Environmental assistance to the child's acquisition of grammar.* Unpublished
    doctoral dissertation, Harvard University, 1965.
Chandler, M. Social cognition: A selective review of current research. In W.
    Overton, & J. Gallagher (Eds.), *Knowledge and development* (Vol. 1). New
    York: Plenum Press, 1977.
Chess, S., Korn, S., & Fernandez, P. *Psychiatric disorders of children with congenital
    rubella.* New York: Brunner/Mazel, 1971.
Clopton, B., & Winfield, J. Effect of early exposure to patterned sound on unit
    activity in rat inferior colliculus. *Journal of Neurophysiology*, 1976, *39*, 1081–
    1089.
Craig, W., & Collins, J. Analysis of communicative interaction in classes for deaf
    children. *American Annals of the Deaf*, 1970, *115*, 79–85.
Dale, P. *Language development.* New York: Holt, Rinehart & Winston, 1976.
Dennis, W. Causes of retardation among institutional children: Iran. *Journal of
    Genetic Psychology*, 1960, *96*, 47–59.
Evans, D. Experiential deprivation: Unresolved factor in the impoverished
    socialization of deaf school children in residence. *American Annals of the Deaf*,
    1975, *120*, 545–554.
Flavell, J. The development of inferences about others. In T. Mischel (Ed.),
    Understanding other persons. Oxford, England: Blackwell, Basil & Mott, 1974.
Fraiberg, S., Siegal, B., & Gibson, R. The role of sound in the search behavior of
    a blind infant. *Psychoanalytic Study of the Child*, 1966, *21*, 327–357.
Frishberg, N. Arbitrariness and iconicity: Historical change in American Sign
    Language. *Language*, 1975, *51*, 696–719.
Furth, H. Conservation of weight in deaf and hearing children. *Child Develop-
    ment*, 1964, *35*, 143–150.
Furth, H. *Thinking without language: Psychological implications of deafness.* New
    York: Free Press, 1966.
Furth, H. *Piaget for teachers.* Englewood Cliffs, New Jersey: Prentice-Hall, 1970.
Furth, H., & Milgram. N. The influence of language on classification: Normal,
    retarded, and deaf. *Genetic Psychology Monograph*, 1965, *72*, 317–351.
Gesell, A., & Ilg, F. *Child development.* New York: Harper & Row, 1949.
Griffiths, C. *Conquering childhood deafness* (1st ed.). New York: Exposition Press,
    1957.
Hall, B. *A primer of Freudian psychology.* New York: Mentor, 1954.
Hess, R., & Shipman, V. Maternal influence upon early learning: The cognitive
    environments of urban pre-school children. In R. Hess & R. Bear (Eds.),
    Early Education. Chicago: Aldine, 1968.

Hobbs, N. *Issues in the classification of children.* San Francisco: Jossey-Bass, 1975.

Hoemann, H. The development of communication skills in deaf and hearing children. *Child Development,* 1972, *43,* 990–1002.

Hoffman, L. Early childhood experience and women's achievement motives. *Journal of Social Issues,* 1972, *28,* 129–155.

Hoffmeister, R., Moores, D., & Best, B. *The acquisition of sign language in deaf children of deaf parents: Progress report* (Research Report No. 65). Minneapolis; Research, Development, and Demonstration Center in Education of Handicapped Children, 1974.

Horowitz, F., & Paden, L. The effectiveness of environmental intervention programs. In B. Caldwell & H. Ricciuti (Eds.), *Review of child development research* (Vol. 3). Chicago: University of Chicago Press, 1973.

Hunt, J. McV. *Intelligence and experience.* New York: Ronald, 1961.

Killackey, H., & Ryugo, D. Effects of neonatal peripheral auditory system damage on the structure of the inferior colliculus of the rat. *Anatomical Record,* 1977, *87,* 624.

Kohlberg, L. A cognitive–developmental analysis of children's sex-role concepts and attitudes. In E. Maccoby (Ed.), *The development of sex differences.* Stanford, California: Stanford University Press, 1966.

Luria, A. R., & Yudovich, F. *Speech and the development of mental processes in the child.* London: Staples Press, 1959.

MacDougall, J., & Rabinovitch, S. Early auditory deprivation and exploratory activity. *Developmental Psychology,* 1972, *7,* 17–20.

McNeill, D. Developmental psycholinguistics. In F. Smith & G. Miller (Eds.), *The genesis of language.* Cambridge, Massachusetts: M.I.T. Press, 1966.

McNeill, D. The development of language. In P. Mussen (Ed.), *Carmichael's manual of child psychology.* New York: Wiley, 1970.

Michael, J., & Kates, S. Concept attainment on social materials by deaf and hearing adolescents. *Journal of Educational Psychology,* 1965, *56,* 81–86.

Mischel, W., & Mischel, H. The nature and development of psychological sex differences. In G. Lesser (Ed.), *Psychology and educational practice.* Glenview, Illinois: Scott Foresman, 1971.

Moore, D., & Aitkin, L. Rearing in an acoustically unusual environment: Effects on neural auditory responses. *Neurosciences Letters,* 1975, *1,* 29–34.

Nass, M. The deaf child's conception of physical causality. *Journal of Abnormal and Social Psychology,* 1964, *69,* 669–673.

Nowell, R., & Liben, L. Linguistic and communicative characteristics of American Sign Language. Paper presented at the meetings of the New England Psychological Association, Worchester, Massachusetts, 1975.

Oléron, P. Conceptual thinking of the deaf. *American Annals of the Deaf,* 1953, *98,* 304–310.

Oléron, P., & Herren, H. L'acquisition des conservations et le language: Etude comparative sur des enfants sourds et entendants. *Enfance,* 1961, *14,* 203–219.

Olsson, J., & Furth, H. Visual memory span in the deaf. *American Journal of Psychology,* 1966, *76,* 480–484.

Piaget, J. *The origins of intelligence in children.* New York: International Universities Press, 1952.

Piaget, J. Development and learning. In R. Ripple & V. Rockcastle (Eds.), *Piaget rediscovered.* Ithaca, New York: Cornell University Press, 1964.

Piaget, J. Piaget's theory. In P. Mussen (Ed.), *Carmichael's manual of child psychology.* New York: Wiley, 1970.

Piaget, J., & Inhelder, B. *The psychology of the child.* New York: Basic Books, 1969.

Pimm, J. The clinical use of Piagetian tasks with emotionally disturbed children. In G. Lubin, J. Magary, & M. Poulsen (Eds.), *Piagetian theory and the helping professions.* Los Angeles: University of Southern California, 1975.

Pitner, R., & Paterson, D. A comparison of deaf and hearing children in visual memory for digits. *Journal of Experimental Psychology,* 1917, *2,* 76–88.

Pitner, R., & Reamer, J. A mental and educational survey of schools for the deaf. *American Annals of the Deaf,* 1920, *65,* 451.

Quigley, S., & Frisina, D. R. Institutionalization and psychoeducational development of deaf children. *Council of Exceptional Children Resarch Monographs,* 1961, *3.*

Reich, P., & Reich, C. *A follow-up study of the deaf.* Mimeographed report, University of Toronto, 1973.

Robertson, A., & Youniss, J. Anticipatory visual imagery in deaf and hearing children. *Child Development,* 1969, *40,* 123–135.

Schlesinger, H., & Meadow, K. *Sound and sign.* Berkeley, California: University of California Press, 1972. (a)

Schlesinger, H., & Meadow, K. Development of maturity in deaf children. *Exceptional Children,* 1972, *38,* 461–467. (b)

Shantz, C. The development of social cognition. In E. Hetherington (Ed.), *Review of child development research* (Vol. 5). Chicago: University of Chicago Press, 1975.

Slobin, D. *Psycholinguistics.* Glenview, Illinois: Scott Foresman, 1971.

Spitz, R. Hospitalism: An inquiry into the genesis of psychiatric conditions in early children. In R. Eissler (Ed.), *The psychoanalytic study of the child* (Vol. 1). New York: International Universities Press, 1945.

Stokoe, W. *Sign language structure: An outline of the visual communication systems of the American deaf.* Buffalo, New York: University of Buffalo, 1960.

Stokoe, W., Casterline, D., & Croneberg, C. *A dictionary of American Sign Language on linguistic principles.* Washington, D.C.: Gallaudet College Press, 1965.

Templin, M. *The development of reasoning in children with normal and defective hearing.* Minneapolis: University of Minnesota Press, 1950.

Thompson, W., & Grusec, J. Studies of early experience. In P. Mussen (Ed.), *Carmichael's manual of child psychology.* New York: Wiley, 1970.

Upshall, C. *Day school vs. institutions for the deaf* (Teachers College, Columbia University contributions to education, No. 389). New York: Bureau of Publications, Teachers College, Columbia University, 1929.

Van der Woude, K. Problem solving and language. *Archives of General Psychiatry,* 1970, *23,* 337–342.

Watson, J. Psychology as the behaviorist views it. *Psychological Review*, 1913, *20*, 158–177.

Webster, D., & Webster, M. Morphological effects of acoustic deprivation on the brainstem auditory system of CBA/J mice. *Anatomical Record*, 1976, *184*, 559.

Weikart, D., Rogers, L., Adcock, C., & McClelland, D. *The cognitively oriented curriculum*. Washington, D.C.: National Association for the Education of Young Children, 1971.

Wiley, J. A psychology of auditory impairment. In W. Cruickshank (Ed.), *Psychology of exceptional children and youth* (3rd ed.). Englewood Cliffs, New Jersey: Prentice-Hall, 1971.

Wolf, A. The dynamics of the selective inhibition of specific functions in neuroses. *Psychosomatic Medicine*, 1943, *5*, 27–38.

Wrightstone, J., Aronow, M., & Moskowitz, S. Developing reading test norms for deaf children. *American Annals of the Deaf*, 1963, *108*, 311–316.

Zigler, E. Mental retardation: Current issues and approaches. In L. Hoffman, & M. Hoffman (Eds.), *Review of child development research* (Vol. 2). New York: Russell Sage Foundation, 1966.

Zucker, I., & Bindra, D. Peripheral sensory loss and exploratory behavior. *Canadian Journal of Psychology*, 1961, *15*, 237–243.

12

The Development of the
Deaf Individual and
the Deaf Community

ADRIENNE E. HARRIS

Within the past decade there has been an important shift in the assumptions that inform research on the deaf. What was seen primarily as a medical problem is now viewed largely as a problem in communication. The gradual and by no means universal changes in deaf education from oralism to total communication and the integration of sign language into curricula for the deaf are manifestations of this conceptual shift. The implications of this change in emphasis can be observed in several monographs and conference reports that project services for the deaf community (Altshuler & Rainer, 1969; Furth, 1973; Hardy & Cull, 1974; Rainer & Altshuler, 1969; Wallace, 1970). This work identifies adequate communication in clinical and educational settings as a central issue, notes the importance of involving the deaf community at all levels in planning services and programs, and recognizes the necessity of adequate supports and encouragement of communicative adequacy between parents and infant or preschool deaf children (Adler & Williams, 1974; Bolton, Cull, & Hardy, 1974; Lane, 1974; Rotter, 1974).

Although support has been growing for the view that deafness is a crisis in communication, work on the physical and medical aspects of deafness has not been abandoned. Developments in technology, both in

DEAF CHILDREN: DEVELOPMENTAL PERSPECTIVES

instruction and amplification, continue and are clearly important in maximizing the deaf individual's exposure to and interaction with the material, physical, and social environment. However, the development of a rich communicative system, shared with critical others in the social network, is identified as the problematic developmental task for the deaf individual. Moreover, deficiencies in communicative competence are seen as important determining factors in cognitive, social, and personal dysfunctioning.

In much writing on nonnormative populations, the concentration on developmental difficulties contains a tendency to blame the victim. Refreshingly, in recent work on deafness there is an acknowledgment that other elements in the social network must bear some of the burden in developing communicative competence. This understanding is apparent in discussions of techniques of family therapy (Robinson & Weather, 1974), of the primacy of parental counseling (McClure, 1969; Meadow, 1969; Schlesinger & Meadow, 1973), of appropriate methodology for psychological tests and clinical evaluation (Schuldt & Schuldt, 1972), and in the view of the deaf child as a potentially competent communicator in a problematic social system (Brown, 1969; Cicourel & Boese, 1972).

However, even within the framework or model of communicative competence, psychological and clinical literature on the deaf presents a paradox. Whatever the root cause, the failure to meet the normative standards (educational and social) of the hearing community has massive and far-reaching consequences for the deaf. That these consequences are often negative is clear when one notes the class and occupational distribution of the deaf population, lower scores (than comparable hearing populations) in reading and school-related skills, and the social isolation of many deaf people (Rainer & Altshuler, 1969).

One is struck initially by the potential for damage and developmental problems in this population. But other features of deaf experience are emerging. There is the beauty, the wit, the metaphoric richness of sign, which Bellugi and Klima render so evocatively in their papers (Bellugi & Klima, 1972). There is the tenacity of a communication system operating virtually underground, a language children teach to children. The survival of communities of deaf adults and the relatively new phenomenon of deaf militancy speak of survival and vigor and cultural richness. I think this paradox can provide a cautionary note for future research and work on the deaf.

A rigorous examination of the hazards and problems of the developing deaf individual needs to be balanced with our respect and awareness of powerful and spontaneous techniques for survival and for the protection of culture and identity. If this balance can be maintained in research on the deaf, the pitfalls of a stereotypic analysis of "cultural deprivation" may be avoided. Taking the example of the analysis of Black English and reflecting on the research trajectory from Bereiter to Labov, I think a useful precedent is available in which we can see that normative assessment of atypical populations can mask resources and dimensions of the experience of nonstandard populations.

If the critical developmental task of the deaf is one of mastering and internalizing some communicative system, we may view the mastery of language skills in the deaf in a new light. Previously, considerable research on the deaf has examined the relationship of speech skills and cognitive performance (Furth, 1966). In this work the performance of the deaf has generally been the terrain in which psychologists or psycholinguists work out some long-standing concern with the relationship between, or independence of, language and thinking. This work rests on at least two assumptions. First, language is equated with speech, correlative perhaps with an assumption that without speech one cannot think. This is an explicit view in the Soviet tradition (see Moores, 1972). Second, this research concentrates on what Halliday (1975) has termed the *mathetic* functions of language. What is under examination is the capacity of language to represent experience, to observe, to conceptualize, and to categorize.

However, language is used both to observe and intrude. In the preoccupation with language in the service of cognitive activity, that is, with the observational or mathetic functions, other important aspects of language activity have been ignored or underplayed. It is important to remember that language also serves intrusive or pragmatic functions. People personalize and identify their experience for themselves and for others. They use language to exert control, to regulate their own actions, and to interact.

A primary aim in this chapter is to suggest broadening the consideration of language competence in deaf populations and to explore its implications for many facets of development. A central assumption of the argument made here is that the principal issue in the deaf community is a struggle over language on both the collective and individual level. Human language systems have special potentialities as mechanisms for regulation and control. Control over language yields the dual possibilities of social control and self control. It is thus appropriate to treat language as a regulatory mechanism on the sociopolitical level, on the interpersonal level, and finally as an internalized system at the service of the individual in the maintenance of cognitive and social activity. The issues of language competence and communicative systems for the deaf can be explored on all three levels.

In analyzing potential functions for language skills and potential problems in communicative competence, several different theoretical perspectives and research traditions will be used. Halliday's functional systemics (Halliday, 1975), psychological work on bilingualism, analyses of infant–caretaker dyads (Bell, 1974; Lewis & Lee-Painter, 1974; Lewis & Freedle, 1974), and the work of Luria (1961) and Bernstein (1971) on the role of language as a vehicle for social and self-control can all provide interesting commentary on the problems of deafness.

INSTITUTIONAL CONTROL

Starting at the macrolevel, the problem of control is played out on the institutional level. Here, control over the form of language is the concern, as the definition or legitimization of modes of instruction and language forms seems to be a powerful motivating force in deaf education and policy in special education.

A number of assumptions are embedded in the institutional opposition to sign, the dominant situation for much of this century in North America and in the Soviet Union. The imperatives of entry into economic or social relations in a speaking community, the suspicion that thinking is somehow intricately implicated in speaking, and the antipathy of parents to any manifestations of damage that may stigmatize their deaf child have combined in this century to support a policy of oral–aural instruction and to relegate manual communication to the status of an underground language. The tenacity of the oralist perspective persists in the face of fairly substantial evidence of advantages of an enriched instructional program in which signing in some form is included. In this volume Liben (Chapter 1) and R. Harris (Chapter 8) review these findings. There is also evidence (Meadow, 1969; Vernon & Koh, 1970) that deaf children in deaf households, exposed to a gestural communication system from birth, are significantly more skilled in intellectual and social tasks than are their deaf counterparts in hearing households.

Thus, deaf individuals find themselves in what must be a classic set of contradictions generated by the majority culture. Measured against the normative standards of the hearing culture, their performance filtered through an often insufficient communication system (deficient either in production, comprehension, or both), the developmental potential of the deaf individuals becomes defined negatively, failing to meet standards derived of the dominant culture. At the same time, deaf students may well be unable to demonstrate intellectual competence through the communicative form lying more clearly within their capabilities, that is, through sign language. They may be the victims of an educational policy that prohibits the use of sign, an inability of educators and researchers to understand it, or institutional and familial prejudice that could inhibit the confident use of that language system. Alternatively, this inability may be determined by the individual history of deaf persons, dependent on such factors as late diagnosis or late entry into the deaf community or special school settings. Whether the linguistic deficit is attributable to an artifact (for example, the person knows sign but is blocked from using it) or is actual (i.e., the person is blocked from acquiring sign), the negative effect on demonstrating intellectual or educational performance is the same.

The problem is not, of course, unique to the deaf. Speakers of nonstandard English suffer the economic and social sanctions of failure to acquire the standard dialect. There is also some evidence (Gumperz & Hernandez-Chavez, 1972) that in school settings, regardless of the complexity or sophistication of the content of answers, teachers may judge the child's cognitive competence as inadequate if the form is nonstandard. The conventional counterargument that school success or standard measures of intelligence are not adequate measures of cognitive competence is irrelevant in this context. Inability to negotiate the tasks and developmental hurdles of the educational system does have economic consequences. The concentration of the deaf in the unskilled and semiskilled laboring class is partially explained by the limited access and control the deaf have over oral speech, the standard mode of contact and performance in school and vocational settings.

Considering the developing consciousness of deaf communities (Galloway, 1969; Hardy & Cull, 1974; Wallace, 1970) and the increasing sensitization of educators, researchers, and clinicians to deaf adults' input regarding social policy and services for the deaf, it is tempting to trace out analogies to problems and issues in bilingualism. One possible resolution to the question of appropriate language format for the deaf would be to assume the necessity of bilingual competence, distinguishing between first language which would incorporate some form of gestural communication and a second language for school instruction (Charrow & Fletcher, 1974). This resolution, in acknowledging bilingualism, would recognize the dual necessity of adequate means of multifunctional symbolic expression and access to the linguistic system of the larger hearing culture.

Studies of bilingualism among speaking or hearing communities (Lambert, 1967; Lambert & Tucker, 1972; McNamara, 1966, 1967) suggest that this strategy has both liabilities and strengths. Hymes (1967) believes that bilingualism should be viewed as one instance of the more general phenomenon of code switching. Under many circumstances, the ability to handle different codes—to respond appropriately to the mix of social and linguistic rules in particular settings—is for most language users both a spontaneous and unconscious occurrence (Bernstein, 1973; Gleason, 1973). It seems then, that bilingualism (i.e., Ameslan and some form of the spoken language, or bimodal codes such as signed and spoken English) is a plausible goal.

However, the efficacy and success of such code switching is highly dependent on the functional context (Hymes, 1967) and upon the value and stigma attached to each code (Lambert, 1967). Here the deaf appear to be analogous to bilingual speakers who must operate in at least one undervalued and stigmatized code. If the use of sign also signals damage, that is, social or cognitive deficiencies to nonsigners, then multiple code maintenance and use may be alienating, difficult, or anxiety-filling for the deaf. In addition, imperfect control over the oral system or use of sign may have (as stigmatized languages do) a negative impact on teacher expectation, which, in turn, can have an interactive effect on classroom performance and school success. The presence of a stigmatized code can be double edged. Ghettoized or socially devalued languages can be devices for boundary maintenance and for ironic commentary when used as a defensive strategy by cultural or social groups.

McNamara (1966, 1967) notes that there may be difficulties and intellectual setbacks when instruction is provided in the weaker language. Bain (1976) also reports that, under certain conditions, school performance by the bilingual operating in a second language may be disrupted. McNamara is sounding a general cautionary note for instructional situations in which students must function in a less practiced language. Bain makes a more specialized statement in examining the effects of class and social esteem on the ability of bilinguals to function intellectually in the weaker language. Both perspectives are relevant to the deaf. Cognitive performance may suffer for those deaf individuals who operate in schools in the weaker language, weaker by virtue both of later age of acquisition and because of the special difficulties in acquiring competence in the oral–aural mode (Cicourel & Boese, 1972).

What is required, then, is a careful assessment of the potential for bilingual competence for the deaf. Is the second language designed to be instrumental (serving educational, intellectual, or mathetic functions) or integrative (pragmatic or social)? Lambert (1967) has demonstrated that different functional criteria for language-learning tap different motivational structures and yield different outcomes in terms of language competence. One must ask under what conditions the possession and demands of two language systems provide the occasion for anomie, alienation, or conflict. Furthermore, will conflicting demands and values in two language systems prove to be dysfunctional for the development of cognitive and school skills? Can teacher preparation and the upgrading of communicative skills among deaf educators promote a positive evaluation and legitimization of sign languages? Can the development of a written form of sign enhance its utility and value? (See Chapter 6 by Sperling, this volume.) These are questions that await some empirical demonstration and indicate the importance of applying a functional analysis to questions of language instruction and language policy.

The struggle to legitimize a visual–gestural as opposed to an oral–aural mode of language is only comprehensible, I suspect, when analogies are made to other struggles for national or cultural identity. There is one crucial difference. In any struggle over minority rights for self-determination, including linguistic determination, it is assumed that parents represent their children. In the case of the deaf, however, 90% of deaf children have hearing parents, meaning that linguistic and cultural barriers may cut across generations and through family structure. Several questions arise. How possible is it and what are the optimal methods to establish adequate communicative lines within natural biological families? Can hearing parents acquire sign with their children? Will they choose to? These are empirical questions, but there is a prior ethical question for researchers and child care workers in this area. How is one to define a constituency? Can one work for parent and child when their interests may not coincide? Who speaks for the deaf child: the biological or linguistic parent? What is the cultural unit *defining* the deaf community?

This issue becomes even more complex when one considers that class distinctions are reflected in sign systems themselves. Stokoe (1972) and I. M. Schlesinger (1971) in studying variants of ASL and Israeli Sign Language (ISL) identify dialectal distinctions of sign with a hierarchy favoring increased approximations to structure of the standard oral system. So the choice of linguistic system within the gestural mode may have real consequences for the educational opportunities and economic prospects of deaf people. I. M. Schlesinger's work suggests a distinct payoff in occupational and educational terms for mastery of a sign system most directly analogous to the speech system of the larger community.

FAMILY DYNAMICS AND SOCIAL INTERACTION

The regulatory power of language and the importance of communicative exchange can be examined in the context of family dynamics, socialization, and the interpersonal domain. In considering communicative competence, it is probably important not to identify communication exclusively with some linguistic system (whether oral or gestural). Much of the current work in communication stresses the multimodel and subtle exchange of information in social encounters (Birdwhistel, 1970). Therefore, we are interested initially in the character of social interactions (verbal and nonverbal) in early infancy. Additionally, the role of language in later socialization will be explored. The critical issues are independence, autonomy, and behavior management. In applying theory and empirical observations from normal populations to deaf children in family settings, we need to be sensitive both to the potential for dysfunction and to alternative strategies for meeting goals, first of attachment and later of independence.

Michael Lewis's work (Lewis, Weinraub, & Ban, 1974; Lewis & Freedle, 1972; Lewis & Rosenblum, 1974) stresses the importance of interactive sequences arising very early in infancy both for language development and adequate social experience. Using extensive observations of parent–child dyads, Lewis and others note the early and ubiquitous appearance of patterns of vocalizing alternations. These vocalizing bouts appear to be the groundwork or practice for later language activity and for social interaction. One of the interesting insights in Lewis's work is that it is not always easy to see who initiates a vocalizing sequence. The role of the infant in eliciting attachment behavior from the parent has been explored further by Bell (1974). The burden of Bell's argument is that the infant produces a great variety of activities—such as eye contact, turning, crying, vocalizing. By incorporating signals from the child with contextual and situational variables, the parent constructs a set of socially derived meanings for the child's behavior. Attachment is thus a bidirectional process in which a range of intricate actions by the child may be crucial in engaging the attention and attachment of the parent.

It is difficult to read this literature on infancy in normal settings and avoid alarmist conclusions about its application to most deaf infants. To state the case most negatively, a child with a sensory loss in which both receptive and productive language capacities are affected may be a limited or atypical participant in the social exchange with the parent. Parent–child interaction may thus be out of phase long before an appropriate diagnosis is made, and the mutual development of attachment seriously compromised. One obvious imperative is the need for early diagnostic techniques. However, Bell's work in particular contains features that permit optimism when applied to the deaf. Bell points out that the process of informational exchange between infant and parent is both multidimensional and overdetermined, and that many nonverbal or nonvocal avenues for exchange are available. What is required is an analysis comparable to that of Fraiberg (1974) regarding blind children, where alternative experiences and tasks were designed to enable blind infants to negotiate critical developmental hurdles. The implications are for very early and creative interventions. A similar argument has been made by Liben (Chapter 11, this volume) regarding the importance of experience in early infancy for cognitive development.

A second critical problem in family dynamics must arise at the point where mastery over some language is expected and, in fact, required to enable the parent to manage the more mobile and independent toddler. A protolanguage or primitive and idiosyncratic gestural system becomes obsolete or insufficient to handle the complex commands through which socialization is effected. Studies of moral judgment, the development of conscience, and social maturity suggest the positive effects of a verbally mediated explanatory and rational style of parenting (Hoffman, 1970; Kohlberg, 1964). Reports of parental difficulty in management and the pattern of impulsive or aggressive deaf children (see Chapter 8 by R. Harris, and Chapter 4 by Schlesinger, this volume) may reflect the insufficiency of the communicative system as a vehicle for instruction and control within the family. There remains the empirical question of what form the language might take and whether a hearing parent and deaf child can develop totally overlapping communicative systems. In the case of the deaf child, the developmental point at which language is expected may be the first point at which the family acknowledges a problem, as this may be the first recognizably missed developmental milestone.

Slater (1971) has written quite evocatively of the way goals and standards for child rearing have a powerful impact, particularly on women. In North America, the child has become the ultimate product. As more and more basic research on children finds its way into the ideology of child rearing, parents faced with socializing a new family member take on an increasingly elaborate and finely tuned task, which must seem, even in normal situations, a distinctly high risk activity. For parents of deaf children, then, there is a need both for counseling and support as the parent accepts the phenomenon of deafness, and for the creation and legitimization of appropriate developmental goals for the child. One must acknowledge that some aspects of parental difficulty in child management may well be the absence of identifiable expectations and endstates.

INDIVIDUAL FUNCTIONING

Finally, language is considered as a source of control on the level of individual functioning. The language system can be a critical and perhaps necessary vehicle for self-regulation. This potential arises by virtue of the power of language to orient, to expand the computing space for problem solving activities, and to offer an elaborate structural system for classification and cognitive organization. At least two distinct theoretical traditions offer support for this perspective.

For Luria (1961), language plays the pivotal role in the formation, installation, and maintenance of individual autonomy and control. The burden of Luria's stage model for verbal regulation is that a developmental progression yields an increased ability to use the semantic or syntactic aspects of verbal messages to plan, inhibit, and organize ongoing behavior. Halliday's (1975) functional systemics contain similar implications.

In characterizing the task of development, Halliday identifies a set of primary functions—goal-directed activities—best described as activities serving to maintain social self, physical self, or cognitive self. These functions (regulatory, interactional, personal, imaginative, heuristic, and instrumental) are derived inductively by Halliday on the basis of the social and physical system in which the child exists. They constitute options for action. In considering language development, then, Halliday, is concerned with the developing ability to realize these functional options through expression.

As children begin to develop an expressive system and gain control over the adult linguistic system, Halliday identifies a set of structural options that arise to serve expanding social and cognitive potential in the child, and in which such primary functions of language as regulations or interaction are embedded in increasingly abstract forms. Grammatical linguistic structures arise to handle developing and differentiated functions. Symbolic structures aid in the integration and organization of experience, in representation, but also in elaborating and identifying social systems. Development of structure in language thus extends the interpersonal functions of language. The assumption here is that the grammatical or lexical level of language systems serves a dual function. It arises to handle increasingly complex information about both the epistemological and the social or interpersonal components of experience. Language is thus the powerful tool for the installation of socialized self-control in the individual. Note that Halliday's model bridges social and cognitive development. Through the development of the pragmatic and mathetic functions of language, the child achieves both entrance into the social fabric and tools for the observation of self and world. Pragmatic functions constitute the manipulative, intrusive, and interactive aspects of speech. Mathetic functions arise as the child separates himself from the environment and comes to interpret experience either for himself or others. Mathetic functions serve in the construction of reality undertaken by the child and most importantly lead the child to learn about language itself.

However, control over language to serve particular functional ends is only one aspect of Halliday's system. As the child comes to adopt a protolanguage and the adult system for serving ontologically prior functions, the internalization of the adult system gives or forces upon the child a social semiotic. The necessary evolution of complex forms to serve increasingly complex functional needs in the child leads the child deeper and deeper into the social and cultural context. The acquisition of the adult linguistic system gives the child access to the social context, its rules, its value system, and its construction of reality. This is not Whorf, however; rather it is the assertion that linguistic forms and interactions are the vehicle for learning about the structures of the social environment.

What implications does this have for the deaf child? We can pursue this question both in the context of cognitive development and personality or social functioning. In examining the role of language skills in cognitive tasks for deaf people, three related questions are asked. First, is the deficiency in the natural oral language critically or artifactually affecting performance? Second, what is the potential of sign as an internal coding system available for cognitive, social, or regulatory activities? Finally, what form might the internal symbolization of sign have?

A detailed critique of the research on cognitive and intellectual skills in the deaf is beyond the scope of this chapter. This literature is reviewed and discussed in this volume by both Liben (Chapter 11) and Moores (Chapter 10). It is sufficient to say that a significant amount of the empirical work on this problem is really uninterpretable either because the researcher did not estimate nonoral linguistic competence or because the format for the empirical research relied too heavily on command of the speech system. Given current understanding of the linguistic attributes of sign (Bellugi & Klima, Chapter 3, this volume; Stokoe, 1972; Tervoort, 1973) there is no a priori reason to assume that a gestural system could not serve mathetic functions as Halliday characterizes them.

Chapter 5 by Brooks on reading problems in the deaf provides an occasion for examining the impact of oral speech disabilities upon cognitive processing. She proposes that the internalized form of the oral speech stream offers ongoing or structural regulation for the reader in that it provides a continuous rhythmic stream with peaks coordinated with high information parts of the graphic message. Skill with a language thus becomes the basis for a strategy of attention suitable to maintain skilled and high speed reading. This is verbal regulation—not in the planning or executive sense, but in the sense of providing the individual with an ongoing spine to activity, which sustains behavior and maximizes orientation toward salient aspects of the graphic message.

An initial reading of Brooks's work might suggest that failure to grasp and "exploit" the intonational or structural features of oral speech may be a serious handicap for the acquisition of superior reading skills. However, English orthography is not analogically mapped to phonology. The relationship is complex. Nickerson and Sperling (Chapter 7 and Chapter 6, respectively, this volume) suggest that certain aspects of the spoken language might indeed, be available to the deaf child with appropriate technology. It is also possible that particular sign systems might provide the same potential for control and direction of attention. What is implied is that maximal effects of sign would occur in those sign systems which are mapped most closely to English grammar.

Both Luria (1961) and Halliday (1975) identify a regulatory function for language. One may reasonably ask, then, how an inadequate command over language or a dysfunctional communication system (i.e., between parent and child, child and school, or child and other socializing agents) will affect the development of this regulatory capacity? Additionally, one may speculate on the effect of difficulties in establishing a regulatory or control function in language upon social and personality development in the deaf.

Robert Harris (Chapter 8, this volume) has reviewed the literature on impulsivity and deafness and suggests a connection between problems of impulse control, language disability, and the characteristic personality profile of deaf children and deaf adolescents. Recently, Schuldt and Schuldt (1972) surveyed personality studies on the deaf. Although noting methodological and interpretive difficulties in the research and the presence of often contradictory evidence, they offer a general summary profile. Compared to hearing controls, deaf children appear more rigid, less well-adjusted, more immature, more aggressive, and less cooperative. There is, in general, underdevelopment of emotional and social skills (measured by conventional instruments) and this underdevelopment is reflected often in insensitivity to the dynamics of interaction and in what the reviewers term an "egocentric life perspective" and "constricted life area [Schuldt & Schuldt, 1972]."

Interestingly, Meadow (1969) has suggested that this characteristic personality profile is less marked for deaf children reared by deaf parents, who, in all likelihood, provide a signing environment. Schuldt and Schuldt also note that better adjustment for deaf children is correlated with such factors as deafness in the family, less severe hearing loss, and nonresidential school placement.

One interpretation of these empirical findings is that a shared, mutually accessible symbol system of some structural and semantic complexity is essential for the development of social control, self-control, and for an adequate conceptualization of the social terrain in which context-appropriate behaviors are embedded. Note, however, that this supposition confounds two distinct explanations.

Following Luria's analysis, an inadequate or inadequately internalized linguistic system leaves the deaf child with fewer and weaker internal mechanisms for inhibition and self-control. Luria's theory presupposes that the initial model for self-control is the instruction and commands of parent to child. It is thus a dynamic interaction that is internalized. If the parent is unable to make linguistic contact with the child, unable to pose increasingly complex demands or reduced to primitive modes of control, that initial model for impulse control and autonomy is unavailable to the child.

Alternatively, one might consider that the language disability has its main effect in limiting the deaf child's access to the social semiotic. Limited access to a communicative system that is both subtle and complex leaves the deaf child significantly less able to read the social demands of the culture, the stereotypic expectations for age-specific, sex-specific, or situation-specific behaviors. If linguistic rules contain or are confounded with social rules, then failure to master language may lead to behavior easily interpreted as nonnormative, immature, or otherwise inappropriate. Currently it is not possible to decide which explanation is more plausible. The somewhat better social, emotional, and cognitive performance of deaf children in deaf households does not clarify our understanding. For, in that situation the child, by virtue of a more functional language, has the potential both for an internal regulatory system and an accurate reading of the social rules because the communicative system is mutually accessible to parent and child.

While the theoretical issue is not resolvable, it is important to note that different implications arise. If the critical problem is failure to acquire an internal code that could guide and control behavior, then any linguistic system may be utilized regardless of modality. If, however, the problem is decoding the social rules of the majority culture, then access to some form of the speech system (in oral or graphic form) is implied. This, as a goal in language learning and development, may be neither desirable nor completely possible for the deaf.

CONCLUSION

I would like to conclude with three general points that are intended both to summarize and to direct attention to future research raised by the chapters in this volume. First, a necessary, though not sufficient, requirement for adequate development in the deaf would seem to be the availability of a shared communication system arising early in family life. Whatever the communicative format, this system must maximize the exchange of information, both social and experiential, between parent and child. The question of language instruction and language activity in the educational setting, though bedeviling and difficult, is probably a secondary concern. Second, in selecting a communication system it would be important to consider its richness, its structural complexity, and its capacity to give the child both access to representational skills and an awareness of social structure.

Finally, the linguistic analysis of sign initiated by Bellugi, Klima, Stokoe, and others needs to be matched with a research program to investigate the potentiality of sign language to operate as an internal code. Is the internal format visual, kinesthetic, or motoric and how will it serve other activities?

Arguments to restrict the input and language usage in the deaf seem frankly bankrupt. The passion that keeps them alive is political and not scientific. Early, enriching, maximal intervention appears imperative and it is inconceivable that sign language will have no role in this process. It is probably important to keep in mind that sign languages are openended systems. To use Levi-Strauss's term they are "hot" and not "cold" systems, evolving and expanding dramatically, adding complexity at least at the lexicogrammatical level. This evolution increases the potential of sign as a tool (both cognitive and social) for the deaf child.

Certain issues and problems facing the deaf seem akin to those of any collectivity seeking self-definition, legitimization, and control over critical institutions of development. Other aspects of deafness seem most clearly understood as problems in discovering normative goals and expectations for performance, social interaction, or personality. These may be problems for the deaf individual or the surrounding hearing community. In trying to derive normative socialization patterns and goals for the deaf, we encounter the problem that taxed Solomon and fascinated Brecht. Should one define normalcy in terms of the hearing parents' needs and standards, the demands and insights of deaf adults, or in terms of the deaf child's possibilities?

REFERENCES

Altshuler, K., & Rainer, J. D. (Eds.) *Mental health and the deaf: Approaches and prospects.* Washington, D.C.: U.S. Department of Health, Education and Welfare, 1969.

Adler, E., & Williams, B. Services to deaf people in the seventies. In R. E. Hardy & J. G. Cull (Eds.), *Educational and psychosocial aspects of deafness.* Springfield, Illinois: Charles C Thomas, 1974.

Bain, B. *The consequences of unilingualism, disruptive bilingualism and creative bilingualism for the development of the body schema: A cross cultural study in Canada, Italy and West Germany.* Paper presented at the First International Christian University Symposium on Pedolinguistics, Tokyo, Japan, 1976.

Bell, R. Q. Contributions of human infants to caregiving and social interaction. In M. Lewis & L. Rosenblum (Eds.), *The effect of the infant on its caregiver.* New York: Wiley-Interscience, 1974.

Bellugi, U., & Klima, E. The roots of language in the sign talk of the deaf. *Psychology Today,* 1972, *6,* 60–64, 75–76.

Bernstein, B. (Ed.), *Class, codes and control I: Theoretical studies towards a sociology of language.* London: Routledge & Kegan Paul, 1971.

Birdwhistel, R. *Kinesics and context.* Philadelphia: University of Pennsylvania Press, 1970.

Bolton, B., Cull, J. E., & Hardy, R. E. Psychological adjustment to hearing loss and deafness. In R. E. Hardy & J. G. Cull (Eds.), *Educational and psychosocial aspects of deafness.* Springfield, Illinois: Charles C Thomas, 1974.

Brown, D. A contemporary psycho-educational approach to mental health and deafness. In K. Altshuler & J. D. Rainer (Eds.), *Mental health and the deaf: Approaches and prospects.* Washington, D.C.: U.S. Department of Health, Education and Welfare. 1969.

Charrow, V. R., & Fletcher, J. D. English as the second language of deaf children. *Developmental Psychology,* 1974, *10,* 463–470.

Cicourel, A., & Boese, R. Sign language and the teaching of deaf children. In C. Cazden, V. John, & D. Hymes (Eds.), *The functions of language in the classroom.* New York: Teachers College Press, 1972.

Fraiberg, S. Blind infants and their mothers: An examination of the sign system. In M. Lewis & L. Rosenblum (Eds.), *The effect of the infant on its caregiver.* New York: Wiley-Interscience, 1974.

Furth, H. *Thinking without language: Psychological implications of deafness.* New York: Free Press, 1966.

Furth, H. *Deafness and learning.* Belmont, California: Wadsworth, 1973.

Galloway, V. H. Mental health: What it means to the typical deaf person. In K. Altshuler & J. Rainer (Eds.), *Mental health and the deaf: Approaches and prospects.* Washington, D.C.: U.S. Department of Health, Education and Welfare, 1969.

Gleason, J. B. Code switching in children's language. In T. E. Moore (Ed.), *Cognitive development and the acquisition of language.* New York: Academic Press, 1973.

Gumperz, J., & Hernandez-Chavez, E. Bilingualism, bidialectalism and classroom interaction. In C. Cazden, V. John & D. Hymes (Eds.), *The functions of language in the classroom.* New York: Teachers College Press, 1972.

Halliday, M. A. K. *Learning how to mean.* London: Arnold, 1975.

Hardy, R. E., & Cull, J. G. (Eds.). *Educational and psychosocial aspects of deafness.* Springfield, Illinois: Charles C Thomas, 1974.

Hoffman, M. L. Moral development. In P. H. Mussen (Ed.), *Carmichael's manual of child psychology.* New York: Wiley, 1970.

Hymes, D. Models of the interaction of language and social setting. *Journal of Social Issues,* 1967, *23,* 8–28.

Klima, E., & Bellugi, U. Poetry and song in a language without sound. *Cognition,* 1976, *4,* 45–97.

Kohlberg, L. The development of moral character and moral ideology. In M. Hoffman & L. Hoffman (Eds.), *Review of child development research* (Vol. 1). New York: Russell Sage Foundation, 1964.

Lambert, W. E. A social psychology of bilingualism. *Journal of Social Issues,* 1967, *23,* 91–108.

Lambert, W. E., & Tucker, G. *Bilingual education of children: The St. Lambert experiment.* Rowley, Massachusetts: Newbury House, 1972.

Lane, Helen. Pre-school education for deaf children. In R. E. Hardy & J. G. Cull (Eds.), *Educational and psychosocial aspects of deafness.* Springfield, Illinois: Charles C Thomas, 1974.

Lewis, M., & Freedle, R. Mother–infant dyad: The cradle of meaning. In P. Pliner, L. Krames, & F. Alloway (Eds.), *Communication and affect: Language and thought.* New York: Academic Press, 1973.

Lewis, M., & Lee-Painter, S. An interactional approach to the mother-infant dyad. In M. Lewis & L. Rosenblum (Eds.), *The effect of the infant on its caregiver.* New York: Wiley-Interscience, 1974.

Lewis, M., & Rosenblum, L. (Eds.), *The effect of the infant on its caregiver.* New York: Wiley-Interscience, 1974.

Lewis, M., Weinraub, M., & Ban, P. *Mothers and fathers, girls and boys: Attachment behavior in the first two years of life.* Paper presented at the meeting of the Society for Research in Child Development, Philadelphia, March 1973.

Luria, A. *The role of speech in the regulation of normal and abnormal behavior.* New York: Liveright, 1961.

McClure, W. Mental health for the deaf in the school setting. In K. Altshuler & J. Rainer (Eds.), *Mental health and the deaf: Approaches and prospects.* Washington, D.C.: U.S. Department of Health, Education and Welfare, 1969.

McNamara, J. R. *Bilingualism in primary education.* Edinburgh: Edinburgh University Press, 1966.

McNamara, J. R. Early manual communication in relation to the deaf child's intellectual, social and communicative functioning. *American Annals of the Deaf,* 1967, *23,* 121–135.

Meadow, K. P. Early manual communication in relation to the deaf child's intellectual, social and communicative functioning. *American Annals of the Deaf,* 1968, *113,* 29–41.

Moores, D. Neo-oralism and education of the deaf in the Soviet Union. *Exceptional Children,* 1972, *38,* 377–384.

Moores, D., Weiss, K., & Goodwin, M. Receptive abilities of deaf children across five modes of communication. *Exceptional Children,* 1973, *39,* 22–28.

Rainer, J. D., & Altshuler, K. (Eds.). *Family and mental health problems in a deaf population.* Springfield, Illinois: Charles C Thomas, 1969.

Robinson, L., & Weather, O. Family therapy of deaf parents and hearing children. *American Annals of the Deaf,* 1974, *119,* 325–336.

Rotter, P. Working with parents of young deaf children. In R. E. Hardy & J. G. Cull (Eds.), *Educational and psychosocial aspects of deafness.* Springfield, Illinois: Charles C Thomas, 1974.

Schlesinger, H. S., & Meadow, K. P. *Sound and sign: Childhood deafness and mental health.* Berkeley: University of California Press, 1972.

Schlesinger, I. M. The grammar of sign language and the problem of language universals. In J. Morton (Ed.), *Biological and social factors in psycholinguistics.* Cambridge, Massachusetts: Lagos Press, 1971.

Schuldt, W. J., & Schuldt, D. A. A review of recent personality research on deaf children. In E. P. Trapp & P. Himelstein (Eds.), *Readings of the exceptional child* (2nd ed.). New York: Appleton-Century-Crofts, 1972.

Slater, P. *The pursuit of loneliness: American culture at the breaking point.* Boston: Beacon Press, 1971.

Stokoe, W. *Semiotics and human sign language.* The Hague: Mouton, 1972.

Tervoort, B. T. *Developmental features of visual communication.* Amsterdam. North Holland, 1973.

Vernon, M., & Koh, S. D. Effects of manual communication on deaf children's linguistic competence, oral skills and psychological adjustment. *American Annals of the Deaf,* 1970, *115,* 527–536.

Wallace, G. *Canadian study of the hard of hearing and deaf* (Technical Report). Department of National Health and Welfare, 1970.

Author Index

Numbers in italics refer to the pages on which the complete references are listed.

Subject Index